Corporate Behavior and Social Change

James E. Post

Reston Publishing
Company, Inc.
A Prentice-Hall
Company
Reston, Virginia

Library of Congress Cataloging in Publication Data

Post, James E.
　　Corporate behavior and social change.

　　Includes bibliographical references and
　　index.
　　1. Industry—Social aspects—United States.
2. Corporations—United States. I. Title.
HD60.5.U5P6　　　658.4'08　　　78-5543
ISBN 0-8359-1083-0
ISBN 0-8359-1082-2 pbk.

© 1978 by Reston Publishing Co.
A Prentice-Hall Company
Reston, Virginia 22090

10 9 8 7 6 5 4 3 2 1

Printed in the United States of America

contents

preface

This book has evolved from a continuing line of research into the behavior of business corporations under various conditions of external change. For more than a decade, there has been an artificial distinction between the manner in which businesses respond to competitive and economic change and the manner in which they respond to socio-cultural and political change. Academically, this distinction has been institutionalized in the development of business policy, and business and society, as two distinct fields of teaching and research. In practice, however, neither field has been able to ignore the subject matter of the other. The business policy paradigms refer to the social responsibility of management as if it were entirely peripheral to the real business of management; the business and society literature refers to corporate social policy as if it were a matter entirely distinct from corporate economic policy. What the real world of practicing managers affirms is that all organizations are confronted with an abundance of economic, political, and social issues that cannot be ignored. Depending on the industry setting and the current state of the external environment, a company's top management may be primarily involved in dealing with regulators and lobbyists, citizens and politicians from local communities, fighting a corporate takeover, or designing the company's strategy for the next decade. The issues are distinguishable, but not separable as categories of items on the day–to–day agendas of top managers. The academic fields may not yet have legitimized the integrated analysis of corporate responses to external change, but management practice has. Rather than speak of business policy and social policy, we are wiser to speak only of management policy, for it embraces both.

This book has both theoretical and empirical roots that deserve explicit mention. The relationship between managed organizations and the society that charters them at one point and thereafter attempts to both control and accommodate them has been a matter of interest since Lee

Preston and I first worked together some years ago. The fruit of that collaboration, *Private Management and Public Policy,*[1] addressed both the nature of the management/society relationship and the implications of a changing relationship for business corporations. Out of that study emerged the fundamental point of view—that corporations and society are social systems that interpenetrate one another—which guided the studies that are the foundation of *Corporate Behavior and Social Change.*

The first of the empirical studies that utilized the interpenetrating systems framework was my analysis of the American insurance industry. Portions of that study (*Risk and Response: Management and Social Change In The American Insurance Industry*[2]) have been used to illustrate some of the concepts discussed in this book. Most importantly, the study of the insurance industry identified several basic patterns of corporate response to change. These patterns have now been tested empirically in a much larger sample of industries, firms, and environmental settings. The outcome has been a confirmation of three general patterns of response—(1) *adaptive,* which emphasizes organizational reaction to external events; (2) *proactive,* in which the organization attempts to initiate, alter, or modify the prevailing environment; and (3) *interactive,* which recognized that corporate purposes and public purposes are both changing, though not at the same rate or in the same direction.

The patterns of response detected in the insurance business seemed to apply to a variety of firms in that industry. Nevertheless, it was not clear whether these patterns also applied to other industries facing other types of public issues and external change. If the patterns of response were to be useful analytical concepts, it was necessary to know whether they existed in other industry settings and in a variety of environmental change cases.

Environmental change touches the core of management activity and policy making. While it appeared that managers in various industries perceived specific problems of change in the same general terms (opportunities, threats, requirements), there was a need to analyze the question of whether managerial perceptions and responses differed when the environment generated economic, technological, or political change issues.

To meet the need for testing the patterns thesis in multiple industries and multiple types of change, a sample of cases was selected that had such variety; current cases were complemented by a number of historical organization/environment conflicts. Public issues were classified as economic, technological, socio-cultural, and political in nature. Industries were clas-

[1] Lee E. Preston and James E. Post, *PRIVATE MANAGEMENT AND PUBLIC POLICY,* (Englewood Cliffs, N.J.: Prentice-Hall, Inc., 1975).
[2] James E. Post, *RISK AND RESPONSE: MANAGEMENT AND SOCIAL CHANGE IN THE AMERICAN INSURANCE INDUSTRY* (Lexington, Mass.: D.C Heath, Inc., 1976).

sified as manufacturing, extractive, service, and trade. While the full scope of this kind of study has not yet been exhausted, the more than fifty cases already analyzed point to a confirmation of the patterns of response thesis. The research framework and methodological issues are discussed further in Appendix A, while the text concentrates on the applied management lessons that stand out from this research.

Chapters are organized by themes (e.g., economic change, technological change, business and political uncertainty) and are clustered into parts which correspond to the basic patterns of response (i.e., adaptive, proactive, interactive). Because there is a discussion of both a type of environmental change and a particular pattern of response in each chapter, one or two cases are used as illustrations of the complexity that exists in such situations. It is not intended to present this as a case book; but rather, to highlight the value of the underlying management policy research by using cases to demonstrate the complexity that characterized the research studies.

Management policy research suffers from two distinct problems, neither of which is easily resolved. First, because policy is an integrative field of study, the number of factors and variables that must be considered in analyzing a particular organizational action or course of action is extremely large. While such quantitative techniques as multivariate analysis offer some hope that this problem can eventually be overcome, the current state of the field is such that simple hypotheses tend to generate simplistic results. The area is complex, but rich; to date, careful case studies remain a proven technique for exploring the richness of management policy problems.

The second problem that confronts researchers in this area is the problem of perspective. Management policy is concerned with the whole organization and the way in which that organization operates, survives, and prospers in a larger social setting. The study of these questions involves research analyzing objective factors such as organizational resources, competitors, and external institutions. But there are also subjective factors involving the personality and personal values of managers involved in decision making. Neither the business policy nor the business and society fields have yet resolved the dilemma of how to blend these objective and subjective elements into integrated research studies.

Concentrating on the general manager, as many business policy studies do, permits an explicit discussion of the personalities and personal values of managers. However, it also too often produces a "great man" approach to the study of management policy. On the other hand, too great a concentration on objective factors or statistical relationships ignores the real impact that a particular manager can have in determining the way a firm responds to change. To combat this problem, the underlying research studies for this book involved some situations where internal managerial factors were considered and others where little subjective personal information was used.

In the following chapters, the case illustrations are mixed, some using subjective information, others not, depending on their relevance to the theme of the chapter. Some may criticize this approach, believing either that subjective information is always relevant or that good policy research should never use subjective information. The best response I have been able to conceive for those criticisms is to welcome others to approach the subject from their particular perspective. For myself, I remain convinced it was necessary to do some of both the subjective and non-subjective analysis in order to formulate and test the patterns of corporate response, and to convey the lessons from that work in a way that is useful to those who read the book.

acknowledgments

Few books, if any, are solely the product of their author. Contributors abound: family, reviewers, editors, supporters, and others. But a book that is born out of a research project as large as this one is a collective effort in ways that exceed the norm. A special group of students, research assistants, and colleagues have contributed to the case studies that are the foundation of this book. Cheryl Alpert, Audrey Fishman, Steven Newman, Edward Baer, and Marilyn Mellis deserve more than a special word of mention for their efforts in data collection, interviewing, and drafting. Their efforts have been both valuable and valued.

The research project and the book have also benefited from the support of a group of understanding and helpful associates at Boston University's School of Management. Associate Dean David Furer, and Professors Henry Morgan and John Russell provided the administrative and moral support so vital to the project. The typing skills and good humor of Mrs. Mary Byron Morrissey and Ms. Kari Estrin bore up admirably under a series of continuing challenges to eyesight and patience. All of these fine people deserve a respite which they will probably not receive.

Gratitude must also be expressed for the critical reviews provided by Lee Preston, Walter Klein, and Alan Beckenstein. Their willingness to carefully review the manuscript in a critical stage produced many helpful suggestions and comments. The management and staff of Reston Publishing Company have also supported and assisted the project in noteworthy fashion. Fred Easter, Stu Horton, and Diane Breunig have been especially considerate and cooperative during the months of preparation and writing.

Lastly, there is a family that has grown accustomed to seeing husband and father amidst bulging files and overloaded desk. It is appropriate that these last few paragraphs be written for them and others who have assisted throughout this entire project.

part one

management and change

chapter
one

the frontiers
of management

THE CHALLENGE
OF UNCERTAINTY

Throughout the twentieth century, a continuing professionalization of management has contributed to both an improvement in the running of our organizational institutions and an elimination of the old frontiers of management practice. In an historical sense, the great challenges have been successfully met in the areas of finance, production, control, marketing, and personnel. Decades of accumulated experience have contributed to a body of knowledge that is the core of the "science" of management. Those areas in which management is still an "art," such as planning and public affairs, are the modern frontiers for professional managers.

Professional management began to emerge in such industries as railroads, steel, and chemicals during the late nineteenth and

3

early twentieth centuries.[1] The first school specifically created for training future managers was established by Joseph Wharton at the University of Pennsylvania in 1881. Gradually, the number of professionally trained managers has grown and their sphere of influence has expanded from large corporations to medium and small-size enterprises, and from the private sector to the public and not-for-profit sectors as well.[2] This transference of skills and knowledge has had its effect, both in the successes such organizations have known, and also in the nature of the failures they now encounter. Louis Lundborg reported that a Bank of America study of business failures indicated that the nature of the critical problems facing an organization varied with its size: small enterprises suffer from problems at the core of their existence such as technical ideas or financing; medium-size entities encounter critical problems in the coordination of purchasing and resource procurement and the marketing and distribution of output. For the large organization, however, the problems that threaten existence and prosperity are the problems of coping with an external environment that is challenging and uncertain in character. The large enterprise, having conquered the technical and administrative problems of production, finance, marketing, and purchasing through professional management, remains critically challenged by those matters that remain the province of "managerial art," not technique.

The most challenging frontiers of professional management today are probably those in which change is occurring most rapidly, where the least is known, where the most speculation occurs, and where the opportunities for imaginative executive leadership are greatest: corporate planning and the management of external affairs. Both areas are given to uncertainty and the managerial challenge is to search for that "technique," as Jacques Ellul called it,[3] which can transform uncertainty into safe prediction. According to both autobiographies and academic studies of entrepreneurs and successful managers, such a challenge provides the excitement that invigorates and moves them.[4]

In a post-industrial society, external affairs management becomes an especially crucial area of organizational activity. Daniel Bell and many others have pointed out the growing extent to which internal management

---

[1] See Alfred D. Chandler, *The Visible Hand* (Boston, Mass.: Belknap Press, 1977).

[2] The "professionalization revolution" is further discussed in Lee E. Preston and James E. Post's, "The Third Managerial Revolution," *Academy of Management Journal* Vol. 17, No. 3 (September 1974) pp. 476–486.

[3] Jacques Ellul, *The Technological Society* (New York: Alfred Knopf Co., Vintage Book Series, 1964).

[4] See for example, Alfred Sloan, *My Years With General Motors* (New York: Doubleday, 1963); Allan Nevins, *Study In Power: John D. Rockefeller* (New York: Scribners, 1953); *Forbes* and *Fortune* both feature articles on successful modern executives which reflect this same theme.

decisions are today being publicly questioned in the political arena. Even Theodore Levitt's optimistic assertion that the structural imbalances that threaten to "immiserize" progress are conquerable because of the art and practice of management,[5] must be tempered by the awareness that managers are participants in a decision-making process that is vastly more political than that presumed in most business school courses.

Organizations of all sizes and types face the challenge of operating in a social setting that is increasingly complex and inherently political. The manner in which organizations respond to this commercial and social complexity is fundamental to their institutional legitimacy and their business survival. Assertions of the need for better ways of coping with this evolving state of affairs are frequent, and even eloquent at times, but rarely offer more. Surprisingly little is known about the approaches organizations actually utilize in attempting to cope with social uncertainty. This book is based on a series of studies that addressed this problem. The remainder of the book focuses on such questions as the types of change confronting modern businesses, the challenges such changes present to management practices, and some of the basic approaches that organizations do employ in attempting to meet the challenge of social uncertainty.

MANAGING THE WHOLE ENTERPRISE

The effects of change on organizations transcend any departmental or line/staff boundaries. Nevertheless, change often occurs in the context of specific issues that at first seem to relate to narrow marketing, personnel, or financial decisions. The responsibility for comprehending the whole "forest" that many specific issues suggest is uniquely the responsibility of top management. This is the same group of managers that have the responsibility for guiding the enterprise as a whole, identifying its purposes, guiding it in its mission, sharpening distinctive competencies, as well as assuming the responsibility for identifying the sources and types of change and preparing the enterprise for the future.

How is this task of coping with external change accomplished? Since the mid-1960's, two basic organizational responses have occurred. One has emphasized the necessity of dealing with external pressure, finding ways to respond more effectively and efficiently to critics, their claims, and their pressures. The emphasis of this approach has been on "external affairs" as a separate organizational activity, one that requires special persons, competencies, and skills to fight the fires of public affairs. A second approach has been to make an attempt to think about the sources of po-

[5] Theodore Levitt, "Management and 'Post Industrial Society,' " *The Public Interest*, No. 44 (Summer 1976) pp. 69–103.

tential public issues *before* they develop, thereby permitting management to better plan its actions in a way that accounts for predictable trends and events and is sufficiently flexible to adapt to a variety of contingencies should they arise. Here the emphasis is on forethought and the principle that good managers know how to handle all aspects of an organization's relationships with the environment. Although these approaches are not mutually exclusive, it has not been common for managements to invest in both approaches. It is only in recent times that firms have adopted *both* the reactive fire-fighting approach and the more proactive anticipatory approach.

The study of *management policy* is concerned with the manner in which organizations as a whole prosper and survive in a larger social setting. It is particularly concerned, therefore, with those matters that affect the organization's ability to meet the basic institutional challenges of the times. In the past, those challenges have related to managing growth, including the coordination and administration of increasingly large bureaucratic structures. By the 1960's those challenges involved the development and articulation of corporate strategies that would facilitate and maximize effective use of organizational resources to meet managerial goals. Strategic planning replaced administration as the cutting edge of the field because administration had been successfully transformed into professional techniques and methods, while strategic planning remained the unconquered "management art." In the 1970's, the fundamental challenge to the prosperity and success of organizations changed again with the recognition that even the best formulated strategic plan could not be successfully implemented without studious attention to the larger environment of which the organization was a part. For nearly a decade, such concerns as equal employment opportunities, pollution control, and product safety were falsely treated as matters of "social responsibility," as if they were peripheral to the "real business" of running the enterprise. Today, most serious students of management history recognize the shallowness of that conception.

The organization is a part of the larger social system. The larger the organization, the more extensive its contacts with the rest of the world, and the greater the dependency of other institutions and segments of the public on it. We speak of this as the *interpenetration* between the entity and its external environment. In a world where more political decisions are made about more things, it is inevitable that the greater the interpenetration between an enterprise and society, the more likely it is to be embroiled in political decisions and decision processes. Indeed, many of the political decisions being made are likely to be made about business or impacts which business is having on other parts of society!

The prominence of this set of considerations and concerns makes it the basic topic of management policy discussion and research for the 1980's. Many still believe that the environment of managed organizations is composed of actors, institutions, and forces about which relatively little can be understood *except* as they relate to business firms and industries. This approach treats the external world as a "business environment," which is relevant to the firm only insofar as it shapes and affects these market matters that directly affect the firm. A more appropriate alternative approach recognizes that there are important trends, structures, and institutions in society as a whole, and that the business enterprise is merely one of a number of actors with interests in where and how society is evolving. Unlike the "inside looking outward" approach, the latter view emphasizes the necessity for a managerial understanding of basic social trends, changing cultural values, and the structural and behavioral shifts occurring in society as a whole. To proponents of this view, study of the social environment is equally relevant to all institutions, because all are a part of the institutional fabric of society.

ORGANIZATIONS AS SOCIAL SYSTEMS

As the public accepts the view that corporations are but units of a larger social system, new pressures develop to force enterprises to meet changing public expectations. Often this takes the form of direct public pressure, though it may also evolve into more formalized public policy as through legislation, court decisions, or administrative regulation. The way in which direct pressure or public policy affects organizations is a complex matter for study and analysis. In this book we have concentrated on describing various patterns of corporate response to pressures and public policy. Thus, the primary concern has been with the development of an understanding about processes of environmental change and patterns of organizational response to change. To accomplish this goal, both the organization and the environment have been treated as social systems that interact and interpenetrate one another.

Organizational Subsystems

As a social system, the corporation has important attributes in common with other types of organizations. Most importantly, from our perspective, it has certain basic subsystems that give it a distinctive organizational character. According to sociologist Talcott Parsons[6], every organization has a *technical subsystem* which is the core of what the entity does and which usually accounts for its distinctive character. If it is a hospital, it is the capability to treat the sick and help the needy; if it is a steel company, it is the capacity to transform iron ore into girders, rolls, and

[6] Talcott Parsons, *Structure and Process in Modern Societies* (New York: The Free Press, 1960) Chapter 2.

sheets of steel for a multitude of uses. These core activities, in turn, typically need two sorts of assistance—coordination of technical activities and the ability to provide support services, including supply of resources on the one hand and distribution of output on the other. An *administrative subsystem* performs these functions. In addition, the organization must have the support and endorsement of the larger society of which it is a part. To acquire this endorsement, every organization also has an *institutional subsystem* which is concerned with maintaining legitimacy and managing the organization's relations with the environment. While the study of management is usually concerned with activities at the managerial (or administrative) level, it is apparent that the institutional function of management is becoming more crucial to firms as the amount of external change increases and the challenges to legitimacy become more frequent.[7]

The relationship between the subsystems can be made clearer if we look at a particular industry. In the insurance industry, for example, the technical core of the business is two-sided, involving the underwriting of risks and the investment of premiums received from policyholders. To coordinate these technical activities there exists a broad array of administrative or managerial activities. To sell insurance policies there are sales and agency relations staffs; there are personnel activities to attract and develop the necessary manpower; there are claims representatives to settle the cases of policyholders who make claims; still other departments are involved in managing real-estate, mortgages, and other forms of investments. All of these activities are administrative in nature, operating to either coordinate the underwriting and investment activities of the insurer or to supply resources (clients and investment dollars) and distribute output (claims and investment opportunities).

Society at large makes a number of demands on the insurance business and to deal with these, every insurance company has staffs of lawyers, public relations personnel, regulatory affairs and public affairs specialists. Together with the company's top management and board of directors, these activities comprise the institutional subsystem. No insurance company can be successful without the activities of all three subsystems and problems in any one of them can disrupt activities elsewhere, thereby injuring the firm as a whole.

Managers, especially those below the top management level, frequently believe that the most serious problems facing the organization for which they work are technical or managerial in nature, problems which involve finance, marketing, product development or internal administration. Often it is only those relatively few top managers or public affairs specialists who comprehend the significance of changing public opinion,

[7] James W. Hurst, *The Legitimacy of the Business Corporation in the Law of the United States, 1780–1970* (Charlottesville, Va.: The University Press of Virginia, 1970).

shifting political winds, or social values in the process of transformation. Yet history has repeatedly demonstrated that these environmental changes have implications that affect the core of the organization's activity. Hence, response to these changes is not discretionary; it is a matter of managerial necessity and organizational survival.

Appearance has much to do with whether or not a manager recognizes an issue as being significant. If a matter appears to be market-related, it will probably interest a marketing manager; if it is finance-related, a financial executive will show some interest; if it relates to employees, a personnel manager may perceive the significance of the issue. But who perceives the overall importance of social change? Too often there is no one who recognizes the indicators of basic social change. Yet, repeatedly, technical and managerial problems arise that, in retrospect, are manifestations of more fundamental social change. In most cases, such change could have been identified and responses planned long before they became pressing personnel, financial or marketing problems. In this broad context, the role of the institutional subsystem of the organization takes on a proactive as well as a reactive character. It is this subsystem of the organization that is entrusted with identifying elements of external change and assessing their impact on the firm before that impact becomes a reality at the technical or managerial levels.

The multidivisional firm has become the dominant corporate structure among large enterprises, replacing the previously dominant integrated firms that operated in only one or a few related business lines. The emergence of conglomerate organizations, with their related and unrelated operating divisions, raises the question of whether the organizational subsystems described above apply to diversified and conglomerate enterprises as well. In general, the organizational components discussed above only vary in minor ways in the multidivisional firm. Each division in such an organization has a technical subsystem that identifies its distinctive competence; an administrative subsystem performs the coordinating and resource procurement and distribution functions; at the least, the divisional manager performs some of the institutional subsystem functions in conjunction with either divisional public relations, public affairs, and legal staffs or with appropriate headquarters personnel. At the level of the multidivisional firms as a whole, there will certainly be an administrative subsystem that coordinates resource allocations among the divisions and an institutional subsystem that is concerned with the legitimacy of the entire multidivisional organization. In some diversified firms, it also appears that a special technical subsystem evolves at the corporate level that is concerned solely with the acquisition and management of financial resources for the entity as a whole, rather than simply coordinating resource allocations among divisions. For the sake of analyzing corporate responses to public issues, however, such a distinction does not appear to be a critical one.

Organizational History

An important aspect of understanding organizations as social systems involves the life history of the firm. Every organization undergoes evolutionary change over time. This life history of the firm is perhaps best illustrated by looking at the succession of chief executives.

In my study of the Aetna Life and Casualty Company,[8] for example, it was found that there were distinct patterns of chief executives. The first five executives of the company spanned the period 1848 to the 1950's and were descendents of the Aetna's founding families. Within this group, however, there were different orientations, some being lawyers and politicians (one was a U.S. Senator), others being skilled administrators or salesmen. In the late 1950's, the first professional manager was selected chief executive. At that time, the greatest challenges in the insurance business involved the emergence of group life insurance. Not surprisingly, the first professional manager to be chosen as Aetna chief executive was an actuary who had spent much of his career developing group life insurance

---

TABLE 1-1. ORGANIZATIONAL SUBSYSTEMS

(A) *Basic Organizational Model*

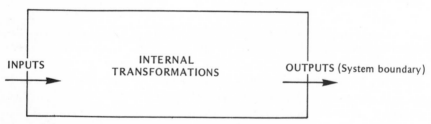

(B) *Basic Organizational Subsystems*

Technical Subsystem	Core activities of enterprise; internal transformation activities; usually the source of the entity's "distinctive competence."
Managerial (Administrative) Subsystem	Coordination of core activities, *and* procurement of input resources and distribution of output products.
Institutional Subsystem	Acquisition and maintenance of public support for the organization's existence and activities.

---

[8] James E. Post, *Risk and Response: Management and Social Change in the American Insurance Industry* (Lexington, Mass.: D. C. Heath, Inc., 1976).

TABLE 1-1. *Cont.*

(C) *Example: Manufacturing Enterprise*

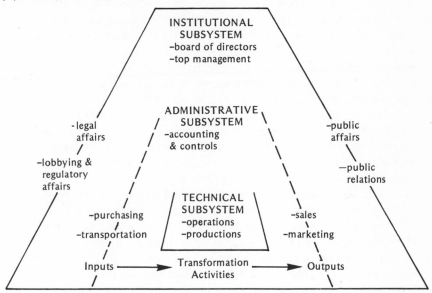

(D) *Example: Multidivisional Organization*

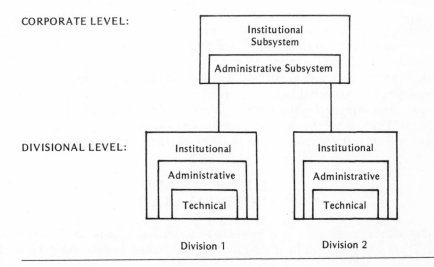

plans. This was a clear case of a representative from the technical core of the business emerging as chief executive by being especially well-suited to deal with key environmental change.

Of course, no chief executive does only technical work. As it turned out, the next chief executive was actually a triumvirate, one of the earliest chief executive offices in the industry. The triumvirate included a representative of the underwriting department, a manager who was primarily sales oriented, and a lawyer representing the institutional component of the firm. For several years this triumvirate functioned as a policy-making group, but out of this experience there re-emerged a single chief executive. In the eighth generation, it was the institutional representative, the lawyer, who emerged as the sole chief executive. This has now continued into a ninth generation, where the chief executive is also a lawyer. These recent selections reflect an awareness that the industry's greatest current problems involve regulatory and public policy change.

Another point of interest linking chief executives and organization systems involves intra-industry patterns of chief executives. Among specific industries, certain routes are known to be traditional paths to the chief executives' office. In the automobile industry, for example, it is rare to find a chief executive who is not an engineer. In banking and in the insurance business, chief executives are frequently lawyers or, occasionally, economists. Similar evidence exists in other industries, and suggests that the character of the firm is a function of the interaction among the component subsystems; the selection of chief executives in turn, is determined both by the character of the firm and the nature of external change.

The point of these observations is simple, yet important. In attempting to understand how, and why, particular firms respond to change in certain ways, it is necessary to appreciate the great diversity that exists even among enterprises in the same industry. While it is true that every organization has a technical, administrative, and institutional subsystem, the historical importance and prominence of those subsystems in shaping the broad strategic and public issues decisions in any organization is likely to depend on historical factors as well as current pressures. The selection of chief executives thereby serves as an illustration of the complex meshing of internal subsystem relationships and external environmental requirements that regularly occurs in all managed organizations.

ENVIRONMENTS AND ENVIRONMENTAL STATES

Organizations are parts or units of larger societal arrangements. Hence, it is appropriate to describe the organization as a social system and the rest of society as the environment of that system. To be sure, not all parts of society are relevant to the organization at the same time, or in the same way, but there are processes at work in the society that do influence and have effect on the enterprise. Perhaps the most important of these processes is the public policy process, which, in most Western democratic societies, is the mechanism through which a society expresses its collective goals and priorities and the strategies for achieving those goals. An understanding of the importance of the environment as a whole to specific organizations, whatever their character (profit, non-profit), size, or structure, is relatively new to management thinking. Managers are often inclined to think of the environment as consisting primarily of those elements that directly impinge on the organization's activities. Hence, managers are more likely to perceive the regulatory agency (e.g., OSHA) with which they must deal as a vital part of the environment rather than the underlying pressures and public interests that led to the formation of OSHA and supported its continued existence. Yet, an understanding of the underlying forces in the environment may be of greatest importance to the manager in terms of comprehending the function of OSHA regulations and assessing the support that exists for expanding or relaxing safety regulations.

Critical Environmental Contents

Our understanding of the environmental setting in which managed organizations operate can be carried beyond a general level by focusing on some of the critical contents in the environment. While not exhaustive, there are a number of specific contents that are especially important to the topic of corporate response to change.

First, there are *means* existing in the environment for transforming the features of the environment and these means are themselves a powerful source of social change. Both physical and social technologies, for example, are increasingly available for use in the alteration of systems. These technologies are an accelerating source of change in society, and breed additional environment-alteration means.[9] While physical technologies have been the more obvious and socially significant form insofar as the alteration of social systems has occurred to date, there is ample evidence that such "social technologies" as re-educative techniques, knowledge-building techniques, and psychological stimulation have immense potential for altering individuals, systems, and the environment of the future.

Second, *structures of authority and power* are also present in the en-

[9] See Robert Chin, "The Utility of Models of the Environments of Systems for Practitioners," in W. Bennis, K. Benne, R. Chin, and K. Corey, *The Planning of Change*, 3rd ed. (New York: Holt, Rinehart, & Winston, Inc., 1976) p. 109.

vironment and their existence is an important element for organizational systems. In one respect, the balance or ratio of power and influence among various systems and forces in the environment is defined for the organizational system. Yet, the ratios of influence confronting the organization's managers are neither stable nor unalterable. The character of the organization and the character of its management become crucial considerations in looking at the structure of authority and power. Does the management accept the existing configuration of power relations? Does it seek to alter that configuration? To what extent will it act to do so? One need only think of ITT's overt dealings with the Antitrust Division of the Justice Department in seeking approval for its merger activities or that same company's efforts to overthrow Salvadore Allende in Chile to recognize the extremes (but not necessarily the limits) of what some organizations will do to alter power configurations in the environment.

A third kind of content in the environment is the *resources* which supply the system with those requirements necessary for survival. If one thinks of the organization as the proverbial "black box" for a moment, it draws upon the environment for various resources which are the inputs into the black box. Some transformation of those inputs or resources occurs within the organization, reflecting the distinctive competence of the entity, and there emerges a set of outputs in the form of goods or services. Among the resources, of course, are those tangible materials and services required for production (e.g., the air which accepts the smoke or the water which carries away the liquid waste by-product of the transformation). That the structure of resource providers, and the configuration of costly and free resources can change, is obvious. As we shall see, when changes such as those signified by the commodities cartels occur, they can have a profound effect on the availability, price, and quality of resources on which the organizational system depends. Thus, in this regard as well as others, stability cannot be assumed to prevail.

Finally, there is an abundance of *information* in the environment existing in the form of events, symbols, and signals. Some of this information will never come to the attention of managers in the enterprise because it needs to be translated or organized in some useful and comprehensible fashion. Other information will be studiously ignored because it does not fit the existing model of what is relevant and important to the organization or to the occupants of particular management positions.

Much has been written about the need for better information systems, systems which are capable of identifying relevant data, trends, and events and decoding them for management use. Indeed, so refined has this argument become that theorists now talk of modifying and refining corporate strategies in response to "weak signals" as well as strong signals and sharply delineated trends.[10] In the field of study that is concerned with the abilities and capacities of an organization to respond to environmental change, information is the most sancrosanct of concepts, and the management message is "more and better"—more information and better analysis of what it means. Whether or not the maxim is valid, it is sufficient to note that information, along with resources, power and authority, and the technologies for system transformation are basic contents of the managerial environment. How they are used in practice, and in response to environmental change will be explored in the remainder of this book.

Environmental States

It is clear that the environment is not static nor is it without a differential impact on different organizations. Hence, it is appropriate to think in terms of various environmental states or conditions, ranging from relatively stable and placid environments to those which are relatively unstable and turbulent. Much has been written about environmental states at a theoretical level,[11] some of which can be usefully introduced to the reader of this book as background toward better understanding external (or environmental) change and the ways organizations can and do respond to it. For our purposes, we will describe environmental states as they actually exist, recognizing that there may be considerable difference between what actually exists (objective environment) and what is believed to exist by managers (perceived environment).[12]

If one were to study the history of the American insurance industry, he would note that insurers of the colonial period operated as independent entrepreneurs on the waterfronts of Boston, New York, Hartford, and Baltimore. Shipowners would approach each underwriter as to the cost of bearing a portion of the risk of loss of the ship or its cargo at sea. Each insurer would make his estimate of the probabilities of loss and set a price for accepting some portion of the value of the cargo and ship. For many years, there was no collaboration among the independent underwriters on the waterfront, each operating separately amidst a changing field of actors. The environment for each insurer was largely placid, with no dominant figures shaping the local market. But it was also an environment in which change was randomized, ships being lost and cargoes de-

[10] H. I. Ansoff, "Strategic Responses to Weak Signals," *California Management Review*, Vol. XIX, No. 2 (1977)

[11] Two classic articles in this area are F. E. Emery and E. L. Trist, "The Causal Texture of Organizational Environments," Human Relations, Vol. 18 (1965) pp. 21–32, and Shirley Terreberry, "The Evolution of Organizational Environments," *Administrative Science Quarterly* Vol. 12 (1968) pp. 590–613.

[12] This is discussed further in Chapter 12.

stroyed without much warning. The optimal strategy and tactic for each underwriter then, was to do the best job of estimating the seaworthiness of the ships, the reputation and competence of the captain, and the probability of pirates, hurricanes, or other threats to marine commerce. Success for the insurer was attributable in part to chance and in part to the competitive wisdom born of trial-and-error learning.

In time, the independent insurance underwriters gave way to syndicates or groups of insurers who collectively agreed to insure person or property against specified types of risk. Connections began to form among parts of the competitive environment and certain syndicates began to compete regularly against one another for particular types of business. The environment was beginning to develop more structure; actors were clustering together and the concept of distinctive competence emerged as a basis for distinguishing among those clusters of insurers. Hence, some syndicates remained exclusive writers of marine insurance coverage; others specialized in fire insurance; still others restricted their business to life insurance. Competition for clients was no longer from any source (randomized competition) but from a predictable group of competitors (clustered competition). From the *placid, randomized environment* of the colonial waterfront, the insurer of the mid-1800's faced a *placid* but *clustered competitive environment.*

Over time, the clustering of insurers evolved from syndicates of independent insurers into integrated organizations or insurance companies. Fire insurance companies began to join with marine insurers and form companies that competed in several lines of the insurance business. Later on, life insurers also began to sell health insurance. This industry-wide clustering of companies and lines of business was coupled with the organizational evolution of the hierarchical insurance company. In time, this continued clustering and evolution created still another distinct environmental state, one which is described as *disturbed* and *reactive.*

When actors in an environment begin to demonstrate internal organizational change, one organization loses its capacity to know what the next movement of other organizations will be. In effect, they may not be playing the same game any longer. The decision of a firm to diversify into new product markets, to set out on a high investment research and development program, or to reorganize its sale activities are simple illustrations of this phenomenon. In such an environment, managers in one organization increasingly focus on the kinds of interactions other entities in the environment have with one another. A favorite example of this phenomenon involved the traditional battle between the "big eastern stock insurers" and the "small midwestern mutual insurers" during the 1880's and 1890's. Residents of midwestern states accused eastern insurers of exploiting policyholders by taking their premium payments and then refusing to pay legitimate claims. As a defensive measure, mutual (policyholder owned) insurers were created in many midwestern cities and towns by local residents. The eastern insurers retaliated with vigorous competitive pressure. But the local insurers went one step further, getting state legislatures to impose a tax on premiums paid to stock insurers (the eastern companies) while exempting mutual insurance companies (the local companies). This improved the local companies' competitive position and preserved their existence. Thereafter, no insurance company (and certainly no eastern stock insurer) ever allowed itself to operate in a state where it did not have a representative (elected, lobbyist, or both) to watch out for its interest![13]

Environments of great complexity are often referred to as turbulent in nature. More precisely, a *turbulent environment* is one in which the organization is confronted by a field of forces, including many clusters and systems, each with its own dynamics, and interacting with other dynamic processes arising from the environment itself, as well as from the interactive forces of the multiple systems.[14] Both the structures and the dynamics change rapidly, and change can emerge from any part of the environment, not only from the traditional or known clusters. The organization in such a state is a bit like the rudderless raft in stormy seas: it is at the mercy of the elements. The instability and uncertainty inherent in such a situation calls for several types of action. First, managers may emphasize the role of the rudder—i.e., some means by which managers may keep the organization "on course," pursuant to strategy and consistent with the organization's mission. Second, attention and energy may be given to bringing about more stability in the environment (e.g., forming coalitions of similar organizations, such as trade associations) and to the process of managing change and environmental uncertainty.

In a turbulent environment, it is likely that there will be a series of revolutions in the structure and organization of environmental contents. Because these are commonplace in a turbulent state, a premium is placed on organizational responsiveness to change. Traditional channels and relationships break down, new ones arise, and still others are in the process of emergence. As Robert Chin has noted:

> These interactions, which are the essence of the complex and turbulent environment, do not appear to have the characteristics of steady-state or even stable relationships. The step-jumps in the equilibrium and the structures of the systems forming the environment interrelate with more and more distant systems, interpenetrating with more and more layers of the environment.[15]

[13] Spencer Kimball, *Insurance and Public Policy: A Study in the Legal Implementation of Social and Economic Public Policy, Based on Wisconsin Records, 1834–1959* (Madison, Wis.: University of Wisconsin Press, 1960).

[14] See Chin, *op. cit.*, p. 107.

[15] *Ibid.*

TABLE 1-2. ENVIRONMENTAL STATES

ENVIRONMENTAL STATE	CHARACTERISTICS	ORGANIZATIONAL BEHAVIOR
Placid, with randomized change	No connections among elements in the environment. Impacts on the organization are random in time, place, and effects.	Optimal approach is to "do one's best" by reacting to change as quickly as possible. Tactics dominate activity. No concept of strategy. Trial and error learning.
Placid environment, with clustered activity and change	Elements in the environment begin to join and have predictable probable effects. Different types of institutions (e.g., competitors) begin to evolve.	Organization can predict change in the environment. Concept of strategy thereby emerges; difference between strategy and tactics is understood. Notion of "distinctive competence" develops within organizations.
Disturbed environment of clustered and interlinked elements	Elements in environment have formed institutional systems of many types. Systems have, in turn, become interlinked clusters. Major structural forms (e.g., oligopolies) develop.	Fewer organizations create more need to accurately anticipate change. Strategy grows in importance; tactics need more coordination to implement strategy. Internal organizational changes are made to better serve strategy.
Turbulent environment of many clusters and many systems	Elements and systems in the environment are creating multiple processes of interaction. Processes as well as actors are now interactive. Exponential increases in dynamic environmental change.	Much greater environmental uncertainty exists while need for certainty grows. More difficult to stabilize environment by individual action; need grows to join in coalitions with other industry and organizational entities.
Turbulent environment which is articulated by some actors	Special actors develop distinctive competence as interpreters of dynamic environmental change.	Decision-making under uncertainty creates new reliance on interpreters of change and early warning systems.

In more practical terms, the larger and more complex the firm's relationships, the more extensive its interpenetration and the more potentially turbulent its environment.

Chin has gone on to note another possible state of the environment, one in which the mechanisms that organize, channel, and process turbulent forces and information about them for the system are identified. He calls such a state an *"articulated turbulent environment"* and its central feature is the existence of system components that focus upon change for the benefit of all units within the social system. The mass media, for example, become articulators of environmental turbulence, indicating its sources, texture, and character. So too can early warning systems, social indicators, intelligence activities, and technical specialists provide the specialized knowledge and interpretation of change and turbulence that permits the organization to be successfully navigated by its managers. If one looks at the roles of trade associations in general, and those in the insurance industry in particular, to continue our example, it is obvious that those associations perform many of the articulating functions to which Chin has referred. Trade associations are often created during periods of special turbulence for an industry and have become part of the industry landscape in insurance as well as in home appliances, pharmaceuticals, manufacturers in general, and countless other clusters of firms and industries.[16] More importantly, they are only a small part of the institutional fabric that has been created to help managers manage under conditions of increasing environmental uncertainty.

APPROACHES TO CHANGING
ENVIRONMENTAL RELATIONSHIPS

Given some understanding of how the environment is organized and what it consists of, we can hypothesize three basic approaches to change in the organization/environment relationship.[17] (1) Change the characteristics of the environment. This involves some direct action to alter or modify features of the environment either directly by the organization or by utilizing other systems in the environment. (2) Change the characteristics or factors within the organization such as its awareness, perceptions, and images of the environment, its functions, or its internal responsiveness to the changing environment. (3) Change the intersystem relationships between the or-

---

[16] According to the Gale Research Company survey, there were 2914 trade, business, and commercial associations to help serve this need in 1976. See *Encyclopedia of Associations*, 11th ed., Margaret Fisk, editor, Vol. 1 (Detroit, Mich.: Gale Research Co., 1977).

[17] Russell Ackoff, *Redesigning the Future* (New York: John Wiley & Sons, 1974) identifies a four-model approach that is similar. According to Ackoff, the four behavior models are inactive, preactive, reactive, and proactive.

ganization and its environment by altering the boundary between them, establishing direct links between features of the environment and parts of the organization, in order to regulate, stabilize, and manage the channels of interaction between the system and the environment, or by lessening the disjunctive connections between the system and the environment. These approaches flow logically from the nature of the discussion about the relationship between the organizational system and its environment. As we shall see in succeeding chapters, these approaches are also confirmed by empirical observation and research; hence, they describe in abstract terms the basic patterns of corporate response to change which the remainder of this book discusses in greater factual detail.

chapter
two

the management
of public issues

PUBLIC ISSUES AND
THEIR LIFE CYCLE

The manner in which all organizations, but especially large corporations, respond to change in the social environment is a matter of great public concern as well as managerial concern. Because of their size and importance to modern economies, large corporations—or "megacorporations" as Phillip Blumberg[1] has called them—are especially deserving of critical analysis by managers and the public alike. The need for such a critique is well recognized in industrialized nations and is reflected in the great number of public issues which involve some degree of corporate/societal conflict. Even in developing nations, where the desire for corporate presence by governments may

[1] Phillip Blumberg, *The Mega Corporation in American Society* (Englewood Cliffs, N.J.: Prentice-Hall, Inc., 1976).

21

mute a serious consideration of the negative impacts of such presence, there has been a growing concern about the pace, process, and direction of development and change.

Large corporations are neither the malevolent Leviathans their severest critics would have us believe, nor are they the benign and gentle benefactors of society their staunchest advocates would have us believe. In truth, they neither control, nor are they completely controlled by, the social environment in which they operate. It is true that corporations influence society, and sometimes in dramatic ways, but they are also influenced—and in dramatic and important ways—by society. What is obvious, but necessary to state explicitly, is that corporations and the environment are parts of a complex interactive system, in which each can and does have important effects on the other.

As the environment changes, its features present to organizations of all sizes and purposes a variety of opportunities, threats, and requirements. The large corporation may face more of these changes, and hence, more opportunities, threats, and requirements than its smaller counterparts, but organizations of whatever size and purpose exist in a general atmosphere that makes external change relevant to them. Out of this systemic interaction of the enterprise and the environment springs the essential need for managers to be capable of managing public issues. But how is that to be accomplished? What is required to effectively manage an organization which is frequently and even continuously buffeted by new kinds of public issues? At the least, effective management depends on an understanding of what is to be managed. Hence, our initial concern in this chapter is with the concept of what constitutes a *public issue.*

Public Issues Life Cycle

Public issues generally appear to pass through a series of phases which, because of their natural evolution, can be treated as a life cycle. Although an issue may not become obvious to us until it is highly politicized and on the verge of legislative action, there is in fact a long gestation period during which time much activity has to occur to make the issue a truly public one. Today, there are many studies of particular issues that have both succeeded and failed in reaching the legislative phase of development. Drawing from these studies, as well as from the body of more than 50 cases underlying this book, we have been able to identify and clarify four distinct stages in the life cycle of a public issue.

Public issues begin their gestation when the expectations of a segment of the public about the performance of a particular firm or industry are not met. This may take a variety of forms, ranging from small groups of local residents objecting to the odor or smoke from a local manufacturing facility to the concern of a person or group arising from their knowledge of a particular kind of corporate performance in some other part of the world. The point is that we do not know what sparks public concern with a particular issue, but we do know that changing public expectations of corporate performance are the key to the growth in absolute numbers of public issues facing companies.[2] Once a gap develops between the actual performance of a corporation and public expectations about what that performance should be, the seeds of another public issue have been sown.

Since the 1960's, individuals and public action groups have learned a great deal about the development of public issues. Indeed, in public action groups in the United States and Europe, there literally exist "managers" of public issues whose responsibility within their organization is to make the issue "happen." Their management tools are the skills of media management, publicity, confrontation, and building public support for holding organizations to new, and presumably higher, levels of performance. If they are successful, their campaigns will generate public pressure against the enterprise or industry in the hope of stimulating the entity to change its behavior. Frequently, such tactics succeed. It is a cliche of sorts, but it is true that "pressure motivates!"

The period of changing social expectations may extend over many months or even years. The point at which the second phase in the life cycle is reached occurs when these new expectations become successfully politicized. It takes the interested citizens and public action groups a long time to generate political interest in some issues, and in many cases it never happens at all, but if political actors such as representatives, Senators, state legislators, regulatory personnel, or even candidates for political office become interested in the issue and committed to some action thereon, the issue will clearly have moved into the political phase of its life history. There is a general impression that one gets from looking at public issues since the mid-1960's that there is more politicalization of social issues than was true in the 1950's, for example, and that politicalization is occurring at much faster rates. Perhaps it is the prevailing political fashion of having attractive candidates searching for issues on which to campaign that has contributed to this state of affairs. It is also possible that society in general has simply become more "issue conscious" than in the past, and political figures are simply responding to that new consciousness. Whatever the case, it seems clear that the character of a public issue changes as it becomes politicized.

The political phase of the life cycle can also be lengthy in its dura-

[2] In my study of the insurance industry, for example, it was found that a large multiple line insurer faced an agenda of more than 250 distinct public issues in 1972. A similar firm would have faced about 100 public issues in 1960, and only about 50 public issues in 1950. The reasons for this increase are discussed in Post, *Risk and Response: Management and Social Change in the American Insurance Industry* (Lexington, Mass.: D. C. Heath, Inc., 1976).

tion. During this time, political actors begin the process of devising a strategy to shape the appropriate legislative context for the issue. In the modern world of state and federal legislative dealings, this can take almost an infinite number of specific forms, reflecting all of the power, personality, and peccadillos of the political cast of characters.[3] Issues such as national health insurance, creation of a consumer protection agency, and federal chartering of corporations have each been in the political phase of the life cycle for nearly a decade or more, with actual legislation always seeming to hinge on unstable political coalitions or the priority given to other, more pressing political issues (e.g., energy). The intricacies of this phase are manifold and are generally beyond the scope of this book. At the least, however, it is vitally important that managers who are entrusted with guiding organizations of any type be sensitive to the possibilities and pitfalls that exist in the pre-legislation phase of a public issue. Just as a knowledge of business law is important for businessmen in order to make them better clients, so too is a knowledge of the public policy process essential for a manager if he is to be more than a prisoner of the company's lawyers and lobbyists. To paraphrase a well-known legal quotation, public policy is too important to be left to the lobbyists!

The third phase of the life cycle is a legislative phase, which generally refers to that period of time surrounding the enactment of legislation pertaining to the public issue and the implementation thereof. This is clearly a turning point in the life cycle (proponents might say the "high point"), but the matter is by no means settled. The actual implementation of the legislative mandate must still occur and that implementation is a matter often subject to considerable interpretation and bargaining. Nevertheless, once the legislative phase has been reached, the ability of management to delay, deflect, or prevent enactment of a particular legislative approach has generally passed. At this point, the appropriate management response is preparation for compliance with the publicly legitimized new set of social expectations. In effect, the rules of the game have been changed and it is the responsibility of managers to prepare themselves to play by the new rules.

The final phase of the public issues life cycle is a litigation phase. Between the enactment of legislation and the litigation phase there occurs a period of time when the exact terms of implementing the legislative objectives are worked out by the administrative agency or other arm of government to which enforcement is entrusted. During this period, there may be negotiations between the industry and the agency on enforcement standards (e.g., OSHA) or timetables for meeting new requirements (EPA and auto emissions). There are many practical management issues to be

---

[3] An excellent introduction to this complexity can be drawn from Eric Redman, *The Dance of Legislation* (New York: Simon and Schuster, 1973).

ironed out and resolved during this period, and it is rare that the agency officials and industry's managers will reach complete consensus on standards, requirements, or compliance. Thus, the potential for litigation inevitably develops. On such matters as equal employment opportunity, environmental protection, and product safety practices, litigation has been frequent and often highly publicized. The decision of a government agency to litigate a case may depend on a number of factors, including the state of the judicial law, the agency's need for a precedent-setting case, and so forth. For the manager, the most significant point is that once a public issue reaches the litigation stage, the opportunities for flexible responses to the underlying social expectations are severely limited. The firm that regularly allows public issues to reach the litigation phase is not a well-managed firm; it is the victim of management by lawyers.(See Table 2-1.)

CORPORATE RESPONSIVENESS TO CHANGE

There are many managerial costs associated with the failure to effectively manage the agenda of public issues facing a firm. Perhaps the most important of these costs is the loss of decision-making discretion. It is absolutely clear that as a public issue evolves through the four stages of the life cycle, the amount of discretion that organizations and their managers have in dealing with the substantive issue decreases. Consider a simple example. If a manufacturer introduces a new product into the market and a number of these items fail to perform as expected, the buyers have several options. They may pressure the manufacturer to return the money they spent, or to correct the defect, or to replace the defective item with one that works properly. The seller, for its part, has a variety of options in dealing with the dissatisfied customer and the defective product. At this point, there is a gap between the actual performance of the manufacturer, as reflected in the defective product, and the customer's expectations. More importantly, the firm's management has great discretion in dealing with the public issue.

If the manufacturer fails to close the gap, however, the irate customer may seek redress in a variety of ways, ranging from lawsuits to letters to congressmen. If the issue becomes politicized, various proposals will surely emerge as possible ways to resolve the defective products issue. It is clear, however, that the range of publicly acceptable resolutions for the issue will be smaller than was true before the issue was politicized. And, even if the manufacturer can still settle the claim with the individual customer, there exists the real likelihood of the issue having developed a life of its own as political actors develop an interest in it. Further loss of discretion occurs as the legislation and litigation phases evolve.

There are several practical implications flowing from the loss of

TABLE 2-1. PUBLIC ISSUES LIFE CYCLE

	PHASE I Changing Public Expectations→	II Political Controversy→	III Development of Legislation→	IV Government Litigation
EXAMPLES				
Civil Rights	1954–60	1960 (presidential campaign issue)	1964 (Civil Rights Act)	1970's (EEOC litigation backlog)
Environmental Protection	1963 (Rachel Carson *Silent Spring*)	1967 (campaign issue; political "sides" developing)	1970 (EPA established)	1970's (Tighter standards; negotiated or court-ordered settlements; nearly 300 cases in Federal courts)
Consumer Protection	1964 (Ralph Nader, *Unsafe at Any Speed*)	1968 (Presidential Consumer Affairs Advisor; proposed legislation)	1972 (Consumer Product Safety Act)	

managerial discretion. First, a loss of discretion seriously reduces the decision-making authority and power that managers possess. It has been widely acknowledged that creative and aggressive managers are often frustrated in industries that operate within an extensive regulatory system. The greater the web of external rules and restrictions, the more limited the opportunities for changing the practices, procedures, and substance of an organization's activities. The second implication is that anticipatory managerial action to deal with changing expectations is generally preferable to reactive managerial action. The enterprise that awaits legislation before dealing with the underlying public expectations will ultimately have fewer options in dealing with the issue. It is true that there may be particular instances where such a stonewalling or footdragging approach seems reasonable, but our research has not discovered a single case in which a company successfully used such an approach for long periods or with respect to many public issues. The third practical implication flowing from the loss of managerial discretion that accompanies the public issues life cycle is that a real need exists for the development of tools for anticipatory management activity.[4] The nature of those tools depends, however, on the approach to corporate responsiveness that the management wishes to adopt.

Corporate Response Process

In Chapter 1 (pages 5–6), it was pointed out that since the mid-1960's, two basic approaches have developed among managed organizations for coping with change. One has emphasized fighting the fires of public pressure, while the other has assumed that it is possible for managers to think about public issues before they move too far along the public issues life cycle. Because these represent very distinct management approaches toward the external environment, there is a need for us to examine these approaches more closely.

There is general agreement among researchers and practitioners that the *corporate response process* involves three basic stages.[5] There is an initial need for some awareness of the issue; there is the need for development of an organizational commitment to respond to the issue; and there is the need for a mechanism to select specific responses and see to their implementation. (See Table 2-2). There is some disagreement however, as to how that response process actually operates in specific organizational situations.

TABLE 2-2. THE CORPORATE RESPONSE PROCESS

STAGE 1   AWARENESS OR COGNIZANCE OF PUBLIC ISSUE
This can be accomplished through external public pressure and legal change or through management scanning for new public issues.

STAGE 2   COMMITMENT TO ACTION
Organizational commitment may develop from either "bottom up" pressures for policy endorsement of coping practices, or, from "top down" policy commitment of senior management.

STAGE 3   SELECTION AND IMPLEMENTATION OF RESPONSE
Organization must determine appropriate action response (including subsystem bargaining) and assign management responsibility for implementation of the chosen action.

---

[4] See Lee E. Preston and James E. Post, *Private Management and Public Policy* (Englewood Cliffs, N.J.: Prentice-Hall, Inc., 1975) Chapters 8 and 9.

[5] Among those whose research confirms this general pattern are Robert Ackerman and Raymond Bauer, *Corporate Social Responsiveness: The Modern Dilemma* (Reston, Va.: Reston Publishing Company, 1976); K. Davis and R. Blomstron, *Business and Society: Environment and Responsibility* (New York: McGraw-Hill, Inc., 1975); Preston and Post, *op. cit.*; G. Steiner, *Business and Society* (New York: Random House, Inc., 1975); and D. Votaw and S. P. Sethi, *The Corporate Dilemma* (Englewood Cliffs, N.J.: Prentice-Hall Inc., 1974).

One view takes as its starting point the proposition that social issues are simply environmental factors to be considered by management when forming a business strategy. A proponent of this view is Robert Ackerman,[6] who found that corporate responsiveness to change involved three distinct phases: (1) the chief executive recognizes the issue to be important and perceives the need for a company policy; (2) the Chief Executive Officer (CEO) appoints specialists to coordinate activities and generate information; and (3) efforts are made to institutionalize the policy by working it into the resource allocation and reward systems of the firm. Edwin Murray, Jr., in a follow-up study of this *business strategy model*,[7] confirmed the general pattern identified by Ackerman, but also recognized that the second stage involved two parts; one involves a period of technical learning about the problem by the specialists; the other involves "administrative learning" about the actual working of the organization. The point that Murray identified emphasizes a point made in Chapter One, namely, that there is a need for new managers to recognize the prevailing power relationships among organizational subsystems and the importance of the organization's previous history in determining current responses to change. More importantly, both the Ackerman and Murray studies assume that the external change occurs first, and that the firm's management has ample opportunity to exercise discretion in the selection of responses to the issue.

An alternative view of management responses was articulated by Votaw and Sethi in an early, seminal piece on the need for a new corporate response to changing social expectations.[8] Their study focused on management responses to immediate pressures ("pickets at the plant gate") and identified three types of tactical responses to pressure: public relations, legalistic, and bargaining. All these tactics, according to Votaw and Sethi, are fire fighting techniques for "cooling off" hostile pressure groups. In terms of the corporate response process, this *pressure-response model* assumes that management commitment occurs incrementally as a series of particular actions are taken in response to specific social pressures. Thus management policy is a result of management practice; actions define commitment when issues are social in nature because managers prefer not to systematically think about such matters in advance. It is a more refined statement of a point mentioned in Chapter One, namely, "pressure motivates!"

[6] R. Ackerman, "How Companies Respond to Social Demands," *Harvard Business Review* (July–August 1973) pp. 88–98.
[7] Edwin A. Murray, Jr., "The Social Response Process in Commercial Banks: An Empirical Investigation," *Academy of Management Review* (July 1976) pp. 5–15.
[8] D. Votaw and S. P. Sethi, "Do We Need a New Corporate Response," reprinted in Votaw and Sethi, *The Corporate Dilemma, op. cit.*

The business strategy and pressure response models differ not only in their assumptions about managements' willingness to think about public issues before the pickets are at the plant gate, but also in the specific order in which the three stages of the response process occur. In the business strategy model, corporate responsiveness occurs by a sequential passing from identification to commitment to implementation. Votaw and Sethi argue, however, that what actually occurs in practice is that pressures force the organization to respond with short-term reactions; policy is formed, if at all, only after a series of actions and practices have created decision-making precedents within the organization. In most organizations, old habits—and precedents from past decisions—are difficult to change. Hence, when management finally recognizes the need for policy development, one cost of implementing the new policy is the organizational cost associated with changing the rules of the game by which personnel operate. Cognizance usually occurs when action is also taking place—i.e., management recognizes the issue or problem at the same time it is being severely pressured to respond to it.

Between the two extreme situations which these models define, there is probably a considerable middle ground where pre-existing corporate policy and current managerial practice interact to redefine both the policy and acceptable practices. It should not surprise us to find that in many organizational settings, there is a continuing tension between the managerial desire to create policy in the traditional "top down" manner and the pressure of immediate circumstances that demands immediate "bottom up" responses.

The business strategy and pressure response models also assume that there are different types of stimuli prompting the organization to respond to change. It has been suggested that all organizational behavior is motivated by three basic types of stimuli, namely, legal compulsion, public pressure, or organizational (management) initiative.[9] The business strategy model, of course, emphasizes managerial initiative and the values of the chief executive as motivators of corporate behavior. In this view, commitment to social policy becomes a manifestation of the managerial identification of the issue and a subsequent decision to make a commitment to do something about it. The pressure response model, on the other hand, argues that legal compulsion and the pressure of external publics are the key motivators of corporate response to public issues. Left to their own devices, management's preference would be to ignore social demands whenever possible, responding only when required to do so by law and/or events. Commitment occurs, if at all, only after a set of action responses have taken place.

[9] G. P. Hinckley and James E. Post, "The Performance of Corporate Responsibility," in Sethi, ed., The Unstable Ground (Los Angeles: Melville Publishing Co., 1974).

Do Organizations Learn?

It is a basic assumption of most business school courses that firms which fail to make proper decisions, and thereby suffer from these failures, learn to make better decisions as a result. Certainly it is assumed that managers who study those failures can learn something from them that is transferable to their own organization by analogy. In practice, numerous courses are predicated on this assumption and an entire school of thought about how to teach management has evolved from the case/analogy approach.

Factual evidence supports both of the responsiveness models discussed in the preceding section. There are countless cases of firms responding to pressure[10] and more than a few in which a firm's management has anticipated external change.[11] Since factual evidence does support both views, an important question is raised about whether, or to what extent, an organization will be consistent in its response to a succession of social issues.

In order to explore this question of organizational learning, one of our research studies focused on the Polaroid Corporation's response to the issue of equal employment opportunity for women.[12] Polaroid was an appropriate case for study since it had previously exhibited behavior that is considered to be an outstanding example of one or another of the models. Its response to the demands for increased minority employment, for example, is an often-cited example of corporate forethought; its response to the issue of investment in South Africa, on the other hand, is well-known as a classic case of response under pressure. The manner in which Polaroid's management responded to the demands for equal opportunity for women can be assessed from these alternative perspectives and an analysis of the process that evolved with regard to the women's issue permits some conclusions to be drawn about organizational learning and corporate responsiveness.

RESPONSIVENESS AND ORGANIZATIONAL LEARNING: POLAROID CORPORATION

An in-depth examination of the interaction between the management at Polaroid Corporation and a coalition of women's groups within the com-

[10] One of the best collections of cases from this perspective is S. P. Sethi's, *Up Against the Corporate Wall*, 3rd edition (Englewood Cliffs, N.J.: Prentice-Hall, Inc., 1977).

[11] A good selection of cases from the manager's perspective, which includes a number of "successes" in the process of response is Ackerman and Bauer's *Corporate Social Responsiveness: The Modern Dilemma, op. cit.*

[12] This study was undertaken by the author and Marilyn Mellis. The following discussion is drawn in part from James E. Post and Marilyn Mellis, "Corporate Responsiveness and Organizational Learning," *California Management Review* (Winter 1978).

pany from 1968 to 1972 on the issue of equal employment opportunity highlights several important aspects of the responsiveness process. Beginning in the mid-1960's, the company was an acknowledged leader in the corporate promotion of equal employment opportunities for minorities. The company's commitment to improving opportunities for minority group members included both internal job-enhancement programs and external community-oriented training programs.[13] The extension of equal employment opportunity to women occurred, however, not as an extension of programs originally aimed at minorities, but rather as the result of a separate line of events.

An article in the company's newspaper in 1969 describing the experience of two women who were concerned about their dual career-family responsibilities attracted the interest of other women at Polaroid who were dealing with the same issue. A group of interested women, blue collar and professional, began to meet regularly to share their feelings about their dual sets of responsibilities.

The group's initial dealings with Polaroid management came when the company established personnel subcommittees to advise management on such employment issues as pensions and retirement. Management also decided to form a subcommittee on women, but ironically, no women were appointed to it. The women complained and a concession was made—the group became the corporate subcommittee on women, scheduled to meet occasionally with a company officer. The "subcommittee" made no great advances on its own, but did achieve one concession in response to the E.E.O.C.'s 1969 *Sex Discrimination Guidelines*. A six-week leave of absence without pay was granted to women for the purpose of childbearing. Interestingly, the women's subcommittee met from the spring of 1970 to the fall of 1971, with its only significant accomplishment coming as the result of legal pressures from the E.E.O.C. Guidelines.

During this period, other women at Polaroid began to act. One woman split off from the original group and began to organize women in the production department. Another group of six professional and nonprofessional women from all areas of the company also joined together, with the intention of setting specific goals and bargaining for change. Meeting in the evenings, they hired an outside consultant for six weeks to help them work on team building and to assist in setting achievable goals. Although there was some fear that they might lose their jobs, each of these women made the commitment to fight until their goals were taken seriously by management. Their objectives were to change the structure of the benefits plans and develop an affirmative action program for women.

Prior to this time, the Civil Rights Act of 1964 had been enacted and the Equal Employment Opportunities Commission had been created.

---

[13] H. M. Morgan, "A Look Back: When Three Businesses Responded to the Urban Crisis, What Happened?" *Journal of Contemporary Business*, Vol. 3, No. 2 (Spring 1974) pp. 61–77.

President Johnson had issued Executive Order 11246 (1965) regarding anti-discrimination efforts and the amendment that included women (1967). The concept of affirmative action for government contractors (which included Polaroid) had been conceived, but guidelines and sanctions had not yet been drawn up and implementation was primarily voluntary. At Polaroid, management had not ignored the unrest among women in the company, but neither had they seriously dealt with the women as a group being subjected to discriminatory practices.

The three women's groups kept sending memos to management, outlining grievances, and identifying desired changes. In response to this influx of complaints, a manager was appointed to act as a liaison between management and the women's groups. Following this, and with the company's support, the women organized into five task forces, each of which was to concentrate on a single area and report its findings to management.

Polaroid's decision to appoint a management liaison served to provide the groups with organizational legitimacy. Presumably the liaison officer would serve to structure the interaction between the women and the company and funnel complaints and grievances through a "routine" channel. The formation of research and action "task forces," however, operated to prevent any "cooling off" of pressures for which Polaroid management might otherwise have hoped. Each of the task forces was charged with diagnosing problems, gathering and analyzing information, and recommending changes to Polaroid management. The activities and success of each group merit some specific mention.

Task Force No. 1—The Status of Women. Using data provided by the personnel department and the company's computer capabilities, this task force analyzed the position of women in terms of jobs and job families, pay, seniority, and so forth. They found that women were over-represented in the lowest level of exempt and non-exempt jobs and that in the non-professional areas, women tended to enter hand assembly or secretarial positions, while men entered the more upwardly mobile areas of machine operations and skilled trades. In professional areas, women were virtually non-existent in department and senior management jobs, line production positions, and the sales force.[14] Moreover, the average seniority for women was higher than or equal to that for men, a fact that helped dispel the myth of high female turnover.

Task Force No. 2—Corporate Policies. This group made some immediate gains. The wording in the company policy book was changed to say "he/she, people, the employee, etc."; job titles were desexed in order to

[14] S. C. Ells, "How Polaroid Gave Women the Kind of Affirmative Action They Wanted," *Management Review* (November 1973) pp. 11–15.

eliminate the assumption that particular jobs were only appropriate for members of one sex; application forms were altered to eliminate questions that might be interpreted differently for men and women (e.g., number of dependents—a large family would be seen as a sign of stability for a man, but as an indication of high rate of absenteeism for a woman).

Task Force No. 2 also effected a change in Polaroid's benefits policy. The revised *E.E.O.C. Guidelines of 1972* played a role in bringing about change. Although the Guidelines were not legally binding, their existence gave the women credibility and support. Childbearing was treated as an incapacitating illness and obstetric coverage for all female employees (single or married) was upgraded to match the benefits given to married female employees and wives of male employees. To this point management appeared to be responding willingly to the demands generated from within the organization. In retrospect, it is clear that the major issues in the overall drive for women's employment equality were yet to come.

Task Force No. 3—Company Practices. This task force revealed that the assignment of new employees to entry level jobs was perpetuating sex discrimination. If a male and female with similar backgrounds and a high school degree applied for employment at Polaroid, the Personnel Department would sex-separate them from the start. Men would be put in positions leading to jobs as crew chiefs or as semi-skilled operators; women would be started off as hand assemblers or, if qualified, as clerk/typists. From the first day on the job, a woman would be earning 10–15% less than her male counterpart. This practice was perpetuated by a system of promotion through job families. Sixteen job families were found to be predominantly occupied by men, while only three were predominantly for women.

Task Force No. 4—Educational Awareness. Management "consciousness raising" sessions for interested departments throughout the company were run by women using role playing, discussion groups and questionnaires in an effort to heighten male employees' knowledge of women's low status within the company. These efforts served to get tradespeople, plant engineers, and managers talking about the issues, an action designed to build a broader base of support within the company. This base, it was felt, would continue to facilitate a lowering of barriers and an improvement of opportunities throughout the firm.

Task Force No. 5—Company Compliance with Equal Opportunity Legislation. This task force was to coordinate the findings of the other groups in response to the issuance of *Revised Order 4* by the Office of Federal Contract Compliance (O.F.C.C.) in 1971 by writing a comprehensive Affirmative Action Plan. In addition to a current utilization analysis, the group prepared numerical goals and timetables for the achievement of goals. Means for achieving these objectives were considered in detail and included promotion, training, hiring, and transfers. Plans were developed for hiring women from the outside as well as promoting from within for managerial and professional positions and skilled trade jobs.

Although successful in achieving management compliance with the E.E.O.C. Guidelines of 1969 and 1972, the women met a roadblock when it came to the Affirmative Action Program. Despite the fact that they were aware of *Revised Order No. 4*, management felt no threat that the O.F.C.C. would bother them, and therefore rejected the women's proposed Affirmative Action Plan in August, 1972. A public relations campaign was undertaken to convince the women that they should be satisfied with the benefits already gotten. The company's position seemed firm.

Two months later, a woman from the compliance agency assigned to Polaroid as a government contractor, visited the company's offices to check compliance with *Revised Order No. 4*. Although encouraged about the accomplishments made in terms of benefits, the officer insisted that the company prepare goals and timetables conforming with government regulations. When some delays occurred in getting the Affirmative Action Plan developed, a final measure of pressure—a "show cause order"—was applied. At that point, *the utilization analysis and affirmative action plan drawn up by the task force was used by the company for meeting O.F.C.C. requirements!* The women had done more than just confront management; they had prepared a policy instrument which the company adopted when pressured by the Office of Federal Contract Compliance. Commitment to an affirmative action plan was accomplished, not through management initiative, but through a combination of internal and external pressures.

Evaluating Polaroid's Responses

The manner in which equal employment opportunities for women became corporate policy at Polaroid illustrates the exceedingly complex process that frequently occurs within companies in responding to public issues. In addition, there is a strong suggestion that this process is neither as rational as that suggested by the business strategy model nor as reactive and incremental as the pressure response model suggests. Being neither wholly anticipatory nor wholly reactive, there is, however, no doubt that management interests and environmental pressures are inherently interactive, influencing one another over the life cycle of the issue.

The interactions between Polaroid management and the coalition of women's groups within the company between 1969 and 1972 illustrate the interplay between the models of corporate responsiveness. Overall, the forces which prompted responses from management took three distinct forms:

(1) public pressure, which stimulated management to take some initiative;

(2) public pressure combined with support and backing from the legal environment;

(3) outright legal compulsion, including legal sanction should the organization fail to comply.

(1) *Public Pressure and Management Initiative.* Between the spring of 1970 and fall of 1971, the company utilized a corporate subcommittee on women as a means of dealing with women's issues. This subcommittee, although not a major factor in retrospect, was created by management because they perceived increasing unrest among the female labor force. The designation of a management representative as liaison to the women's groups was also a management initiative. Finally, the willingness of Polaroid's management to recognize, cooperate with, and receive the findings of the task forces was responsive to an environment that was changing.

The Polaroid experience points out quite clearly that there are gradients of pressure on the company, especially in defined areas ("policies," "practices," "educational awareness") and with respect to specific remedies being sought (e.g., changed wording in the company policy book, desexed job titles, redesign of application forms). The response called for by management was a specific one, but considerable managerial discretion still existed. The decision to develop an educational consciousness-raising program for employees, for example, was responsive to the women and provided an opportunity to work for positive change within the organization without being forced into a long-term commitment.

(2) *Public Pressure with Legal Support.* The decision to grant leaves of absence for childbearing was made at the request of the women's groups. The company did not have to fear legal action in the event of their refusal, since the E.E.O.C. Guidelines of 1969 were not mandatory in nature. Similarly, when the task forces recommended that childbearing be treated as a temporary disability and that obstetric coverage for female employees be comparable to the coverage being received by the female family members of male employees, the company acted in a manner consistent with the 1972 Guidelines. In neither instance was the company required to agree to such accommodations. Yet, in both instances, the women's demands for change were reinforced by a clear public policy recommendation (the E.E.O.C. Guidelines) for private sector action.

(3) *Legal Compulsion.* The situation in which managerial discretion is most limited, of course, is one in which the law requires an immediate response to a specifically defined problem. Polaroid's dealings with Task Force No. 5 illustrates a situation in which the legal environment became a source of specific legal direction. The failure to negotiate an affirmative action plan constituted a management failure because it then allowed the company to be placed in a situation where discretionary action was foreclosed.

Polaroid's reaction to the recommendation of Task Force No. 5 raises a question that is central to the issue of corporate responsiveness—*Why did a company which had a record of support for minority affirmative action plans, which had already made a considerable number of concessions to the women's groups, and which had shown a sensitivity to developing public policy, refuse to move in the direction of an affirmative action program for women?* The failure of Polaroid's management to respond in a positive way to the proposed affirmative action plan advocated by Task Force No. 5 can be explained on one of several grounds. First, it is possible that management felt that it had already been both generous and reasonable in responding to the women's demands for change by modifying a number of its practices and policies, by granting new rights to women employees regarding maternity leaves, and by supporting and promoting the educational awareness workshops. It is possible that Polaroid's management simply concluded that "enough is enough" and that a commitment to specific goals and timetables was beyond reasonable expectations. This rationale is plausible if one realizes that the concessions previously made to the women did not, for the most part, have a direct effect on the company's employment structure. On the other hand, difficulty of implementing a minority affirmative action plan had been substantial; to adopt another set of goals and timetables would have further constricted management's discretion in employment matters. Thus, despite an awareness of *Revised Order No. 4,* management may have perceived the costs of committing itself to such a plan as too great.

The theory that the women's demands were illegitimate seems less plausible. Even if one adds the additional consideration that Polaroid's management may have feared that to go further in making concessions to women would encourage other groups to make demands on the firm, it must be noted that once required to formulate a plan, the company's management utilized the plan developed by Task Force No. 5. This usage of the task-force proposal was more than a matter of convenience. If committing an organization to a major new employment policy thrust is a matter of serious consequence, then a management is not going to endorse a plan to which it has no commitment. If this is true, then neither the idea that "enough is enough" nor the fear of other groups demanding similar treatment provides a rationale for Polaroid's action.

The most logical explanation for Polaroid's rejection of the affirmative action proposal seems to be its prior commitment to minority affirmative action. The company's commitment to programs for minority group members was substantial and it was regularly reaffirmed by Polaroid's top management.[15] Women's rights, conversely, was not a well-developed movement at the time and the company's commitment was not reinforced by the emotional factors that were at work with the minority issue. As long as the demands of the women's groups could be satisfied without cutting into the minority action budget, management was able to satisfy both commitments. When a choice had to be made, the minority programs were given first priority.

What factors might have changed these priorities? Certainly the emotional commitment of top management is one variable that might have changed the priorities or eliminated the need for choosing between minority programs and women's programs. Polaroid's long-standing commitment to improve opportunities for minority group members contrasted sharply with the responses given to the women. Not only is the contrast between the two situations unmistakable, but it underscores the difference between the two responsiveness models described earlier in this chapter.

Promotion of minority group opportunities had become a "top down" process, involving top management awareness of the problem, the articulation of values and goals, and the development of a strategy to accomplish those goals. The implementation of that strategy involved affirmative action, including the setting of hiring quotas and the establishment of timetables. Promotion of women's opportunities, on the other hand, was primarily a "bottom up" process, wherein pressures and demands led to modified actions, practices, and procedures. Only gradually, did the pressure "percolate upward" to a top management level. And in particular, it was the failure of the organization to respond fast enough to this process that resulted in the O.F.C.C. order for an affirmative action program. Commitment to an affirmative action plan came when the company had to acquiesce to legal pressure.

Learning and Responsiveness

The manner in which Polaroid's management responded to the demands and expectations of its women employees for improved employment opportunities fits neither the business strategy nor the pressure response models of the corporate response process. Yet the three stages of the general responsiveness model—(1) awareness, (2) commitment, (3) implementation—did occur, though not in a sequence or manner sug-

[15] Morgan, *op. cit.*

gested by either model. Thus, the experience at Polaroid suggests two important conclusions.

First, corporate responses to change are never entirely based on anticipation and forethought or on pressure and threat. The response process that actually occurs with respect to a single issue (e.g., equal employment opportunity for women) may develop in a series of phases, each of which itself follows a somewhat different pattern. At Polaroid, management's response to issues with low cost and low organization impact diffffered significantly from its response to demands which required a commitment to structural change within the organization, such as the affirmative action program. The different gradients of pressure felt by Polaroid's management (direct pressure from the women employees, E.E.O.C. Guidelines, legal pressure from O.F.C.C.) certainly underscore the selective importance of pressure in determining the nature of the managerial response elicited by the demands of a relevant public.

A second conclusion relates to management commitment and organizational learning. Commitment is not a unitary concept, either wholly present or totally absent, but one that involves various threshholds. Specifically, management learns not only which responses will be acceptable under given circumstances, but also, how much commitment is necessary to satisfy its critics without having to undergo a fundamental reordering of organizational priorities and goals. At Polaroid, management initially committed itself to a series of changes which had minimal organizational impact. When changes with more serious organizational implications were proposed, management's commitment to be responsive waned. To develop that level of commitment necessary to create an affirmative response, new pressures were required. Hence, forethought and management initiative seem to hold for a period, but only until management is unwilling to seriously rethink organizational priorities and objectives in light of the new public expectations.

PATTERNS OF RESPONSE

The Polaroid example provides a tantalizing introduction into the complexities surrounding organizational responses to a changing environment. Pressure, management initiative, and changing public policy all combine as stimuli to provoke an organizational response to new environmental realities. In our research studies, a number of patterns of corporate response have emerged as basic approaches which managements pursue in attempting to cope with change. External change can be perceived by management as providing new opportunities to improve its performance, or as creating new requirements for improving that performance. In either event, when management perceives external change (the awareness stage) some action must be taken to keep the gap between the organization's actual performance and that which is expected by the many external publics as narrow as possible.

How can that gap be closed? Our answer to that question is conceptually similar to the theoretical approaches to environmental change discussed at the conclusion of Chapter One. Action may be taken to modify organizational behavior so as to meet the new performance expectations; action can be taken to change the public expectations; or some combination of organizational change and environmental change may simultaneously take place to narrow the gap. These three possibilities are abstractions which have been confirmed by the body of empirical cases that contributed to this book. What that body of research suggests is that while there are numerous variations, there are three basic patterns of corporate response to change. Some of the more prominent variations are presented as case illustrations in this book.

The cases discussed in this book, therefore, are developed along two main dimensions. The first is the type of environmental change involved. In general, this involves either economic, technological, socio-cultural, political change, or combinations of these. The second dimension involves the pattern of response to environmental change evidenced by the organizational entity. Three broad patterns are utilized for discussion purposes: *adaptive*, which emphasizes organizational reaction to environmental change; *proactive*, which emphasizes organizational action to promote change in the environment; and *interactive*, which emphasizes simultaneous change in both the organization and the environment.

A basic question is what constitutes a pattern of response. How does one know that a pattern exists? What evidence does the researcher sift to determine which pattern is actually in effect? To define a pattern of response three key terms must be understood. They are terms which relate to the manner in which an organization copes with change. The first term is *tactics*. Tactics are organizational actions which are immediate in their nature, short term in their time horizon and intended to have an immediate effect on the environment. Tactics for coping with change include actions such as the issuance of public relations statements, bargaining with various groups in the environment, and actions to enforce legal rights. A second term is *strategy*. A strategy is more long term in its time horizon and implies coherence among a set of tactical actions which are purposeful in an overall sense and consistent with the organization's goals. Discussion of goals, in turn, forces us to take note of the difference between the *operative goals* of the organization (those which are really being sought) and the stated goals which are often proclaimed in formal statements. The mention of formal statements leads to the third key term, *policy*. Policy refers to those overall objectives and goals which identify the purposeful directions of the entity. In many respects, the word policy is often misused to describe subelements in an organization's activities, such as personnel policy, marketing policy, and so forth, which are more appropriately referred to as operating policies. Policy must be sufficiently general to guide the entire organization, and all operating policies taken together must contribute to the accomplishment of an overall purpose and mission of the organization.

The patterns of response to change are inductively developed from evidence of the firm's behavior. That development requires that the observer not rely solely on a policy statement or solely on a single action (tactic) in generalizing about the pattern which the firm follows. For example, a policy statement articulating a position against the making of bribes or illegal business payments to potential clients in return for their business would not by itself constitute a pattern of response. Indeed, one would have to look at specific actions (tactics) and the specific business strategy taken as a whole to determine whether actual behavior supported or undermined the policy statement. In brief, then, *a pattern of response is equivalent to an operative policy*. It is that policy which an overall set of organizational actions manifest and with which they are consistent.

part two

adaptive patterns of response

chapter three

adapting to economic change

INTRODUCTION

Investors, managers, and students of management have long prized and favored those organizations which are most adept at responding to new economic conditions. Economic change can present threats or new requirements for a corporate management; but there are times when it also offers new opportunities for economic growth and success. In some respects, the degree of threat or opportunity that changing economic conditions present depends on the perceptions of corporate managers. There are many manifestations of economic change, ranging from relatively clear quantitative shifts in population to the more imprecise expectations of consumers or the unpredicted actions of competitors.

Even though changing economic conditions represent the kind of change to which

43

managers are most accustomed, and probably best able to cope, there are new elements in the character and nature of economic change that make it more challenging and difficult to deal with. Adapting to economic change is increasingly complicated by the complex interaction of economic trends, varied governmental institutions, and changing economic aspirations. Neil Jacoby, former Dean of the Graduate School of Management at UCLA and a business economist with many decades of experience, has looked ahead to the 1980's and perceived six major challenges for managers. They are (1) the challenge of high political turbulence and uncertainty; (2) slow economic growth; (3) expensive capital and credit; (4) weakening industrial discipline; (5) rising public demands for governmental regulation; (6) growing challenges to the legitimacy of profit-seeking enterprise.[1] John Paluszek, in his book, *Will the Corporation Survive?*[2] develops an even longer list of manifestations of economic change. It is most significant that these authors recognize the increased interrelationship between economic conditions and political climates. It is probably no longer permissible to speak of the "economic environment" of business and the "political environment" of business as if they were independent of one another. To be sure, there are still instances in which demographic shifts or consumer expectations change without a direct political implication. Two such cases are discussed below. More familiar in recent years, however, has been the kind of eco-political change represented by the emergence of cartels. In more complex economic-political environments, the success of conventional adaptive responses by organizations is more tentative. As we shall see in the discussion of the bauxite cartel, in Chapter Four, the traditional managerial approach of *reacting* to new eco-political conditions takes longer and is less likely to succeed as a strategy for coping with change.

In the cases presented below, different facets of economic change and conventional adaptive responses are discussed. Demographic change in the form of declining birth rates is the environmental condition in the Gerber Products Company case: the company's reaction involved a very basic business strategy shift. Changing consumer preferences are discussed in the Variable Life Insurance case, where a traditional product innovation response is discussed in the framework of regulated industry. Finally, the International Bauxite Association case, which is discussed in Chapter Four, focuses on a changing market relationship between supplier nations and aluminum manufacturers in which the operative factors are both political and economic in character.

[1] Neil Jacoby, "Six Challenges to Business Management," *Business Horizons* (August 1976) p. 29.
[2] John Paluszek, *Will the Corporation Survive?* (Reston, Va: Reston Publishing Co., 1977).

DEMOGRAPHIC CHANGE
AND STRATEGIC REACTION:
GERBER PRODUCTS COMPANY

Following World War II, a tremendous post-war baby boom occurred. In 1945, the birth rate was 20.4 births per 1000 population; in 1950, the rate was 24.1; in 1955, the rate was 25.0; in 1960, it was 23.7; it has generally continued to decline since that time.[3] By the late 1960's, however, the post-war babies were beginning to marry and start families of their own. In 1968, marriages exceeded 2 million, a new high. At the rate of ten marriages per thousand population, the marriage rate was the highest since 1950. However, while the number of marriages increased, the fertility rate (numbers of births for women between ages 15 and 44) declined substantially. The growing acceptability of family planning and the more effective and widespread use of birth control measures were believed to be major factors in the declining fertility trend.

According to the Bureau of Census, marriage statistics indicated that the average age of women getting married was rising, and that they generally expected to limit the size of their families. Statistics also indicated that there was a longer interval between the date of marriage and the birth of the first child. Among the factors believed to be contributing to this trend were the rising income levels of young families and the growing reluctance of young married couples to sacrifice this income at an early age.

Gerber and the American Baby Food Industry

The implications of these trends were significant for the American baby food industry. According to many observers, the implications of these trends were felt nowhere more than at the Gerber Products Company, the undisputed leader in the manufacturing and distribution of strained and junior baby foods in the United States.

Gerber's involvement in the baby food business began almost by accident. In 1927, Dan Gerber was attempting to strain some peas for his seven-month-old son in the family kitchen. After much difficulty he concluded that the food could be better prepared utilizing equipment at the family-owned cannery. At the time, the cannery processed fruits and vegetables for the adult food market. From that homey beginning, the Gerber Products Company evolved into the nation's leading preparer of baby food products.

Dan Gerber played a leading role in the development of the baby food business. With the approval of his father, who was president of the

[3] U.S. Bureau of the Census, *Statistical Abstract of the United States; 1975 (96th edition)* (Washington, D.C.: U.S. Government Printing Office, 1975).

cannery, Dan Gerber instituted a new canning line that was used to produce five strained baby food products. In 1928, the company invested in the first advertising designed to introduce mothers to strained vegetables and vegetable soups.

The first strained baby foods in the United States were developed by Harold Clapp, a restaurateur who in 1921 successfully experimented with straining adult foods for use by babies. However, it was the Gerber company that shaped the baby food industry in the United States.[4] Gerber was the first company to shift distribution efforts from drug stores to supermarkets, outlets through which the cannery had successfully promoted and sold their canned soups. In 1938, the Gerber family launched another marketing innovation when it created a direct sales force to sell the company's products and replaced existing food brokers. These salesmen not only sold the company product but also serviced all aspects of the retailers' inventory including reordering when shelf stock was low.

These efforts proved successful in establishing a national baby food market. As demand rose, sales volume of this product line outranked all other products prepared by the Fremont Canning Company. By the early 1940's the importance of the baby food line to the company led to a decision to discontinue the other products and concentrate solely on the production and sale of baby foods.

The entire market for baby foods (including strained and junior foods) developed rapidly after World War II. Retail sales volume escalated dramatically from 88 million dollars in 1948 to 275 million in 1958. Unit supermarket sales for this product group amounted to $2.7 billion in 1958 and were second only to the sales of soft drinks. During the same ten-year period the average per capita baby food expenditures increased from $31 per year to $65 per year. This sharp increase in usage was attributed to the post-war increase in births, a better educated population not bound to traditional feeding practices, and rising disposable income. The modern mother was willing to budget more money for convenient foods such as baby foods and the industry prospered in an environment that favored convenience products and aggregate increases in births.

Gerber's Strategy

By 1959, Gerber Products Company was the leading national manufacturer of baby foods. It accounted for approximately 45 percent of the industry's sales volume. The decision to concentrate the company's efforts on baby foods proved successful for two decades after World War II. The "Gerber Baby," a registered trademark, identified the company and its

---

[4] The company name was changed from Fremont Canning Company to Gerber Products Company in 1941.

products and conveyed an image of quality and concern for babies that bred success. This identification of a distinct market and a concentration of production and distribution efforts in servicing it enabled Gerber to outsell competitors and establish a dominant market position.

In the 1950's most of Gerber's competitors were diversified firms such as H. J. Heinz and Beech Nut, which offered smaller lines of baby foods. Gerber had a special expertise in distribution. The company's goal was to achieve a significant profit margin by maintaining high sales volume. To do this, they drew on their experience in supermarket distribution by developing a technique that maximized their products' visibility: domination of available shelf space. Shelf space is allocated according to the number of products a manufacturer has to offer. Therefore, by offering a large variety of baby foods, a company such as Gerber received proportionately more shelf space than competitors with more limited lines. Gerber's market strategy was tied to product development. The company developed new varieties of foods and introduced combinations of vegetables, fruits and dinners in both the strained and junior foods lines. By 1959 they marketed 105 varieties and expanded the original line of strained fruits and vegetables to include meats, desserts, and cereals. Each new product provided additional shelf space in the supermarket. Additional shelf space, in turn, guaranteed expanding sales volume.

To further distinguish their products, Gerber also emphasized innovative package techniques. Juice cans, for example, went from paper labels to lithographed cans, which permitted better color reproduction and prevented scuffing in transit and on the shelf. The company also shifted to glass jars and introduced small multipacked units that allowed greater diversification of the baby's diet and provided greater purchasing convenience for the child's mother.

Production

As a food processor, Gerber was fully integrated from the field to the supermarket. In the plant, automatic production techniques allowed the company to gain considerable economies in production and packaging. The volume achieved through the sale of many varieties of baby foods translated into efficiencies in the production, sales, and distribution operations.

Quality control has also been a major factor. All products are required to meet strict nutritional standards and the company has established a large research department to oversee quality control in production and new product development. Each year the research department conducts audits of all plants to insure that testing and quality control procedures established by the company are adhered to and that a high quality product continues to be offered in the market.

Advertising

Gerber became very adept at using a selective marketing approach in the selling of their baby food products. In general, the company relied on informational advertising of two types: medical advertising and mass advertising.

Direct mail campaigns have long been an integral part of the promotion of new and existing products. The company compiles extensive lists of birth registrations. Approximately three weeks after a child is born, it sends the mother samples of its products together with coupons to be redeemed at neighborhood stores. A follow-up mailing usually includes additional coupons. Although expensive, this marketing effort has produced excellent results for Gerber. The company boasts a 20 percent follow-up rate on mail advertising and estimates that they distribute over nine million pieces of mail each year which reach 75 percent of all new mothers. The company's quality image has been stressed throughout its advertising campaign. A personalized letter goes to all new mothers from a fictional Mrs. Gerber whose picture and personality are central to this facet of the company's advertising. Gerber is also believed to be the first firm in the industry to recognize the potential of special baby magazines and the women's magazines sold in supermarkets as vehicles for carrying baby food advertising.

To further enhance its quality image, the company has undertaken to communicate with the medical profession. For many years they were the only company in the industry to employ a professional relations department with employees calling up physicians and hospital staffs to discuss Gerber products. These efforts were started as early as 1929, only shortly after the first production of baby food products. Interestingly, the introduction of baby foods in 1928 coincided with a tendency on the part of pediatricians to recommend earlier feeding of more solid foods for infants. To contact the pediatric community, the company also sponsored a scholarly professional journal known as "The Pediatric Herald." The company has long made it a practice to publicize to pediatricians all information concerning Gerber products—their content, composition, and related factors. At a somewhat more general level, this information is included in millions of educational child care books which have been distributed in doctors' offices, to mothers and expectant mothers. On the whole the company cultivated both a selected mail advertising approach toward new mothers and a broad appeal to the pediatrics community.

Facing the Future

As the Gerber Products Company faced the late 1960's, it was argued by some that the company should prepare to react to the changing demographic environment. However, the company sales had persevered well and a future course of action was not readily evident. Dan Gerber, who had succeeded his father as chief executive officer of the company, considered several major alternatives as early as the early 1960's. Since the company had strength in the processing and preparation of food products, they could turn to the adult food market and expand their product line from baby foods to adult foods. A second broad set of options was to expand into other infant and baby-related products. A third possible course was diversification. In the midst of the company's continuing success, Mr. Gerber attempted to chart a future course for the company.

The Industry's Response to Change

As the aggregate demand for baby foods began to slacken, retail sales volume fell, thereby affecting the manufacturer's ability to achieve the economies of scale in distribution and production operations necessary to the maintenance of profit margins on these products. Realization grew that the national market for baby foods was maturing and that continued success lay in the ability of the manufacturer to maintain a market share sufficiently large to generate production efficiency. Several companies began to cut prices in an effort to gain market share. In 1969, H. J. Heinz and Beech Nut Baby Foods entered into a price war which affected the entire industry. The price reductions came at a time when production costs were being fueled by increases in the cost of raw materials, quality control, and new product development. The Heinz-Beech Nut price war was an effort on the part of those firms to seize market share from one another or at the expense of Gerber. The price war continued for five years, during which time profit margins became increasingly thin. Swift & Company, which had been producing strained meats as a sideline to its meat products business, dropped out of the industry, leaving its 3 to 4 percent market share to Heinz, Squibb–Beech Nut, and Gerber.[5] The price war continued until national price controls were imposed in 1974, at which time prices were frozen at the lowest level in five years. Swift's departure from the industry was a simple acknowledgment that there was very little profit to be gained in the baby food business. Indeed, during the previous year, Squibb had been searching for a buyer for the Beech Nut division, including the baby food product line. Negotiations with a British firm, Lyons Limited, were terminated without a deal. Later Baker Laboratories, a privately held pharmaceutical firm, reached an agreement with Squibb to purchase Beech Nut baby food for 16 million dollars, including 11 million in cash. The remaining 5 million was to be paid in annual installments through 1976.[6] In 1971, Squibb had withdrawn the baby food product line

[5] *Business Week*, July 13, 1974, p. 46.
[6] Squibb *10-K Report*, 1972.

from several unprofitable markets in the United States and was rumored in 1972 to be considering closing down baby food production permanently if a buyer could not be found.[7]

Both Squibb and H. J. Heniz derived their major sales from other products in 1972. Neither had a large stake in keeping their baby food divisions strong and viable. Both companies are highly diversified and indeed are defined as pharmaceutical and food processing companies, respectively. With the withdrawal of Swift and the sale of Beech Nut Baby Food to Baker Laboratories, the industry balance tipped in Gerber's direction. Business media stopped covering and publishing information on Baker/Beech Nut and H. J. Heinz. Almost by default, the industry became defined as the Gerber Products Company. Gerber moved aggressively into the vacuum created by these industry changes with noticeable self-confidence. Gerber launched a positive public relations campaign about its business that helped obscure the fact that Baker/Beech Nut and H. J. Heinz still had considerable capital facilities tied up in the production of baby food.

Gerber's Strategic Response

Gerber's market share in the industry during the late 1950's and early 1960's hovered at about 50 percent of national baby food sales. Indeed, the price war in the late 1960's and early 1970's was, in part, an effort by competitors to take away Gerber's share. The company's ability to survive these competitive threats and maintain prosperity based on baby food made a strategic response both necessary and difficult. True, the demographics suggested the need to position the company for a declining baby food market; however, to shift capital out of baby food into some other competitive area would cost Gerber some share of the baby food market they dominated. Hence, the company was caught between the Scylla of a birth dearth and the Charibdas of capital needs.

The first strategic move occurred in the early 1960's as Gerber sought a means to broaden its revenue base. New products were being developed by the research department, and the company initiated efforts to market a broader set of products to a clientele that had already come to know and trust the "Gerber baby." The key concept in this response was to extend the "cycle of use" of the company's products. To do this, Gerber's research department developed foods for infants too young for baby food (e.g., infant formula and baby cereal) and toddlers beyond the strained and junior food age (e.g., toddler meals, pretzels, and cookies). The effort to build on the basic Gerber image was generally successful, though a decade of effort failed to produce success in the infant formula business.[8]

[7] Squibb 10-K Report, 1971.
[8] The infant formula industry is discussed in another context in Chapter 13 of this book.

Expanding the cycle of use was only the first step in what would become a continuing response to changing demographic and competitive conditions. Gerber next sought to expand the cycle of use by distributing other products which served a broad range of baby needs. Through a series of acquisitions, the company introduced waterproof pants and bibs under the Gerber name to nearly 50 percent of the supermarkets carrying Gerber baby food. Where others had failed, Gerber's name and image generated a great success in the supermarket marketing of these products. In a related effort, the company began distributing a line of infant shirts, socks, training pants, and crib sheets. All were distributed through supermarkets under the Gerber name and alongside the baby food line.

Gradually, the concept of Gerber as a "baby-needs company" rather than a baby-food company began to develop. Additional acquisitions were made which seemed to complement existing baby products and thereby expand the "umbrella of baby needs" to be met by Gerber. A manufacturer of stretch wear garments for infants to be sold through department stores and infant specialty shops was acquired; a leading manufacturer of vaporizers, humidifiers, and other nursery products sold through drug stores, department stores, and other mass merchandising outlets was acquired; in 1968, a life insurance subsidiary was established to sell life insurance coverage on newborns to their parents; and in 1970, the company established a Children's Center Division to operate day care centers under the Gerber name. The thrust of this strategy was to build on, in the words of one executive, "what Gerber knows best"—babies, children, and their parents!

Not all of these acquisitions and moves were successful. The life insurance activity, for example, proved very costly for Gerber for nearly eight years before it became profitable. Despite the short term costs, the insurance business offers the company a cash flow that will provide a capital base from which other potential acquisitions might be financed. The day care centers also encountered difficulty for a time, but seem to have been rendered sound by the creative application of Gerber philosophy about children and tight financial controls.

The transformation to a "baby-needs company" was one leg upon which Gerber's response was built. A second leg was to build on the company's competence as a food processor. Part of Gerber's original effort to develop manufacturing expertise in foreign countries involved acquiring small food processors in several Latin American nations. While this was originally to be a base for future baby food manufacturing as part of the company's international marketing effort, it gave the company a product base with such products as tomato catsup. Today, Gerber has encouraged its research department to develop new adult food products which it can market to supermarkets in the United States. Ironically, where the demands of the baby food market led Gerber to abandon the adult food market and concentrate on baby food in the 1940's, population changes forced a new effort to reestablish the company's presence in the adult food market thirty years later.

The third leg of Gerber's survival strategy for the 1970's has emphasized vertical integration as a means of improving economies in the basic businesses (especially food) to which it is committed. In this context, it has acquired a large farming operation and a meat processor. Similarly, it has begun the captive manufacture of metal cans and glass jars, both of which are used for packaging of baby foods.

Summary

Gerber's response to the basic economic problem of a stable or no-growth market for baby foods was based on a reaction to perceived change at various points in time. Beginning with an effort to build on its customer base by expanding the cycle of use during the mid-1960's, the company ultimately redefined its basic business as being "baby needs," not baby food. Although this led to several far-flung ventures (life insurance and day care centers), it was predicated on the management assumption about what that customer class valued in choosing products and services for their children.

When opportunities seemed to beckon in the environment, Gerber reacted by committing itself to baby-related activities. Both the life insurance and day care ventures were initiated from outside the company by entrepreneurs who sought Gerber's name and investment. It is noteworthy that the company perceived an opportunity in those overtures that was consistent with their own objectives of diversification. It is also noteworthy that such diversification was far more reactive in nature than the efforts to vertically integrate and develop the company's international market. In retrospect, there seems to be good reason to surmise that at least part of Gerber's initial difficulty with the insurance and day care businesses occurred because they were conceived and managed by outsiders. This meant that in their beginning years, the goals of their subsidiary managers and those of Gerber top management had to be more closely harmonized. That was a significant task that ultimately affected the speed with which the company's adaptation to economic change could occur.

COMPETITIVE CHANGE AND PRODUCT INNOVATION: VARIABLE LIFE INSURANCE[9]

Aetna Life & Casualty is a large multiple line insurance company with major market shares in the life and health sectors of the American insur-

---

[9] This is a revised version of material initially presented in J. Post, *Risk and Response* (D. C. Heath, Inc., 1976).

ance industry, as well as the property and casualty sectors. The broad scope of its operations does not obscure the importance of life insurance business to the company's success, however. In the evolution of the company, life insurance was the hub around which the component member companies in the firm were organized. In the 1970's, Aetna's status as a diversified financial company with more than $12 billion in assets is anchored by its $100 billion of life insurance in force.

During the 1960's, the company's management was concerned about the life insurance business for two reasons: (1) The firm had $27 billion of insurance in force in 1962, yielding premium income of $165 million (12.2 percent of total premiums). The investment income from these premiums, however, accounted for 87 percent of the total investment income earned by the company. To the extent that a multiple line insurer depends on investment income to sustain itself, this meant that Aetna was crucially dependent on the life insurance business. (2) The threat to Aetna's life insurance operations came from the continuing impact of inflation, which tends to erode the real worth of a fixed amount life insurance policy. As early as the late 1950's, Aetna's management had concluded that it was necessary to carefully monitor inflationary trends and prepare to respond. The nature of that response is discussed below.

Background

In 1950 total life insurance in force in the United States exceeded $234 billion. By 1959 that amount had increased to over $542 billion, as both individual life and group life insurance sales increased.[10] Given that history of growth, industry spokesmen were optimistically describing the potential for future life insurance growth during the 1960's. Yet industry optimism was also tempered by a deep concern about the impact of inflation.

Although life insurance is generally promoted and advertised as a basic form of family financial protection rather than as an investment device, there are investment aspects to many types of life insurance policies. Ordinary life insurance is usually issued in amounts of $1,000 or more with premiums payable on an annual, semiannual, quarterly, or monthly basis.[11] Ordinary life is the basic form of life insurance in force. It is usually purchased by individuals through agents, and it is the oldest and most widely used form of life insurance coverage. These policies offer more than the protection features normally associated with insurance. All but the term insurance type of ordinary life policy build cash values against which the policyholder can borrow. Ordinary life policies also frequently have a participating feature, which refunds a portion of the

---

[10] Institute of Life Insurance, *1971 Life Insurance Fact Book* (New York: Institute of Life Insurance, 1971) p. 24.
[11] *Ibid.*, p. 120.

premium to policyholders in the form of dividends based on the insurer's annual investment earnings, administrative expenses, and cost experience.[12]

The investment aspects of the life insurance policy operate to place life insurance in competition with other forms of financial investment, especially savings accounts and mutual funds. During periods of inflation, returns on investments such as common stock and mutual funds tend to rise with corporate profits. Fixed return devices, such as savings accounts, may be permitted to increase their interest rates to depositors in an effort to maintain savings levels. Because of restrictions on the size of reserve levels and the permissible types of investment that they can make, life insurers have frequently argued before regulatory agencies in favor of standards that would permit them to more effectively compete for investors' funds. Such a situation existed in the 1960's when life insurers were especially concerned because returns on mutual funds were comparatively high and because banking regulatory authorities had permitted an increase in the interest rates paid to depositors.

The changing role of life insurance as an investment, and the crux of the problem facing life insurers, is reflected in the fact that in 1948 life insurance companies accounted for 47.1 percent of the growth in savings; but in 1967, when institutional savings increased by $64.1 billion, life insurance accounted for only $8.6 billion or 13.4 percent.[13] And although the net rate of interest earned by life insurers on invested funds did increase annually throughout the 1960's (4.11 percent in 1960; 4.61 percent in 1965; 5.12 percent in 1969),[14] the rate was not sufficient to materially change the dividend returns to policy holders.

Inflation's Impact

Inflation had been a recognized problem for the industry since the 1950's. The industry was affected in several ways by inflation, and these impacts shaped the responses of member firms. First, inflation obviously affected the quality of the insurance product as an investment. In this regard, it was a matter that affected the technical core of the business. The technical alternatives were to improve the investment return for policyholders by either securing a higher return on invested premiums or by making it possible to treat more of the insurance premium as an invest-

[12] *Ibid.*, p. 26.
[13] Douglas G. Olsen and Howard E. Winklevoss, "Equity Based Variable Life Insurance," *Wharton Quarterly* (Summer 1971) pp. 26–40. Raymond Goldsmith, *Financial Intermediaries in the American Economy Since 1900*, National Bureau of Economic Research Study (Princeton, N.J.: Princeton University Press, 1958).
[14] Institute of Life Insurance, *op. cit.*, p. 55.

ment rather than a purchase of protection. Regulations on permissible sources of insurer investment limited the first alternative; and the fixed return guaranteed by a policy's face value limited the latter. The ability to pursue the first alternative depended on a relaxation of regulatory standards, the second on the development of new products.

A second impact of inflation involved the changes it produced in the flow of investable funds going to insurance companies. If this continued to decrease, in actual dollars or in proportion, the traditional role of life insurers as suppliers of credit, including mortgage funds, would necessarily change. This, in turn, would affect the profitability of an industry that depended upon investment returns, not underwriting, for its overall profit. These concerns primarily touched the managerial subsystem of the insurer; that is, the subsystem that is entrusted with coordinating the flow of resources into the organization and generating the net profit from the provision of actual services. Like the technical alternatives, the managerial alternatives were dependent upon a loosening of current restrictions on investment alternatives and on the creation of new products for attracting a continuing flow of premium dollars to the insurance enterprise.

The third impact of inflation was an institutional one. Since the viability of an insurance enterprise is tied to public confidence in the service provided as well as in the financial integrity of the firm, anything that erodes public confidence in the insurance product has to be a major source of concern. Inflation, of course, had precisely that effect on the life insurance industry. As the investing public became increasingly conscious of the shrinking value of life insurance policies, in real dollars, alternatives for protecting families were more frequently pursued. The responses available to the industry were limited: campaigns could be undertaken to show the continuing value of life insurance; doubt could be cast on the future solvency of investment alternatives; or the adverse social impact of inflation could be publicized and a call made for a campaign to maintain stable price levels.

At the industry level, the top managements of the leading insurers agreed upon a concerted, industry-sponsored public relations campaign to make the public more conscious of the dangers of continuing inflation. A proposed program of government action to control inflation was publicized, and public support was sought for balanced governmental budgets and wage increases that were limited to actual improvements in worker productivity.

By 1960, the industry's prized weapon in this public relations campaign was a twelve and one-half minute film entitled "Trouble in Paradise." The film portrayed the manner in which the members of a mythical kingdom awoke to the dreadful dangers of inflation and responded by balancing their government's budget and tying their own wage increases to productivity improvement. The film received an enthusiastic endorsement from delegates to the 1959 Institute of Life Insurance annual meeting, but alas, several years of showing served to attract neither a film critics' award nor public support for the industry's program. As the industry continued to attract proportionately fewer savings dollars, it became apparent to the managements of some companies that alternative strategies of response were required.

The strategy selected by a number of companies, including the Aetna, concentrated on the development of new products that could overcome the fixed-return aspects of ordinary life policies. One early product in this regard was the variable annuity. Annuities had been sold in the United States since the 1800's, usually providing that the beneficiary receive a fixed number of payments or a fixed amount of money based on contributions to the annuity fund and estimated investment returns. The variable annuity is based, in whole or in part, on common stock investments or on a cost-of-living index. Part or all of the invested funds are placed in separate accounts to be invested in ways restricted to normal life insurance investments. Because of the long-standing connection between life insurance companies and fixed annuity contracts, state regulatory authorities raised minimal objection to variable annuity programs. By 1968, life insurance company variable annuities covered 317,300 persons; in 1969 the number swelled to 426,800, an increase of 109,500 persons.[15]

Variable annuities were not sufficient to compete with the growing popularity of mutual funds, however. Thus pressure existed on insurance company managements to develop still other inflation-resistant products. Aetna's basic strategy during the early 1960's had been one of joining new product development and its large life agency force. This would permit the agents to better function as financial consultants, directing a client toward the most advantageous financial package. Since variable annuities could not meet all these needs, Aetna sought to expand its product line still further.

In its 1966 annual report the company announced its intention to expand into the individual annuity contract market by acquisition, rather than by direct business development. The announcement was brief, only stating that to expedite this matter Aetna was seeking to purchase all of the outstanding shares of the Participating Annuity Life Insurance Company of Little Rock, Ark., which had been founded in 1954.[16] Underlying Aetna's announcement was a story of a decade-long struggle to secure regulatory approval of insurance products with variable components.

[15] Ibid.

[16] Letter to Shareholders, 1966 Annual Report, Aetna Life & Casualty.

In Search of New Products

During the mid-1950's a number of small insurance companies had attempted to sell to restricted segments of the public, insurance products that included a variable component permitting adjustment of the dollar value of the policy under specified conditions (e.g., inflation) and terms (e.g., adjusted premiums). One of the leaders of this movement was John D. Marsh who, after experience with TIAA-CREF, founded the Participating Annuity Life Insurance Company (PALIC) in 1954.

PALIC began its operations by training a group of agents who would be qualified to engage in the sale of variable annuity products. The Securities and Exchange Commission had moved to restrict the sale of such products by unregistered salesmen under the Securities Acts of 1933, 1934, and 1940. Thus the issue was joined as to whether insurance agents would be permitted to sell annuities that had such variable features. A test case was prepared by the various insurers involved, PALIC being one of those that joined in the fight. Eventually the test case was appealed to the United States Supreme Court, and in 1959 the Court ruled that variable annuities may be sold by insurance companies, provided that salesmen also qualify as registered representatives under the Securities Act.[17]

The case was a victory for the insurance companies, since it established their right to sell annuity products to the public. It was also a victory for Marsh, since he had previously undertaken to train PALIC's salesmen for this new business. While the test case had moved through the courts, PALIC had continued to train and register salesmen who were qualified to sell variable annuity products under the SEC's registration requirements. Thus, once the Supreme Court established the right of insurers to offer such products, PALIC was prepared to enter the market with a fully trained and registered sales force. Marsh had recognized, however, that large sales of variable products could not be expected without a major advertising effort, including a nationwide system for servicing the accounts. For these reasons, he began to market PALIC to a larger company that was attuned to the variable market and possessed a national market system.

The marketing of PALIC took a considerable amount of time. But as the mutual fund business continued to worry insurance executives,[18] the interest in acquiring PALIC began to grow. PALIC had two principal assets: an agency force of more than 6,000 SEC-registered salesmen and the expertise of a management team headed by John Marsh. Relying on

---

[17] *Securities and Exchange Commission v. Variable Annuity Life Insurance Company of America*, 79 S. Ct. 618 (1959).

[18] By the mid-1960's, a number of insurance companies had reorganized as holding companies so as to control subsidiaries that could sell equity products, especially mutual funds.

the worth of these two sets of assets in an area of the financial services business that was almost entirely unknown to insurance companies, Marsh was prepared to sell PALIC to the highest bidder.

An acquisition of PALIC fit well with Aetna's strategy of improving return on investment by moving into more lucrative investment areas than those permitted life insurers under traditional regulation. Moreover, as Aetna moved broadly into the financial services industry, Marsh's experience could prove increasingly valuable. Eventually, an agreement was reached whereby Aetna would purchase the total outstanding shares of PALIC with Aetna shares. The actual sale was consummated in March 1967 after Aetna had itself legally become a holding company.

As an Aetna subsidiary, PALIC's immediate task was to embark on a program of training Aetna's national field organization in the variable annuity business and to prepare them for licensing as securities salesmen by the SEC. By late 1967 the Aetna field force had begun selling variable annuities to the public.

Aetna was one of the first large insurers to enter the variable annuity market, and with PALIC's expertise and sales force, Aetna's share of the market began to grow rapidly. In 1968 the company reported outstanding first year sales of variable annuities; in 1969 PALIC's premium income increased 270 percent to $30.8 million; in 1970 premium income rose an additional 27 percent to $39.1 million by the end of the year. The field organization's enthusiasm for the variable annuity product was understandable: 25 percent of the first-year premium was paid as commission on each sale. As several sources who were interviewed noted, some field people became millionaires in those first few years and all the field people knew it! Aetna continued to sponsor PALIC's growth and market expansion by making a $6 million capital contribution to the subsidiary in 1970.[19]

Variable Life Insurance

A name change transformed PALIC into the Aetna Variable Annuity and Life Insurance Company (VALIC), which continued as a subsidiary of the parent Aetna Life and Casualty Company. By 1972 premium income had grown to $80 million, though start-up costs continued to create net losses on the business. The company had also succeeded in expanding its sales force, establishing a substantial premium base, and gaining actuarial and sales experience with variable products. The competence and confi-

[19] Technically, Aetna was suffering a loss on the variable annuity business because of a statutory underwriting requirement that stipulated that the entire cost of writing new business must be absorbed in the year of the sale.

dence that the company had acquired with variable products was reflected in the 1972 annual report, when variable annuities were distinguished from other types of variable products that the company was engaged in developing. Among the prospective products then identified was variable life insurance.

In contrast with traditional life insurance policies, the variable life insurance contract has a provision whereby death proceeds are contingent upon the actual investment performance of the company. Unlike the normal investment portfolio, which consists primarily of bonds and mortgages, the assets representing variable life contracts are predominantly invested in common stock. The ultimate obligations of the insurer are, therefore, directly related to the investment performance of a specifically designated portfolio of common stock. Aetna had been engaged in developing a life insurance policy along these general lines.

Product Innovation and Regulation

An important regulatory question arose with regard to variable life insurance: was it to be regulated by the states, as were other forms of life insurance, or, because of its ties to securities, by the SEC? For Aetna, that decision had to be made by the SEC. Because of its involvement in the variable annuities business, Aetna (VALIC) had become a registered SEC company. Under the terms of the Securities Acts and the rules of the SEC, registered companies cannot sell any product that itself is unregistered. While this presented no problem with regard to variable annuities, it did mean that Aetna had to secure registration of variable life insurance, a step that would thereby bring the product under SEC regulation. Since the state insurance commissions would also regulate the product because of its insurance characteristics, the potential existed for a system of dual regulation.[20] Because of the problems inherent in such a situation, and because of the prospectively inhibiting effect of reduced sales commissions, Aetna applied for an SEC exemption for its variable life insurance contracts.

The SEC responded by granting Aetna an exemption in 1972 that permitted the company to sell variable life insurance as an exempt product, available for sale only with qualified pension plans. The SEC reserved decision on the question of whether individual variable life insurance policies would receive an exemption. The SEC decision thereby allowed sales of variable life insurance on an exempt product basis before a final resolution of the question of whether or not variable life would be regulated as a

---

[20] The effect of SEC regulation was likely to include disclosure requirements, a review of sales literature and techniques, and a limitation on the sales commission that would be substantially lower than the commissions normally paid on life insurance contracts.

security. In July 1972, Aetna sold the first variable life insurance policy issued in the United States as part of a qualified pension plan.

Receipt of the SEC exemption eliminated one half of the regulatory problem. The other half involved securing state insurance commission approval of the variable life insurance contract. The approval of the insurance commissioner of each state in which the company sought to sell the policy had to be secured before any actual sales could take place. The process of securing such approval, at a time when the state commissions themselves were unsure about SEC's course of action, was predictably slow. As of January 1974, only 23 states had passed the necessary enabling legislation allowing such sales and had approved specific variable life insurance contracts for sale within the state. Moreover, as of that date, the large insurance-purchasing states of New York, New Jersey, Pennsylvania, Illinois, and California had neither passed enabling legislation nor approved any specific variable life contracts.

In January 1973, the SEC ruled that the individual variable life insurance policies would be exempt from SEC regulation. However, the Commission quickly reconsidered when securities interests objected, thereby further halting any sales of individual variable life insurance policies. Throughout 1974 Aetna management continued to lobby with the SEC for an exemption of individual variable life policies. It also continued to sell variable life insurance where permitted as part of qualified corporate pension and profit-sharing plans and continued to pursue state insurance commission approvals of variable life products. Nevertheless, the limited conditions under which variable life insurance could be sold, and the limited number of states in which it could be sold, effectively precluded the product from the market.

Epilogue

In October 1976, the SEC adopted regulations that permitted life insurance companies to sell individual variable life insurance policies. Of the eighteen insurers that once indicated an intention to sell the product, only one (Equitable Life) indicated an intention to actually market the product. With investor confidence having declined precipitously during the mid-1970's, the late approval of variable life insurance was not seen as a panacea for the insurer's competitive problems. As one executive commented, "It's a fine step—only five years late!"

In fact, the SEC's late approval is but the final act in a play that took sixteen years to reach its denouement. Reaction through product development proved to be a failure as a response to inflation during the 1960's and 1970's. The attempt to react through product innovation consumed considerable resources and management effort but produced a largely unsuccessful result. The failure to get timely regulatory approvals was, in the final analysis, an industry failure to effectively manage its external affairs.

ADAPTIVE RESPONSES TO ECONOMIC CHANGE

A changing economic environment probably represents the most conventional situation calling for managerial responses for coping with change. The cases presented in this chapter raise several important questions and point toward several conclusions about coping with economic change. These are explicitly considered below.

Environment As a Source of Opportunity

One clear case of opportunity presented above involved the Gerber Products Company's decision in the early 1940's to specialize in the business of baby food production and abandon the adult prepared food market. By the late 1940's, a post-war baby boom presented an immense opportunity for the company to develop a major market position. Indeed, throughout the 1950's and 1960's, Gerber had the largest share in the American baby food market.

The company's response to this set of opportunities was essentially reactive in nature. The critical environmental conditions occurred before Gerber's decision was made to specialize in baby food production. The growing acceptance of prepared baby food had been proceeding throughout the 1930's; the public demand for convenience in food preparation was exacerbated during World War II when large numbers of women were employed in factories and were no longer able to spend long hours in food preparation; and the company's ability to simultaneously operate both baby food canning lines and adult food canning lines had been pushed close to their limits. In this context, Gerber's management (the Gerber family) was forced to make choices. In retrospect, the decision to stake the company's future on baby food was one of great strategic importance because it defined a new purpose for the company. No longer was Gerber a food products firm; rather, it became a *baby food company*.

When the post-war baby boom came in the late 1940's, Gerber was well-positioned to take advantage of the new market. But the company's decision to become a baby food producer was not made in anticipation of such a baby boom. Indeed, in 1941, few could have foreseen the eventual conclusion of a world war that had just begun. What the Gerber family did perceive was a set of environmental conditions that required it to make choices about manufacturing and marketing. Hence, this strategic decision was a reaction born of necessity, not anticipation. When oppor-

Figure 3-1. Coping with the Environment

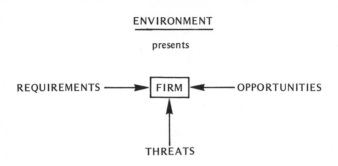

tunity did occur, the firm was ready to respond again with aggressive marketing and sales efforts.

Environment As Threat

If the population boom of the 1940's and 1950's was a great opportunity for the Gerber Products Company, the population decline of the 1960's was a serious threat to its prosperity and success. Recognition of the imminent decline did not spur significant responses by the company or the industry at large until the late 1960's, however. Then a series of price decreases, in a competitive move to establish market share positions before the ultimate birth decline, injured several of the major baby food companies, even forcing two to seriously explore ways of withdrawing entirely. Gerber resisted the price competition during the five year price war, always cutting its price reluctantly and well after other firms had done so. This reactive approach to competitive moves had its detrimental side; Gerber was always on the defensive in terms of coping with its competitors. On the other hand, this reactive approach ultimately proved helpful when national price controls were imposed in 1973. The fact that Gerber's prices were somewhat higher at that point than their competitors gave them a measure of flexibility in their own marketing efforts. They could cut their price still further to meet competitors' prices if necessary. If such cutting was not necessary to maintain market share, however, Gerber would be making an extra penny or two on every jar of baby food which it sold in comparison to its competitors. The net effect was to provide a revenue cushion from current sales which could be used for other types of marketing effort.

Gerber's decisions to expand the international side of the business and to diversify into other product areas were the other components of the company's response to a declining birth rate. Both were basically reactions to the changing demographic and market environment in the baby food market in the United States. The sequence of actions leading to these two operations clearly indicate that they were undertaken, not in anticipation of change, but as reactions to the threat which change posed for the company.

As part of a plan to add additional products to the Gerber line, and thereby expand the "cycle of use" whereby Gerber products were used from about six months of age until two or three years of age, the company made some initial forays into international production in the 1960's with the establishment of two small Latin American operations. Before that time, Gerber had concluded that it could not properly market its baby food in Europe without an investment much larger than it was willing to make. Hence, a decision was made to enter a joint venture in Europe with a large food marketing company, CPC International, whereby the latter bore responsibility for developing sales volume and Gerber concentrated on production from its United States plants. The Latin American plants gave Gerber a resource acquisition base for such foods as bananas and an opportunity to acquire international production expertise. Only gradually did the company come to view Mexico and Latin America as major markets for its baby food products.

The diversification efforts at Gerber followed an incremental response route as well. It began with the "cycle of use" concept, whereby the company tried to make it possible for children to use Gerber products from about six months of age to about three years of age. This led to such new products as rubber pants, baby bibs, etc. When the new venture proposals came to the attention of management, as in the case of the life insurance and day care center ideas, the company's role was one of reaction to the idea, not initiation. Eventually, this reactive posture led the company to oversee these operations in only a general way. When difficulties arose with these operations in turn, significant corrections were unable to occur until new managers were installed whose management loyalty was to Gerber, not the subsidiaries.

The series of threats posed by the changing economic environment, and the Gerber Products Company's reactive approach to coping with change illustrate a common situation. It is often easier for management to simply continue doing what they do best, reacting to the external world only when required to do so. The alternative—change for the sake of change—is certainly not a preferable course of action for a sensible management. But there is a certain poverty in a wholly reactive approach to change. Such an approach never insulates the organization from the unpredicted exogenous event. The imposition of national price controls in 1973 was one such event in Gerber's case. Of course, that unpredicted event worked to the company's advantage, but not because it was anticipated or because contingency plans had been made. Rather, it could be argued that the positive impact of the price controls on Gerber's market position was wholly serendipitous. Reaction didn't produce the positive market effect; it was luck and chance and factors beyond the company's control.

If exogenous change can produce a positive effect occasionally, it cannot be expected to occur repeatedly. That is the ultimate danger of a reactive posture toward change. No matter how fast the company's adaptive mechanisms work, there is likely to occur some form of change to which it cannot react fast enough to avoid harm. Gerber's success story on this score seems to have finally come to an end in 1977. Amidst the company's continuing plan to diversify and acquire other firms, it suddenly— and unexpectedly by all accounts—found itself the victim of a takeover attempt by Anderson-Clayton, a large food company. Gerber has utilized a battery of the legal devices at its immediate disposal to resist the takeover bid in the courts, in the press, and in the Federal Trade Commission (alleging the takeover would have anti-trust implication in several product markets). Although the takeover has been temporarily stalled by these maneuvers, it is not yet clear whether Gerber will be successful in its ultimate effort to resist the takeover attempt. Most importantly, however, the reactive posture adopted by the company has only served to produce considerable internal turmoil within the organization during this most recent event. That may be the greatest negative impact of all from a reactive approach to change—people and organizations cannot adapt with infinite skill and ability. Eventually, the threats of external change will take their toll on the ability of people within the organization to perform their normal tasks and functions.

Environment Establishes New Requirements

If threatening conditions are one kind of negative impact that the external environment can have on an organization, another is the imposition of new requirements on the entity. This was the situation when the life insurance industry sought to develop variable life insurance during the 1960's and 1970's. As seen in the description of Aetna Life & Casualty's efforts to secure regulatory approval for its variable life insurance policy, the environment imposed multiple sets of requirements. The company's traditional way of dealing with insurance commissions at the state level was rendered much more difficult by the necessity of dealing with the Securities and Exchange Commission at the federal level.

Dual regulation is not the only circumstance in which new requirements emanate from actors in the external environment. As pointed out in Chapter One, it is possible for virtually any group of committed people to organize themselves in such a way as to influence and affect the activity and behavior of other social institutions. We have referred to this as the phenomenon of becoming a "relevant public" to a particular organization. The ability of a relevant public to influence, impede, restrict, delay, or otherwise obstruct the normal activities of a firm or organization is a measure of its relevancy to the firm. (Obstruction is not the only condition that makes a group "relevant" to a firm, but it is the way *new groups can most readily interject themselves into the consciousness of a management that would prefer to ignore them.) In this context, the task of coping with the demands of these groups is less a matter of dealing with threats than a matter of meeting new requirements. The difference between threats and requirements is more than semantic differe*nce. When the environment poses a threat to an organization, as did the declining birth rate for Gerber, it is something to be dealt with on a somewhat immediate and even ad hoc basis. When that threat is a relatively permanent one, as in dealing with regulatory agencies or contending with such relevant publics as customers, shareholders, and employees, it can be considered a management requirement. Indeed, a threat is usually specific to a narrow issue; a requirement refers to a body of specific issues (a regulatory agenda or an employee list of demands).

In the life insurance case, the firms in the industry attempted to treat the issue of inflation as a limited threat to their business. In that context, product innovation was a traditional and conventional response to economic change. But the conventional response failed because it required that the corporations involved dealing with a new relevant public, the Securities Exchange Commission. The intrusion of the SEC into the product innovation process produced several byproducts. First, it established a new set of requirements (multiple threats) for all products with variable or investment components. Secondly, it introduced a new actor into the institutional system of relationships between the industry and its regulators. Even after the SEC had granted qualified permission to Aetna to sell VLI, the state regulatory commission proceeded slowly because they were unsure of the implications of the SEC's decision on the federal/state relationship with regard to life insurance. Against this background, the "simple" adaptive response of product innovation failed to produce a timely approval from the federal and state regulatory agencies.

chapter four

the political context of economic change

INTRODUCTION

The interpenetration between government policy and corporate activity is probably no better seen than in the choices that nations must make about the organization of their economies. Increasingly, nations are acting to deliberately influence and determine the manner in which economic activity will be undertaken. The options range from a free market of private sellers and producers at one extreme to a government enterprise at the other. Shifts in the organization of economic activity are usually slow to develop and often confined to a single industry. The evolution of industry-based regulation in the United States, for example, has progressed in a steady, but largely incremental fashion. In other national settings, however, the pressures for reorganization of economic activity have been greater and the resultant shifts in industrial organization more dramatic. Often proceeding under the banner of national honor or economic justice, developing countries have increasingly sought to define, articulate, and press for a *new economic order.* While the meaning of the phrase has not always been clear, the manifestations of economic change have been unmistakable: a political movement to redefine the terms of trade between host nations and the multinational corporations that have developed and processed the LDC's natural resources.

The efforts of the LDC's to gain a greater measure of control over the resources of their own nations, and to extract a higher price from the industrialized nations which rely on these resources, is epitomized by the successful formation and operation of OPEC, the international oil cartel. Less well known, but more typical of the interaction between developing nations that aspire to greater economic development and multinational corporations that have an interest in maintaining the prevailing market relationships is the story of the International Bauxite Association. For the aluminum industry, the formation of the bauxite cartel represented an environmental change of great economic significance. To nations such as Jamaica, the cartel offered the hope of increasing national wealth and a "larger pie" from which to base social plans for progress.

CARTELS IN OUR FUTURE:
INTERNATIONAL BAUXITE ASSOCIATION

Background

In the early 1970's, high world-wide inflation left most less developed countries with poor balance-of-payments position. While importing industrial and finished goods at increasing prices, they maintained only a steady level of revenue from the export of raw materials at relatively flat rates. Some raw material prices, in fact, plummeted. Refining sugar, which sold for 72 cents per pound in the New York cash market in November 1974, sold for 23½ cents only eight months later. Copper wirebars selling for $1.52 per pound in London in April 1975 sold for 56 cents in July. Exacerbating the inflation, while perhaps encouraging other raw material producers to organize into producer associations, OPEC (Organization of Petroleum Exporting Countries) quadrupled the price of oil beginning in 1973.

Inflation and uncertain prices for their exports led raw material producing countries, especially the developing nations, to demand a redistribution of the world's wealth. Jamaica and ten other bauxite producers began taking collective, as well as individual, actions to obtain a greater share of the income generated by bauxite. Their actions were constrained, to some degree, by technological and political factors, as well as by the market potential, which in turn was affected by the demand for aluminum in the developed world and the possible alternatives to bauxite in aluminum refining. Corporate response, on the other hand, was constrained by the reliance on bauxite, at least in the short run.

The Product

Bauxite ore is refined into alumina—white, powdered alumina oxide—which in turn is smelted into aluminum. Caustic soda is used to selectively dissolve the alumina for recovery in the Bayer process. Many clays and shales contain alumina as well, but the alumina is usually bound to the silica in the form of aluminum-silicate or silica-aluminate. These compounds must be disassociated in order to extract the alumina. Bauxite presently remains the most feasible material for extracting alumina, with approximately four pounds of bauxite required to produce one pound of alumina.

Jamaica

Independent from Great Britain since 1962, Jamaica is an island of two worlds. One is the world of tourists, attracted by the dazzling beaches, smooth rum and colorful limbo dancers. The other is the economic and social reality of most of the two million inhabitants. While inflation in 1973–74 climbed by 25–30 percent because of the almost total reliance on imported oil for energy, average per capita income remained at about $700. About 25 percent of the population was unemployed, and nearly 50 percent was illiterate. With most families in Kingston and Montego Bay cramped into small squalid quarters, the birth rate was expected to soar in the next ten years because of an increasing percentage of the population under 19 years of age. Many of Jamaica's economic problems seemed to be rooted in its government's tax and trade policies.

Prime Minister Michael Manley was elected on a reform platform in 1972 and proceeded to institute comprehensive literacy and family planning programs. These, however, were expected to fall short of their goals. The government had also instituted a land-lease program, in which small plots of arable mountainous land were leased by the government from private owners and assigned to small farmers. Although only 1 percent of the arable land had been used in this way, the government expected to purchase 8 percent of its total land area from aluminum companies and assign it to small farmers. Moreover, the government was putting about two-thirds of the $200 million expected revenue from the aluminum industry into a capital development fund for further growth; it must, however, withstand pressures for immediate spending in order to work toward long-term growth. Jamaica, at the same time, was seeking compensation for past destruction that industrialization had brought.

The Aluminum Industry 1972–74

In 1972, the aluminum industry began to experience a slippage in output which executives blamed on additional capacity that occurred in 1970 and 1971 just as the market began to decline as a result of the recession. Aluminum Company of America (Alcoa), the largest and most successful producer in the country, announced its strategy. "Alcoa has aggressively gone out and cut prices and has sharply increased its market share for the first time since World War II," reported an analysis by Oppenheimer & Company.

While most of Alcoa's competitors' earnings dropped, Alcoa's income rose 25 percent in the first three quarters of 1972 to $54 million, and its shipments increased about 19 percent, or nearly double the industry average for the year. Compared to the other producers, Alcoa had the highest level of inventories and excess plant capacity. Their role had become one of price disciplinarian.

Within the industry, producers felt that their largest problem was energy, which accounted for 25 percent of production costs. They felt they could get this situation in hand by:

(1) Making greater use of the nation's coal reserves. This would probably lead to increased capacity.
(2) Increasing the smelting efficiency. Alcoa, for example, built a 30,000 ton-a-year pilot plant in Palestine, Texas, to test a new smelting process that was projected to cut power consumption by 30 percent.
(3) Recycling more scrap aluminum.

The developing countries began investigating the possibility of bauxite refineries in their own countries. At first glance, this greatly appealed to the price-concerned industry. The powdery alumina would be cheaper to ship than bauxite. Also, by refining the ore elsewhere, U.S. producers could circumvent restrictive United States pollution laws. Alcoa and Reynolds Aluminum invested heavily in refineries in Jamaica. But the appeal needed to be balanced against the threat of nationalization; too frequently political unrest was directed against the larger industries.

Jamaica and the Aluminum Companies

Although bauxite was the island's main source of revenue, supplying 40 percent of the United States' needs, the government remained virtually ignorant of the aluminum industry until 1973. At that time, Dr. Garnet Brown, Permanent Secretary of Mining and Natural Resources, began a year and a half study of the industry and pried loose much information held in confidence by industry firms.

In May 1974, the government entered into negotiations with six large aluminum companies regarding terms for government participation in the ownership of the bauxite ore facilities on the island. The government walked out of the talks and in June legislated a new tax system which increased the levy dramatically. The new tax increased Jamaican revenues from less than $3 per ton to between $7 and $11 per ton. Before the new tax, the total cost of bauxite ranged between $9 and $15 per ton. Manley said,

> "Within the context of budgetary priorities and in the face of the urgent needs for economic development, the government cannot allow the negotiations to continue indefinitely."

The "Jamaican formula," which was quickly imitated by the other bauxite producers in the Caribbean, levied a fixed percentage of the fluctuating price of the end product, aluminum ingot. In 1974, the tax was 7.5 percent of the realized price of ingot. Hence, Jamaica's share was indexed against inflation and, conversely, was vulnerable to recession.

While paying the increased tax, the companies were appealing to international arbitration. "We will pay the additional revenues . . . but will do so under protest" acknowledged the chairman and Chief Executive Officer of Alcoa.[1] Alcoa, with five other companies, requested the International Center for Settlement of Investment Disputes (ICSID), a body formed under the auspices of the World Bank, to rule on the legality of the Jamaican government's increased tax and royalty action, which, the companies claimed, breeched long term contract agreements.[2] "Bauxite may well be pricing itself out of the market," argued Alcoa's chief executive.[3]

Meanwhile, Alcoa agreed to pay the Dominican Republic, with whom the company was also engaged in heated debate, an additional $6.8 million in bauxite taxes from April 1, 1974 until the end of 1975. The new agreement would substantially increase the country's revenue. The agreement and the company's announcement that it wouldn't have a "material effect" on Alcoa's earnings because its accounts provided for such payments was not lost on the Jamaicans.

Because the aluminum companies paid their local employees well by

---

[1] Harper, *Business Week*, June 22, 1971, p. 29.

[2] This was actually a defensive action should shareholders take it upon themselves to sue the managers for dereliction of duty. The State Department seems to have just shrugged its shoulders when asked for help.

[3] Harper, *op. cit.*

local standards and produced substantial revenue for Jamaica, it was difficult for the government to take uncompromising stands that could lead to
operating losses. Hence, later, in 1975, the government agreed to reduce
the minimum tonnage on which six companies had agreed to pay tax in
1974. The aggregate cut was 14 million long tons (2,240 lbs. = 1 long ton),
and the companies affected included Kaiser Aluminum and Reynolds
Metal Company. The Jamaican government publicly attributed the necessity for the reduction to the "reality" of the U.S. economy and the decreased demand for aluminum.

The International Bauxite Association (IBA)

In October 1973, middle level government officials from major
bauxite producers, including Australia, Guinea, Guyana, Jamaica,
Surinam, and Yugoslavia met in Belgrade to discuss the possibility of collective action in order to maximize revenues from bauxite. A preliminary
IBA charter was drawn. In March 1974, the same nations, plus Sierra
Leone, met again to formally create the IBA and to designate Kingston, Jamaica, as headquarters. In November 1974, the members, joined by Haiti,
Ghana, and the Dominican Republic, met to approve the first annual budget—about $1 million—and to assign each country's contribution. The
staff consisted of the Executive Director Henri Guda, who was Surinam's
Permanent Secretary of Taxation and Finances, Dr. Brown of Jamaica,
who headed the Department of Statistical Research and Technical Information, two other top aides and about 20 supporting clerical and professional people.

The primary concern was the acquisition of information by the various governments concerning the functions of the industry. In order to do
so, the government intended to purchase major ownership in the firms,
thereby allowing full access to company statistics and plans.

IBA's second objective was to formulate a common pricing system in
time for the November 1975 meeting of the Board. There were technical
and political difficulties that needed to be overcome. Under Dr. Brown,
technical experts from all IBA countries compiled data relating to each
country's reserves, pricing policies, mining costs, and other variables. Preliminary studies had shown that because there were many differences between bauxite deposits, a single floor price would be impractical. Hence, a
pricing formula was needed to account for the quality of the ore, the dis-
tance of the deposits from the ore's destination, and mining and shipping
costs.

The third goal was the coordination of production levels. This would
help to avoid excessive supplies. It would also assure equity for each
country within an agreed level of total output.

Once the technical constraints could be met, the political reality would then be considered. The members of the IBA had different government forms and different relationships with the ore deposits. Yugoslavia and Guyana owned the ore outright. Australia merely reviewed the export contracts to determine if the transaction price was fair. The others levied a tax on production. Although issues of national sovereignty were involved, members were generally optimistic that an acceptable formula could be worked out by the November meeting. There was some discussion about pressuring foreign companies into hiring more host-country people, especially in upper management positions. An inter-governmentally-owned shipping fleet was also being explored. Furthermore, all the technical data would be made available to member countries if they wanted to build their own processing plants on aluminum smelters.

Like all producers' associations, the IBA faced major obstacles, and its success would hinge on how effectively the association could manage its market. One problem was that new sources of bauxite could undermine the current producers. Secondly, other raw materials could be substituted for bauxite in aluminum production. And third, if aluminum became too expensive to produce as a result of bauxite costs, other end products could be substituted by aluminum users.

The Industry's Alternatives

With the increasing cost of producing aluminum from bauxite, and the collective actions of the IBA, the aluminum industry began to seek alternatives. While the IBA did not anticipate an embargo, Henri Guda said that member countries should reduce production to keep prices firm. Guda anticipated that alternatives to bauxite would be found. But bauxite was the cheapest source for alumina. Morever, alumina refineries were designed and tooled to use specific grades of bauxite. Substantial capital investment would be required to adapt the refineries to different grades and/or different ores.

The companies expected no further shocks like the cartel and the formation of the IBA since steep new exactions would make bauxite from Jamaica and the other countries noncompetitive. This, as mentioned above, would endanger the payrolls and the foreign exchange for which the mines accounted. But as the expense of transport, power, interest, and wages and salaries grew, aluminum producers' concerns turned from prices to availability. The threat of increased taxes was not the only uncertainty surrounding bauxite. Studies revealed that bauxite depletion would occur in 50 years, leaving the only remaining deposits in obscure locations.

In early 1974, Pechiney Ugine Kuhlmann, through its subsidiary,

Aluminum Pechiney of France, and Alcan Aluminum Ltd., through its subsidiary, Aluminum Company of Canada, Ltd., announced that they would jointly pursue a process which would extract alumina from clays and shales widely available throughout the world. In the future, this might increase world supplies and even enable aluminum manufacturers to avoid the high tax bauxite-producing countries.

Alcoa's cost of bauxite ore had increased by 89 percent during a five-year period; its fuel and power costs had climbed 105 percent in the same period. In early 1974, the company disclosed that it had acquired anorthosite deposits in Wyoming that contained more alumina than all the bauxite reserves in the world. An Alcoa spokesman said "Our 8,000-acre deposit could supply the aluminum industry with all its alumina needs for the next 75 years at the present rate of consumption."[4]

On another front, seven U.S. producers and one Canadian firm announced a program whereby they would join with the U.S. Bureau of Mines in an effort to develop a non-bauxite process. Rather than increase bauxite supplies, this action could eventually eliminate the need for bauxite.

By mid-year, however, the industry was growing more anxious for new bauxite supplies as the price of the aluminum ingot jumped up to 36 cents a pound, an increase of 2½ cents. Reynolds Metals Company and Kaiser Aluminum were the most heavily hit by the increased tax and royalty payments on the Jamaican bauxite. But even Alcoa was pressed into pushing up its prices. Increased industry capacity was the only thing that would slow the price hike in the short run. Perhaps with this in mind, Alcoa initiated plans to expand its smelter in Badin, North Carolina, a multimillion dollar project.

The Industry, 1975

In 1975, the weakness of the domestic economy remained the greatest deterrent to the aluminum industry. The drop in the construction and automobile activity would trim the industry's 1975 shipments by as much as 9 percent below 1974. Producers still said that they would cut production before cutting prices, which rose to 39 cents per pound; companies were operating at less than 80 percent of capacity.

Prices remained strong throughout the year for several reasons:

(1) Producers moved to cut production more quickly than in previous years.

(2) Producers also elected to keep larger ingot inventories rather than cut prices.

[4] *Industry Week*, January 23, 1974, p. 21.

(3) Customers, still hurting from the shortages of 1973 and 1974, were willing to accept higher prices in order to assure themselves of long term supplies.

(4) The government no longer had a big aluminum stockpile with which it could beat back the price increase. The stockpile was almost totally depleted in 1974. Approximately 11 percent of the total aluminum shipments had been coming from the stockpile of the General Services Administration. The threat that the government would put more aluminum onto the market had kept prices down, but that threat appeared more remote than in the past.

Alcoa's new president, William B. Renner, reported a decline in profits, nonetheless, of 31 percent or $31.5 million for 1974. Overall, the industry tried to be optimistic. David P. Reynolds, of Reynolds Aluminum, believed in a quick recovery. An industry analyst observed, "Watch those ingot prices rise. For once, aluminum producers have played a recession right. A year from now, there will again be severe aluminum shortages in the U.S. and this time, this industry will be in proper position to capitalize on them."[5]

But the end of the year brought a sagging demand and a price strategy that backfired, plunging producers into a vicious price war. As the demand declined, the producers sought to keep prices high and stable by cutting production and withholding the already bulging inventories from the market. They had looked to the summer (air-conditioners and recreational vehicles) for recovery and thus borrowed heavily to carry the inventories. Alcoa's debt ratio climbed from 39 percent to 45 percent. In an effort to get back below 40 percent, the company cut its capital spendings. Many producers were operating in the red. The profits of the big three (Alcoa, Kaiser, Reynolds) had fallen an average of 47 percent. To prevent declining prices, close to $500 million had been borrowed to finance the swelling inventories, which amounted to a six-month supply at the end of 1975.

Discounts of 8 percent to 15 percent were offered on list prices of products which accounted for about 20 percent of the aluminum output; mostly sheet, coil and plate products. (Justice Department investigators, who had been conducting a study of the industry behavior during this time, were carefully studying data on the makers' pricing and production policies.) The industry did anticipate price cuts by smaller producers early on, but these would not have held as total demand increased. Hence, the big firms continued to believe that the prices would remain firm. But such was not the case. The summer upturn was mild at best. List prices looked

---

[5] *Business Week*, July 7, 1975, pp. 15–16.

shaky. In early fall, Martin Marietta Aluminum Inc., the seventh largest United States producer, offered a 3 percent discount on coil to distributors. Ranks broke as other companies moved to compete; profits and shipments plummeted. Alcoa estimated that its inventory run-off would be 800 million pounds. Buyers became extremely cautious, however, and didn't rush to fill their depleted inventories. Production was cut even further in order to move inventory and halt price erosion. Some analysts predicted that the only way producers could restore their credibility would be to lower the prices. The major producers did not agree.

Late in 1975, both producers and bauxite exporting countries were still trying to deal with the pricing problem. The IBA urged its eleven members to adopt an "interim" minimum pricing formula for ore in 1976. Although details were not made public, one source implied that the "organized price"[6] was lower than Jamaica's, which had raised its levies again. Jamaica's Prime Minister Manley "emphasized that the Third World wasn't fully satisfied with the present developments of the new world economic order."[7]

New Developments, 1976

Prices. Since 1973, Jamaica and ten other countries forming the IBA had increased taxes and royalties on bauxite from $2 to $11 per ton. Under that formula, the price of bauxite increases each time the price of aluminum ingot rises. The principal reason for the weakening of the cartel-like campaign to raise ore prices centered around a severe slump in demand during 1975. Insiders saw bauxite prices rising moderately once world demand recovered from the recession, but too many pressures led to a slackening of price. Primarily, the device necessary to keep aluminum companies from playing one country against another was a common-pricing formula acceptable to IBA members. This could not be easily reached, however.

As demand began to strengthen, the price of aluminum rose to catch up with the cost increases incurred during the industry's slump. Producers looked for shipments totalling 6.1 million tons, 30 percent more than the 4.7 million in 1975. By 1977, they predicted a 12 percent rise in consumer demand, and by 1980, a growth of 28 percent. Predictions of a price rise were at 4 cents per pound or approximately 10 percent. Buyers insisted that the market wouldn't bear an increase of more than 2 cents except with a sharp slowdown in the industry's rate of capacity expansion. Even though aluminum's domestic ingot price held stable for six months, prices of some fabricated aluminum products had eroded.

[6] The price which was suggested by the IBA, but which was not binding on its members.
[7] *Wall Street Journal*, November 10, 1975.

As the cost of energy soared, aluminum prices continued to climb. The aluminum industry used approximately 4 percent of the total U.S. output of electric power, and most of this went to operate the smelters. Production costs in 1976 ranged from 6 cents per pound to 8 cents per pound. Paradoxically, as energy costs kept rising, bauxite remained cost competitive as a source of alumina on the one hand, but also spurred development of aluminum-containing oil shales on the other.

Supply. Aluminum is the third most abundant element in the earth's crust, but for economic purposes, it is primarily commercially processed from bauxite. The United States has only sparse reserves of bauxite and remains highly dependent on Australia, Guinea and Jamaica.

The aluminum industry and the federal government have spent approximately $1.2 million a year developing and supporting research into alternative refining and finding new sources of bauxite as the threats of cartelism continue to rise. The companies have threatened to locate sources of supply in other than IBA countries, but they have also made heavy investments in the cartel countries. According to N. H. Krome George, Alcoa's chairman, the company can't walk away from major investments like those in Jamaica.

Jamaica, the prime United States supplier, has produced close to 43 percent of the bauxite used worldwide for aluminum production. But while it tripled bauxite charges to keep up with the quadrupling oil costs, a world surplus was expected to bring a drop in bauxite demand during 1976.

Dealing with LDC's

Jamaica was the center of much activity during 1976. It was there that the International Monetary Fund (IMF) met during January to discuss the provision of additional financial help for developing countries and to grant loans equivalent to 75 percent of the country's contributions to the fund. The main disagreement revolved around the relative needs and financial positions of the poor nations versus the industrial nations. Originally, the developing nations demanded a tripling of unrestricted IMF credit but conceded to less severe demands. Their compromise encouraged support from other countries and enabled the meeting to continue constructively.

During the IMF's meeting on the balance-of-payments problem, Jamaicans protested outside the conference site and fighting broke out in the streets. The disparity between Jamaica's many destitute and few wealthy persons gave rise to violent conflict and demand. Jamaica, it appeared, was leaning toward a civil war with Michael Manley's People's National Party fighting the Jamaican Labor Party. Much of the rioting was anti-American, bringing fear and anxiety to visitors, and thereby gravely injuring Jamaica's prime industry, tourism. Many believed Jamaica was living inside a time bomb.

After two years of sharp increases, the price of bauxite began to level off. "We don't intend to price ourselves out of the market," stated Guda, Secretary General of the cartel. Jamaica, itself, lowered the taxes on bauxite under agreements with foreign companies that they would give the Kingston government part ownership in the mining and refining facilities on the island.

In rolling back the tax rate on Alcoa's bauxite production, Jamaica froze the levy through 1983. The government would own 6 percent of a joint venture with Alcoa to operate all installations on the island. It would also guarantee 40 years supply of bauxite for Alcoa's present refining capacity. According to Alcoa's Chairman George, the plan established a new, stable, relationship with the Jamaican government.

At the 1976 aluminum list price of 48 cents per pound, the agreement would lower bauxite levies by $2.6 million per year for Alcoa when the company's Jamaican refinery opened at full capacity. Reynolds and Kaiser, both dependent on Jamaica for two-thirds of their bauxite, expected to receive similar tax treatment in the final versions of the preliminary contracts drawn up in 1974 and 1976. The aluminum industry hoped that Jamaica's hold on taxes would influence other producers in the Caribbean.

Jamaica and its constituents protected themselves against worldwide inflation by "indexing" their bauxite revenues to aluminum. Although the agreement disallowed future abrupt bauxite price hikes, by basing the bauxite levies as such, Jamaica guaranteed that its tax would follow ingot price rises in the U.S. This protection against deterioration was a goal sought by most Third World countries, but reached by few.

The Alcoa agreement, and similar ones under negotiation, reflected a rising concern in Jamaica that surging bauxite taxes could put the island at a price disadvantage in competition with other suppliers of the raw material. Aluminum companies could neither move existing facilities, nor immediately alter worldwide patterns of supply.

Industry Responses

With producers' costs soaring, resulting from the increasing costs of raw materials and electricity, and the threat of the cartel, the industry's primary concerns were to identify material substitutions and to locate alternatives. Rising aluminum prices gave profits a "healthier look," but were not enough to facilitate significant expansion or modernization. Profits of the big three's—Reynolds, Kaiser and Alcoa—fell an average of 47 percent in 1975. They had managed to hold the operating rate of their plants just above the breakeven point, but at a very heavy cost. The three had borrowed approximately $500 million to finance swelling inventories of the metal. But high debt-to-equity ratios continued to plague the companies; Reynolds had been at 49 percent, Kaiser's at 47 percent and Alcoa's at 45 percent.

Gains in actual shipments also accelerated in the first quarter of 1976. Domestic shipments were expected to rise 25 percent to 30 percent. If projections held, there would be better prices for producers. There might even exist a shortage of metal resulting from the government's stockpile depletion.

It was hoped that accelerated recycling would help to alleviate the squeeze. As the industry became "supersensitive" to charges that it was squandering the nation's energy on beer cans and domestic foil, there developed a strong emphasis on recyclability.[8]

Reynolds Metal Company

Reynolds' long term plans were battered in 1976. The company added 20 percent additional capacity in 1971 and claimed that it had full use from this big investment in the plant for only one brief period two years ago. Reynolds stated intentions of building a pilot processing plant in Arkansas.

The main concern in the company was prices. Reynold's long term debt was 51 percent of its invested capital, i.e., the long-term debt plus the shareholders' equity, which didn't include an off-balance sheet debt. Reynolds hoped to raise prices an average 6.4 percent for aluminum ingot and most fabricated products during 1976. "We're not discouraged," according to one executive. As prices go up, "it's closing the gap."

Sympathetic, Arkansas gave its biggest user of electricity a break on sales taxes in hopes that the company would recall some of its 1,400 laid off workers and help ease the 7.3 percent unemployment rate. As plans evolved to further increase primary aluminum output, boosting the U.S. smelter operating rate to 77 percent from 74 percent, Reynolds recalled 210 employees.

By April, the company reopened two production lines to "meet improving demand for aluminum" and raised the producing rate to 81 percent capacity. It began to negotiate for a plant in Brazil while still considering the building of a smelter in Paraguay. As Reynolds announced plans to further hike prices up to 48 cents a pound, news of questionable payments to Canada, Jamaica, Guyana and Surinam became known.

[8] It takes only 5 percent as much energy to melt down old aluminum as it does to produce virgin metal from ore.

Kaiser Aluminum Corporation

During 1976, Kaiser Aluminum remained optimistic as it studied its options and possibilities for increased production and alternatives to supply. It continued a feasibility study on bauxite production in Ghana as it checked into the economics of turning clays from Georgia and Alabama into aluminum.

T. F. Preece, Vice President of Planning, said that the company received far greater returns from its chemical operations. He stated that there were good payoffs in modernizing existing smelters, making alterations that conserved energy and installing fabricating capacity, such as rolling mills, to add value to metal that otherwise might be sold in ingot form.

Kaiser expected to increase its domestic aluminum production rate on May 1 to 77 percent of capacity from 73 percent. It predicted that the 1976 net income would exceed $81.2 million. By April, the concern had raised the international price of primary aluminum ingot 4 cents a pound to 43 cents. Domestic shipments in March had been the highest in the previous sixteen months, and with prices expected to continue to climb to 48 cents a pound in August, the outlook was positive.

In June, the Kaiser company told the Securities and Exchange Commission that it had contributed approximately $90,000 to two major political parties in Jamaica since 1970. They claimed that these were made, however, in a manner consistent with both Jamaican and U.S. laws, and were properly authorized and accounted for in the company's books.

Aluminum Company of America (Alcoa)

Although one quarter of Alcoa's production capacity was idle, the first phase of a new 300,000-ton-per-year smelter, which would cut costs between 4.5 cents and 5 cents per pound was put into effect. The plant at Palestine, Texas, would provide the company with more profitable production. The key was a chemical catalyst in the smelting process which would help reduce the amount of electric power needed by 30 percent. It had taken 15 years and $25 million to perfect the process.

In July, the refinery in Jamaica closed due to a production vessel which had burst. There was extensive damage to the key unit. However, Alcoa claimed that its shipments would not be affected. There was no indication of sabotage.

To partially replace lost production, Alcoa said that it intended to restart an unspecified amount of alumina-refining at its Point Comfort, Texas, facility. This plant had been left idle due to low smelter operating rates resulting from the industry's 1975 slump.

Price boosts took effect with shipments on June 1, causing the "appropriate adjustments" in prices of other ingot products and of "approximately a quarter" of its aluminum mill product tonnage. Alcoa's debt ratio climbed from 39 percent to 45 percent in 1975 alone. To get back below 40 percent, the company planned to cut capital spending throughout 1976. W. H. Krome George, Alcoa's chairman, in a statement announcing the price increases, said that costs had risen very substantially, while aluminum prices remained relatively stable. The growth of costs and the essential usefulness of the product fully justified improved prices. Alcoa's return on investment was claimed to be far short of capital needs to meet the demand the company and the industry saw ahead.

As with the other major companies, Alcoa took stock of its possible courses of action. Alcoa purchased a vast deposit of anorthosite—the nation's largest domestic aluminum resource—in Wyoming in 1972. There had been some problems in processing, but the outlook remained positive. Alcoa's subsidiary, Surinam Aluminum Company, reached a three-year agreement covering the levy it would pay on bauxite to the government of Surinam, where Alcoa receives 25 percent of its bauxite requirements. But the company's main concern was its involvement in Jamaica.

It was brought to light that a controversial U.S. Ambassador to Jamaica had prodded Alcoa to make a $25,000 payment to a political party there in 1971. The Ambassador was Vincent De Roulet, a Nixon administration political appointee who had served from 1969–73 and died in 1975.

Roulet asked the company to make the contribution to an "educational program" in a foreign country to explain to the citizenry the advantage of U.S. investments. Alcoa made the payment in a cashier's check for $25,000, but the company was unable to determine whether any such educational program ever became a reality.

Alcoa proceeded to make two more payments of an additional $25,-000 and $5,000. There was no evidence of a bribe or any improper payments to a government employee. Corporate political contributions were legal in Jamaica.

It appeared that Roulet was concerned about the nationalization of U.S. assets. The U.S. aluminum industry gets 10 percent of its aluminum requirements from Jamaica. Alcoa, alone, through its subsidiary operates a $155 million, 550,000 ton-a-year aluminum refinery there.

Roulet said he had made a "deal" with Prime Minister Manley prior to the 1972 election. In exchange for Manley's guarantee that he wouldn't nationalize the bauxite industry, Roulet promised not to intervene in the elections. Manley denied the allegation.

In testimony before the Senate Multinational Subcommittee in July 1973, Roulet said that he thought a Jamaican politician had "got the impression that the President of the U.S. in those days was a good man to have as a friend and the bauxite boys were nice people to have as friends . . . and it might make more sense to go along with the U.S., which wasn't madly in love with the prospect of expropriation. . . ."

THE POLITICAL CHARACTER
OF ECONOMIC CHANGE

One conclusion that seems clear from cases such as the bauxite cartel is that as additional relevant publics and political actors are introduced into the familiar economic decision-making framework, the amount of managerial uncertainty increases. The formation of the resource cartels is perhaps the most extreme example of this phenomenon in recent managerial history.

The bauxite cartel case presents a series of managerial responses to this new economic-political development. The initial environmental change was the effort of the bauxite producing nations to form the cartel. The reasons for its formation were certainly economic in nature, although the steps taken to form the cartel were definitely of a political nature. The industry's initial reaction seems to have been one of bargaining with the producer nations in order to keep the bauxite levies low, and to actually undermine the formation of the IBA. Indeed, Alcoa's payment to the U.S. Ambassador in Jamaica is a throwback to the early effort to buy off, or bargain away, the social and economic aspirations of the developing nations. The failure of this bargaining approach, and the relative success of the IBA, eventually forced a new course of action on the industry's members. There were some who chose to resist at all costs, and eventually forsake their investment in the developing nations.[9] The three major firms in the industry, however, apparently recognized the inevitability of the cartel and searched for alternative courses of action that would either assure new sources of bauxite or new production processes that would allow the industry to replace bauxite with a substitute product.

In the variable life insurance case (chapter 3), the political system provided a *context* in which economic change and response had to occur. The underlying change involved investor movement away from life insurance and toward mutual funds and common stock. To this change, the life insurers responded with a conventional economic response, new product innovation. The difficulties that ensued were attributable to the tension involved in harmonizing economic adaptations, which depend on flexibility and speed, with political requirements of regulatory consistency, standardization, and approval.

---

[9] Revere Copper, for example, relinquished its mining facilities in Jamaica and submitted a claim with the Overseas Private Insurance Corporation (OPIC) for damages due to expropriation.

By comparison, the International Bauxite Association case is a situation in which the underlying change is political and economic in *character*. The decision about how economic activity is to be organized in a society is both a political and an economic decision. The complexity of the interpenetration between the aluminum industry and the developing nations, such as Jamaica, is well illustrated in such a case. For Jamaica, the industry represents an important, even critical, source of revenue. It cannot be jeopardized too much; yet, the political perception that motivated the nations to create the IBA was one of insufficient revenue for a natural and limited resource that the industrialized nations prized and for which they seemed able to pay considerably more. Despite their prominence as providers of revenue for the developing nations, the industry's members seem to have been unable to present the united front required to deal more effectively with the IBA. Hence, it has now become necessary for each company to accept the inevitability of the cartel and plan their own strategic responses to the new realities of political economy in the bauxite producing nations.

chapter five

the promise of technology

TECHNOLOGY AS A SOCIAL GOOD

In the evolution of the American economy, technology and technological innovation have been the principal engine of change. Because technological innovation assisted men in accomplishing their tasks, and then enabled them to become more productive and efficient, it has generally been favored and cultivated. Since the industrial revolution, America has celebrated its inventors, tinkerers, and engineers. Institutions have been created to organize and stimulate the evolution of technology. Universities, research laboratories, and government funding have characterized the scientific establishment. Indeed, financial support for technology and science by the federal government has been one of the principal stimuli of twentieth century technological development.

Technology has the potential of bringing broad and sweeping change to a society. Historian Thomas Cochran has pointed out that technological innovation needs supporting roles and institutions to reach its full measure of accomplishment.[1] He makes the point that new forms of art and music won acceptance in France in the late nineteenth century because it had a number of institutions which encouraged such innovation; no such acceptance occurred in the United States because there were few institutions to support the ideas. American culture, however, offered little resistance to new machinery or methods of organizing work. Businesses not only accepted technological and scientific change, they sought it out and were founded on it. It was the wellspring of production efficiency, increasing output, expansion of markets, and new products. Business has been one of the central institutions in American society, and American businessmen have endorsed and favored change based on technology since colonial times.

For businessmen, technology was favored because of its potential as a source of profit opportunities; for society as a whole, technological innovation was the foundation for social improvement. Life was made easier, more fun, and less burdensome when new innovations appeared. Refrigeration, washing machines, electricity, automobiles and countless other manifestations of technology made America a wealthier and probably a happier society. Technology was a social good because it provided economic growth, new jobs, and an improved quality of life.

It is only in the past decade that large-scale public concern with technological change has become a normal part of the American business environment. Concern with atomic energy existed during the 1940's and 1950's, it is true, but the impact of technology did not really emerge as a major item on the American public policy agenda until the 1960's. The environmental movement was founded on a concern for preserving the natural environment from the intrusion of technology. Where there had been a positive attitude toward any new technology, the 1960's produced a plethora of questions and objections, concern and disillusionment. The secondary impacts of technology were noteworthy and publicly discussed. The natural environment developed a broad array of supporters and protectors, and technology seemed to lose her promise.

TECHNOLOGY AS A SOCIAL THREAT: FLUOROCARBONS AND THE OZONE LAYER

Concern for the physical environment has produced many public issues since the 1960's, touching nearly every manufacturing industry. Among

[1] Thomas C. Cochran, *Social Change In America: The Twentieth Century* (New York: Harper & Row, 1972), Harper Torchbook Series, p. 26.

the many issues which the development of the supersonic transport (SST) aircraft brought to the forefront of public discussion was the impact of technology on the earth's upper atmosphere. The impact of the SST on the ozone layer of the earth's atmosphere may not have been the central objection to its development and commercial use, but the emergence of the issue led a number of scientists to concentrate their research on the ozone layer. One finding was that one of man's most ubiquitous technologies, the aerosol spray can, was generating quite as much damage—perhaps even more—to the ozone layer as would the SST. This finding created a serious public issue for the many consumer products companies that used aerosol spray cans for their products and, no less so, for the relatively few companies that manufactured the critical aerosol propellant, fluorocarbon gas. For both groups, their basic business activities (marketing in the first case, manufacturing in the second) were so intimately associated with this issue that management responses were essential. Those responses are discussed below.

Nature of Problem

Fluorocarbons are used as a propellant in aerosol spray cans and are discharged into the atmosphere when the product is used. Fluorocarbons do not react chemically with other compounds nor with the people who consume the products, and they vaporize quickly. Because fluorocarbons are insoluble in water, removal from air by rainfall does not occur. The very stability of fluorocarbon is its most dangerous aspect because this allows it to reach the ozone layer before decomposing.

Ozone is an oxygen gas whose molecules consist of three oxygen atoms rather than the two atoms which constitute ordinary oxygen. A seven-mile band of the stratosphere, about 22 miles deep, containing a high concentration of naturally occurring ozone, is known as the "ozone layer." The ozone layer is formed when sunlight strikes oxygen. Most scientists agree that life on earth did not evolve until after the ozone layer was formed.[2]

There are two properties of the stratosphere which are instrumental in producing the ozone layer and are also important in considering the effects of pollutants introduced into this area. First, the stratosphere is thermally very stable; this has allowed ozone to build up in relatively high concentrations because it is not rapidly mixed with the lower portions of the atmosphere. This also means, however, that pollutants introduced into the area tend to accumulate and remain there. Second, chemical reactions among gases in this region are heavily influenced by high-energy radiation from the sun; this radiation can decompose compounds which are rela-

[2] Allen L. Hammond et al, "Stratospheric Pollution: Multiple Threats to Earth's Ozone," *Science*, Vol. 186, No. 4161 (October 25, 1974), p. 337.

tively inert under other conditions. It is just this condition which has created the ozone layer and can decompose fluorocarbons. One breakdown product of fluorocarbon is chlorine, which is a major catalyst in destroying ozone.

These chlorine atoms which are released when fluorocarbons interact with ultra-violet light are chemically active. One molecule of fluorocarbon can destroy many molecules of ozone by initiating a chain reaction. Thus, the presence of even small quantities of fluorocarbon molecules can have a magnified effect resulting in the reduction of thousands of ozone molecules to common oxygen. It is not so much the presence of these reactions which is in question, but the speed at which they take place.

The amount of ozone in the stratosphere varies with the time of day, the season and the latitude. These changes are considered to be naturally balanced; it is only when these natural balances are disturbed that there is a chance of ozone depletion and the resulting increase in radiation which adversely affects the biosphere.[3]

There are two potential sources of penetration and decomposition of the ozone layer:

1) Nitrogen Oxides: this gaseous element is released by supersonic airplanes, by nuclear explosions and fertilizer.

2) Free Chlorine Atoms: these are derived from the chlorofluorocarbons in refrigerants, coolants and aerosol-can propellants.

One major problem arising from the depletion of the ozone layer is that the excess amount of ultra-violet rays reaching the biosphere can cause skin cancer in humans and seriously affect all other forms of animal and plant life. Increases in surface temperatures, severe climactic changes, sunburn leading to premature aging of the skin, allergic reactions, and mutations are also predicted.

There are approximately one million Americans working in chlorofluorocarbon related industries with sales of nearly $8 billion.[4] The breakdown of products using the chemical is as follows: 50 percent aerosol cans, 35 percent refrigerants and coolants, and 15 percent foam for cushions and insulation, fire extinguisher agent, and cleaning solvents.[5] Although

---

[3] The biosphere is that zone of living organisms at or near the earth's surface, extending from the subsurface of soil and water areas into the air.
[4] Janet H. Weinberg, "Ozone Verdict: On Faith or Fact?" *Science News*, Vol. 102, (May 17, 1975), p. 322.
[5] "We've Been Asked: Why the Worry Over Spray Cans?" *U.S. News & World Report*, Vol. LXXVIII, No. 18 (May 5, 1975), p. 41.

aerosol propellants (which are used in 55 percent of all aerosols[6]) account for only one-half of the fluorocarbon production in the United States, they account for close to two-thirds of the harmful emissions into the atmosphere.[7] Freon-11 and Freon-12 (the DuPont trademark for fluorocarbons) constituted almost 80 percent of the total fluorocarbon production in 1974.

Aerosols may use either one of two principal propellants, fluorocarbons or hydrocarbons. Hydrocarbons are more reactive and more flammable, not odorless or tasteless, though they are less expensive than fluorocarbons. Therefore they may be used in products with a water base that protects against flammability and in products not used on people. Hydrocarbons are generally not dangerous to the environment. There are two other alternative compounds, nitrous oxide and carbon dioxide. Nitrous oxide is principally used as an anesthetic, also known as laughing gas. It too is soluble in water, flammable, and has the same disadvantages as hydrocarbons. Carbon dioxide is a compressed gas that does not have a fine even spray. Since the pressure of this gas as a propellant weakens with the decreasing of can ingredients, large amounts of this propellant are needed in comparison to the product ingredients.

When compared with other forms of packaging, aerosols seem to have a long list of advantages:

1) Efficiency: most effective application for some products.
2) Reliability: formulated for optimum characteristics and delivered ready-to-use without variance with each application.
3) Application: controlled direction, concentration and amount; uniformity of dispersion; even metered dosage where that is important.
4) Convenience: quick and easy, of course, with no preparation, no clean-up.
5) Hygiene: sealed container, no product contamination; lack of direct contact at point of application permits common use of personal products by other family members.
6) Stability: no evaporation or dilution; little deterioration.
7) Economy: very little waste or spill; uniformity of application often provides better mileage.

---

[6] *Economic Significance of Fluorocarbons*, U.S. Department of Commerce, C57.502:F 67, released July 1976.
[7] "Preliminary Economic Impact Assessment of Possible Regulatory Action to Control Atmospheric Emissions of Selected Halocarbons," draft report prepared by A. D. Little, Inc. for U.S. Environmental Protection Agency, released December, 1975.

8) Performance: application as foam; uniform coating on sur-
                   faces whether smooth, porous or rough.
9) Aesthetics: dry or pleasantly moist application; avoids un-
                   desirable wetness or stickiness.
10) Safety: no accidental spillage or ingestion; (fluorocar-
                   bon can reduce flammability which may be in-
                   herent in some products.)

History of Rising Concerns

The first ozone controversy involved the development of the SST. The SST was accused of emitting nitrogen oxides which would have had a substantial effect on the reduction of the ozone layer, influencing both the weather and health factors. This ozone depletion was the key environmental argument to restrict the supersonic transport. The position finally emerged that it was the job of the SST supporters to prove that the plane would not have the effects that were postulated.

In 1971, Dr. James E. Lovelock of the University of Reading, England, while doing a routine air-sampling, identified a significant concentration of fluorocarbons in the atmosphere up to ten miles above the surface. Dr. Lovelock recorded his findings and was aware of the inert nature of fluorocarbons and their possible usefulness in tracing air movements.

In mid-1972, two chemists in California, Professor F. Sherwood Rowland and Dr. Mario J. Molina, having heard of Dr. Lovelock's findings, began to investigate the implications of fluorocarbon presence in the upper atmosphere. They presented a paper in the June 28, 1974 issue of *Nature*, which noted that chlorofluoromethanes were being added to the environment in steadily increasing amounts. Chemically inert, these compounds can remain in the atmosphere for 40–150 years, and concentrations can be expected to reach 10–30 times present levels. The paper suggested that continued increases in fluorocarbon usage could result in a 10 percent decrease in ozone within 50–80 years.

A second paper by two University of Michigan scientists using the same process model, appeared in the September 27, 1974 issue of *Science*. This paper predicted a 10 percent decrease in ozone by 1985 or 1990. Other papers supporting these findings have predicted ozone layer depletion up to 40 percent by 1995, depending on the growth of fluorocarbon usage.

An early theorist of ozone destruction, Harold S. Johnston of the University of California at Berkeley, stated that the controversy was more philosophical than scientific: is there ever enough data to confirm an unpopular scientific theory, a theory that could put a halt to a major industry and change the habits of millions of consumers? Rowland and Molina, together with Dr. Johnston, were able to determine that free chlorine atoms destroy the ozone six times more efficiently than the nitrogen oxides emitted by the SST.[8]

In October 1974, the National Academy of Sciences (NAS) reviewed the published papers and recognized a need to further investigate the matter. They selected two committees to study the problem for one year or longer and render a report to the Academy. The two committees consisted of the (1) Panel on Atmospheric Chemistry—leading chemists in the field to determine the present state of the ozone layer and (2) a group of people concerned with determining the overall potential impact of the problem. Although both groups were leaning towards acceptance of the ozone destruction theory and were suggesting that a 5 percent depletion in the ozone layer might produce an additional 8000 cases of skin cancer per year among Caucasians,[9] they recommended a slow approach to the problem and urged that any action wait until the completion of their study in 1976.

In late 1974, the Natural Resources Defense Council, a public environmental protection group, petitioned the Consumer Product Safety Commission to ban fluorocarbon use. The CPSC deferred judgment until the results from the NAS were completed and published.

A federal task force was established in early 1975. Its membership was composed of representatives from twelve federal agencies and a report was published in June 1975 supporting the scientific findings behind the ozone depletion theory. This group suggested January 1978 as the target date for controlling legislation, depending on the findings of the NAS in 1976.

Other governmental action also began in 1975. In February, several bills recommending studies of the problem by NAS and NASA were introduced in Congress. NASA launched its Atmospheric Explorer Satellite on November 19, 1975 to make direct measurements of ozone. Six weeks earlier another satellite was launched to measure nitric acid in the ozone.[10] The NASA study was not expected to be completed until 1978. Several congressional committees held hearings on the ozone topic, but no action resulted. In June 1975, Oregon passed the first legislation to control aerosol use. The bill banned the sale of products containing fluorocarbon propellants after March 1, 1977. In August 1975, a government research team released results of atmospheric tests that strongly supported the

[8] "Fluorocarbons and Ozone: New Predictions Ominous," *Science News*, Vol. 106, No. 14 (October 5, 1974), p. 213.

[9] Hammond, *op. cit.*, p. 337.

[10] "Ozone from Orbit: A Lowdown Look," *Science News*, Vol. 108, No. 22 (November 29, 1975), p. 341.

ozone depletion theory. It was discovered that the fluorocarbon levels at different altitudes corresponded closely to those predicted.

The debate over ozone destruction involved many levels of government because "cancer—even the more benign types of skin cancer—evokes strong public responses. And when the threat comes from the skies and the entire population of the earth is exposed, a public forum is assured."[11]

The Industry and Its Responses

Just over one billion pounds of fluorocarbon products were manufactured in the United States in 1974. There are six primary manufacturers who account for virtually all the United States production. DuPont is the largest manufacturer, with close to 50 percent of the market; Allied Chemical has about 25 percent of the total, Union Carbide, 17 percent, while Pennwalt, Kaiser Aluminum, and Racon produce the rest. The exact amount that each company produces for the aerosol industry alone cannot be determined. Only Racon depended on fluorocarbons for a major portion (100 percent) of its sales, while the other producers derived less than 10 percent of their sales from fluorocarbons (in the case of DuPont, only 1 percent) in 1974. The United States accounts for roughly one-half of the total world fluorocarbon production.[12]

Manufacturers and marketers of personal care products have the biggest stake in the fluorocarbon/aerosol business. These include Gillette (Right Guard, Adorn, The Dry Look), Bristol-Myers (Ban, Vitalis, Clairol), and Carter-Wallace (Arrid). The total value of fluorocarbons produced for aerosol use in 1974 in the U.S. was about $250 million. In 1975 DuPont announced that its fluorocarbon sales were increasing for the industry by 8–9 percent annually.

The DuPont Company had been in the process of constructing the largest fluorocarbon plant in the world, in Corpus Christi, Texas. The cost was estimated at $100 million and it was expected to be completed by 1980. This will allow DuPont to double its production of Freon *if* it is still legal. When asked what would happen if Freon loses the battle, DuPont's plant manager, A. B. Rhodes, answered, "You got me, I guess we'll just be out of business."[13]

John Dickinson, Vice-President of Gillette North American, states that although the company recently introduced Right Guard Roll-On,

[11] E. M. Leeper, "Spray Cans Must Go . . . Bumpers Promises Bill Banning Nonessential Fluorocarbons," *BioScience*, Vol. 25, No. 11 (November, 1975), p. 755.

[12] *Economic Significance of Fluorocarbons*, U.S. Department of Commerce, C57.502:F 67, released July, 1976.

[13] Sean Mitchell, "The Politics of Freon," *The Nation*, Vol. 220, No. 25 (June 28, 1975), p. 775.

there could be a shortage of molded plastic parts and other components, if sprays are banned and people flock to buy roll-ons. This is because plant conversions rarely take less than one year.

Fluorocarbon manufacturers initially resisted the reports about the ozone destruction, believing them to be sensational and premature and foreseeing economic damage if fluorocarbon production were limited. A leading manufacturer provided $3 million to fund research at three universities under the direction of the Manufacturing Chemists Association. DuPont assigned their own research and development department to study replacement formulas and predicted that through early 1976 they would spend more than $5 million studying alternatives. Manufacturers of fluorocarbon consumer products also began studying their alternatives such as pumps, sticks and roll-ons. By June of 1975, Gillette and Bristol-Myers had placed pump-top hairsprays on the market as alternatives to their sizable aerosol-spray product lines.[15] These new sprays and new roll-ons were being heavily advertised; Bristol-Myers spent $6 million during a three-month campaign to promote its Ban Basic non-aerosol deodorant.[16] Most marketers positioned their fluorocarbon aerosol products side by side with the new substitutes.

In June 1975, the Johnson Wax Company announced in a three-quarter page advertisement that "Effective today, our company has removed all fluorocarbon propellants from our product lines in the United States, and we are aggressively reformulating our product ingredient world-wide to achieve the same goal."[17] The Johnson company converted the propellant in its floor wax to hydrocarbons. All Johnson aerosol products were labeled "Use with confidence, contains no Freon (R) or other fluorocarbons claimed to harm the ozone layer." It is possible that Johnson Wax could afford to be so dramatic because it carried only three fluorocarbon products. On June 30, 1975, the DuPont Company also bought an almost full-page advertisement in the *New York Times* to express its "dual concern" for the survival of the ozone layer and the American aerosol industry. In September 1975, Alberto-Culver noted, "In response to the environmental question, a new propellant system using naturally occurring compressed gases was put into operation . . ."[18]

On September 26, 1975, a summary report of the Fluorocarbon Research Program[19] identified two time scales for the basis of determining future actions:

[14] E. M. Leeper, *op. cit.,* p. 755.
[15] *New York Times,* June 22, 1975, Sec. 3, p. 3.
[16] *New York Times,* May 12, 1976, p. 29.
[17] *New York Times,* June 20, 1975.
[18] Alberto-Culver Annual Report, September 30, 1975.
[19] "Effect of Fluorocarbons on the Atmosphere," a summary of the Fluorocarbons Research Program, sponsored by the Fluorocarbon Industry and administered by the Manufacturing Chemists Association, September 26, 1975.

(1) Longterm Scale: requires many years to completely and accurately measure which compounds actually affect the ozone layer and to what extent, as well as the resulting effects on public health and the environment.

(2) Short-term Scale: two or three years are necessary to obtain sufficient data to predict the outcomes of the longterm studies, to determine the accuracies of such predictions, and to decide when action, if any, must be taken to prevent possible harm to humans and/or environment.

By the end of 1975, Gillette reported to its stockholders that "As a result of intensified R & D efforts, the company has introduced products which provide highly effective non-aerosol alternatives to consumers. . . . All major Gillette aerosol products which use fluorocarbon propellants are also available in non-aerosol forms."[20] During 1975, when marketers of spray products were moving rapidly to bring out substitutes, the various federal regulatory agencies were consistently turning down requests for restrictive actions against fluorocarbon products.

By early 1976, the Manufacturing Chemists Association conceded the general validity of the ozone depletion theory but insisted that two more years of study was needed before any bans were imposed. In March 1976, the MCA outlined three conclusions in a technical report:

(1) Research gaps will take years to fill.

(2) Ozone decreases during the next few years of production will be minimal; and

(3) Research should continue through 1978 at least without regulation on production.[21]

DuPont's Response

DuPont developed and patented Freon (fluorocarbon) in the early 1950's, which stimulated the aerosol boom. By 1954, consumer usage had increased to nearly 200 million cans and expanded to nearly 500 million by 1958; products included hair sprays, shaving creams and the traditional insecticides. By the end of the 1960's usage exceeded 2.3 billion cans and covered a wide range of home and personal care products. Their convenience of use, combined with expensive and wide advertising, made aerosol packaging one of the most popular consumer product technologies.

[20] Gillette Annual Report, December 31, 1975.

[21] "To Ban or Not To Ban: Data for the Ozone Question," *Science News*, Vol. 109, No. 12 (March 20, 1976), p. 180.

DuPont is the leading manufacturer of fluorocarbons with about 50 percent of the market, followed by Allied Chemical, Union Carbide and others. In 1973, DuPont began constructing its Corpus Christi plant in order to double its Freon production to meet the expected 8-10 percent annual growth in fluorocarbon demand. In July 1972, DuPont served as catalyst for a research program to investigate the effects, if any, of fluorocarbons upon the environment. This was supported by all of the free world's 19 producers of fluorocarbons, six being from the United States (See Table 5-1).

That program was to be administered by the industry-sponsored MCA and directed by a technical panel which included one member from each supporting company. Thus, industry's concern existed before the Rowland/Molina study was issued. After the Rowland/Molina study identified the potential seriousness of the problem in 1974, the MCA's research program was expanded still further, concentrating on determining to what extent, if any, fluorocarbon affects the ozone layer.

DuPont's immediate response to the controversy involved three parts. First, they increased their research to find suitable alternative products. Secondly, they began a publicity campaign to convey two messages:

TABLE 5-1.

FLUOROCARBON MANUFACTURERS
REPRESENTED ON THE
MCA TECHNICAL PANEL ON FLUOROCARBON RESEARCH

Akzo Chemical nv (Holland)
Allied Chemical Corporation (U.S.)
Asahi Glass Co., Ltd. (Japan)
Australian Fluorine Chemical Pty. Ltd. (Australia)
Daikin Kogyo Co., Ltd. (Japan)
E. I. DuPont de Nemours & Co., Inc. (U.S.)
DuPont of Canada Limited (Canada)
Farbwerke Hoechst AG (West Germany)
Imperial Chemical Industries Limited (England)
I.S.C. Chemicals Ltd. (England)
Kaiser Aluminum & Chemical Corporation (U.S.)
Kali-Chemie Aktiengesellschaft (West Germany)
Mitsui Fluorochemicals Co. Ltd. (Japan)
Montedision S.P.A. (Italy)
Pennwalt Corp. (U.S.)
Racon Incorporated (U.S.)
Rhone-Poulenc Industrie (France)
Ugine Kuhlmann, Produits Chimiques (France)
Union Carbide Corporation (U.S.)

---

(1) they are a reasonable and responsible corporation which is intent on furthering the public good, and (2) restrictive regulation of fluorocarbon products was unwarranted because (in their opinion) the controversy is still subjective rather than scientific. Finally, DuPont employed three outside agencies to trumpet its viewpoint, two of which existed before the issue (the Manufacturing Chemists Association and the Aerosol Education Board). The third agency, the Council on Atmospheric Sciences, was created specifically to address the issue. The 1975 DuPont Annual Report noted that "through the CAS, DuPont has helped to oppose restrictive state legislation before all facts are known . . ."

DuPont's basic argument was that a sound scientific case against fluorocarbons had not yet been presented. Philosophically, it was an "innocent-until-proven-guilty" position. It was conveyed publicly when DuPont ran an advertisement in June, 1975, which claimed that "there is no persuasive evidence" that fluorocarbons harm the atmosphere. "In the meantime, aerosol products suffer under a cloud of presumed guilt and other fluorocarbon-dependent industries are seriously threatened. We believe this is unfair."[22] In this and subsequent ads, DuPont wanted loftier motives than pure self-interest to prevail. The willingness of the company to stop production of products when proven to be harmful was stressed. "DuPont wants to do what is right . . . (but), the nation cannot afford to act on this and other issues before all the facts are known.[23]

By the end of 1975, DuPont's argument had changed in a slight, but significant way. Instead of trying to bury the issue due to lack of evidence, they urged that several years more be devoted to further study of the problem, despite the fact that the harmful effects of fluorocarbons on the ozone layer had already been fairly well established. When the National Academy of Sciences reported, in September, 1976, that fluorocarbons were probably dangerous substances and that their use should probably be severely restricted, DuPont emphasized that "there is no significant risk to the public . . . in taking time to complete the industry and government sponsored research programs."[24]

During 1975 and 1976, DuPont hinted in very explicit ways that a major economic crisis could be expected if the use of fluorocarbons were banned. Curiously, while inflating the industry stake, DuPont consistently implied that its own economic stake was negligible; dollar figures were never mentioned, only percentage terms. DuPont sales of fluorocarbon aerosols were reported as 1 percent of total company sales, conveniently overlooking the fact that this still amounted to $100 million!

[22] *New York Times*, November 2, 1974, p. 59.
[23] *New York Times*, June 30, 1975, p. 28.
[24] DuPont Corporate News, September 13, 1976.

TABLE 5-2.

WHAT THE FLUOROCARBON BAN WILL COST THE INDUSTRY

INDUSTRY SECTOR	ESTIMATED LOST SALES, 1977–80 (MILLIONS OF 1976 DOLLARS)
Marketers and captive fillers	$ 573
Chemical manufacturers	299
Container manufacturers	132
Valve manufacturers	37
Independent fillers	26
TOTAL	$1,067

Data: International Research & Technology Corporation

Gillette's Response

Gillette produces consumer personal care products that employ fluorocarbons as propellants in their aerosols. These products totaled 66 separate items and accounted for 10 percent of the company's $1.3 billion sales in 1975. The consumer products containing fluorocarbons included:

(1) Underarm deodorants and antiperspirants: Right Guard Line, Soft & Dri Line
(2) Men's hair products: The Dry Look Line
(3) Hair sprays: Adorn Line, White Rain Line
(4) Foot spray: Foot Guard

All of these products are leaders in their respective markets. They also market some aerosol products that use hydrocarbon or carbon dioxide as propellants. Gillette has also introduced alternatives for those who choose to use a non-aerosol product:

(1) Roll-ons: Right Guard, Soft & Dri
(2) Pump hair sprays: Adorn, Firm & Free, White Rain, Dry Look, Max Hold.

Gillette faced a situation in which if aerosol products were banned, and consumer demand for non-aerosol alternatives reached existing levels of aerosol demand, the cost of additional tooling and equipment would be $1–2 million, and the time necessary to reach existing levels of production would be 12–15 months. This conversion time would have been greatly increased if the entire industry were forced to do it simultaneously. Book value of capital equipment rendered useless with a national ban was estimated at $6 million. Loss of inventories (product materials, work-in-process, and finished goods) would amount to an estimated $15 million.

Inventories in the hands of wholesalers and retailers nationwide would amount to $40 million (Gillette's selling price) if Gillette were forced to buy them back.

Gillette's management conceived and implemented a three-phase response to the controversy. During Phase I, in mid-1974, they created a task force comprised of sales, research, manufacturing and other departments to study the problem and to recommend a course of action. The recommended course of action included the following elements:

(1) Development of alternative propellants for aerosols other than using fluorocarbons.
(2) Expansion of aerosol product lines to include non-aerosol packagings.
(3) Identification of the activities and priorities required to reach a position where fluorocarbon use could be discontinued.
(4) Estimates of the personnel and expense required to reach that position.

Hence, the thrust of their recommendation was that Gillette must be ready with alternatives if fluorocarbon use was actually banned.

The main activities for Phase II involved the research and marketing departments. They tested some 40 different propellants until they found "acceptable" alternatives. New manufacturing processes were planned and purchase orders were placed for the necessary new production equipment. The research department found a few problems Gillette would encounter if they employed hydrocarbon as the new propellant. Since hydrocarbon aerosol production is more expensive than fluorocarbon, the company's production costs would be higher if fluorocarbons were discontinued. These higher costs would ultimately be passed on to the consumer. However, a can of hydrocarbon aerosol will last up to one third longer. Therefore, assuming a constant level of consumer use, the retail turnover will decrease, tending to push retail prices up. The higher price was not seen as necessarily implying a decrease in total market share, but there was uncertainty about the impact. Overall, detailed plans were prepared for the initial production, market introduction, and retail distribution of the new non-fluorocarbon aerosols.

Phase III of the Gillette plan was to begin with the fluorocarbon ban. A plan was drafted to ensure that non-fluorocarbon aerosols entered the market at the appropriate time. These plans include:

(1) Installation of the new manufacturing equipment.
(2) Conversion of the manufacturing processes to nonfluorocarbon.
(3) Notification to company customers concerning product changes.

(4) Nationwide consumer advertising to promote the new brand formulas and to ensure consumer acceptance.

Finally, the regulations resulting from United States legislation will most likely have an eventual influence on worldwide regulatory policy. This could take many years however. Gillette, which has significant international sales, has pledged to stop using fluorocarbons internationally if credible scientific evidence establishes the case against fluorocarbons.

Government Action and Regulations

On April 26, 1977 the Food and Drug Administration formally ordered that warning labels be placed on aerosol products containing fluorocarbons. The action, which was proposed in November, 1976, applies to fluorocarbon-powered products marketed after October 31, 1977. At the same time, the Consumer Product Safety Commission proposed a similar labeling requirement for the products under its jurisdiction. The label will state: "Warning: Contains a chlorofluorocarbon that may harm the public health and environment by reducing ozone in the upper atmosphere."

The FDA warning label will affect primarily spray deodorants, antiperspirants, hair-care products, colognes and fragrances. The Consumer Product Safety Commission's ban, which was to take effect 60 days after a 30-day comment period, would apply to certain household products. The warning label is expected to affect about half of the aerosol containers sold each year. Unaffected would be aerosols that use other propellants for such products as shaving cream, spray points, and food toppings. Also, essential uses of fluorocarbons would be exempt; these include bronchial inhalants, contraceptive foams and cytology fixatives that are medical devices used in a cancer diagnostic procedure.

The FDA regulates about 85 percent of all products containing fluorocarbons and the remaining 15 percent are regulated by the Consumer Product Safety Commission which has previously required a label warning on certain pesticides under its jurisdiction.

On May 11, 1977, the FDA, the Environmental Protection Agency and the Consumer Product Safety Commission joined in announcing a plan for banning fluorocarbons from most aerosol spray cans within two years. Under a proposed timetable laid out by the FDA and EPA, manufacturing fluorocarbons for the aerosol market must cease by October 15, 1978. Companies cannot use the gas as a spray can propellant after December 15 of that year, and spray cans containing the gas cannot enter the market after April 15, 1979. However, cans on the shelf on that date won't have to be recalled. The agencies announced a period for receiving public comment and planned a public hearing before the final regulation is adopted.

It has been anticipated that the phase-out would cost the industry several hundred million dollars annually, but that it might save consumers money in the long run because alternatives to fluorocarbon propellants are cheaper. Those aerosol and other fluorocarbon products which are to be exempt from the warning label would also be exempt from the ban. Douglas M. Costle, administrator of the EPA, noted that the exemptions accounted for only about 2–3 percent of the total aerosol propellant used in the United States.[25] He also noted that although the United States is the major producer of fluorocarbon, the ozone depletion problem is global and will require international cooperation and action.[26]

It is estimated that a ban would eliminate 60 percent of all fluorocarbon emissions in this country. The remaining 40 percent comes from non-propellant uses, such as in air-conditioning and refrigerant equipment. Gas escaping from these closed systems is regarded as less of a threat than from spray cans. However, the EPA has announced a tentative plan to issue additional regulations for fluorocarbon coolants in June, 1978.[27]

Industry Response to the Ban

The four-year fight over a ban on fluorocarbon as an aerosol propellant came to a close and the industry's response was muted for two reasons. First, the ban allowed fluorocarbon propellants to be sold until April 15, 1979. Secondly, alternative propellants seem to be emerging that are cheaper and potentially as effective.

Just one day after the Environmental Protection Agency, the Food and Drug Administration and the Consumer Product Safety Commission jointly announced the ban, Robert H. Abplanalp, president of Precision Valve Corporation and inventor of the first workable aerosol valve, introduced a new design he claims "could have wiped out fluorocarbons even if the controversy had not arisen."[28] The new valve, called Aquasol, uses a dual-duct system (conventional aerosols have only one duct) which lets fillers use propellants that are not soluble in the product. The valve uses such refinery derivatives of natural gas as butane, isobutane or propane.[29] Abplanalp claims that fillers can get twice as much product into a can with the new valve and that they can dispense all existing aerosol products with less costly hydrocarbon propellants.

[25] *New York Times*, May 12, 1977, p. 1.
[26] *Ibid.*
[27] *Ibid.*
[28] "The Aerosol Ban Has Lost Its Sting," *Business Week*, May 30, 1977, p. 30.
[29] *New York Times*, May 13, 1977, p. D-1.

The ability to use less costly propellants such as hydrocarbons may also wipe out the ban's negative economic impact. Economists at the International Research & Technology Corporation did a detailed economic analysis of the impact of a ban for the EPA and concluded that much of the impact on marketers could be eliminated if they retained current unit prices.[30]

John Vinton, chairman of Gillette's aerosol task force for the personal care division, said that before the ban was proposed, the company had been busy introducing other systems for dispensing its product. "By year-end most of our products will be using non-aerosol propellants and the pricing is exactly the same," he said, adding that Gillette's technical people have been in contact with different suppliers—"anyone who says he has a different, acceptable system."[31]

Consumers, many of whom did not previously differentiate between fluorocarbon and nonfluorocarbon aerosols, are increasingly turning away from aerosol products. Consumer product advertising has even begun to emphasize the pump spray or non-aerosol products. It is not a case of environmental protection selling deodorants; it is that you can't sell deodorants without a statement about protection of the environment.

TOWARD "APPROPRIATE" TECHNOLOGY

The fluorocarbon case illustrates two aspects of the new questioning of technology. First, there is the question of whether or not a product is so important to a society that it should be banned entirely. Aerosol cans may be terribly important to the manufacturers and marketers that make and use them, but the public reaction to this case seems to indicate that there are some products or technologies the public is willing to give up. Aerosol cans are not alone in this respect. Public opinion polls indicate a growing public sensitivity to the "forcing of technology" upon them. Public opposition to the supersonic transport, for example, revolved around the social value of being able to go from New York to London in three and one-half hours rather than six hours at the risk of permanent damage to the upper atmosphere. No doubt there was a group of persons who so care about speed that they would be willing to justify such a risk. Their preferences, however, have not prevailed. If the SST does become a widespread form of air travel, it will probably be less the result of public support than the economic need of the French and British governments to recoup some of two billion dollars of development costs by forcing the SST on other governments, or at least forcing other governments to allow the SST to land.

---

[30] "The Aerosol Ban Has Lost Its Sting," p. 31.
[31] New York Times, May 13, 1977, p. D-1.

Because alternatives exist, the aerosol can is probably not a vital product in American society. The existence of other propellants and other non-aerosol technologies for consumer products have the practical effect of making the loss of aerosol cans considerably less than a serious blow to the American quality of life. That is not true with respect to the use of Freon as a coolant for refrigeration and air conditioning systems. For these uses, few satisfactory alternatives exist and the willingness of the public, the industry, or the regulators to force a ban is noticeably less. Whether the argument that the "closed system" nature of such fluorocarbon usage is as true as the industry has argued, the point remains that public expectations still support the use of fluorocarbons for refrigerant and air conditioning uses while they do not support their use in aerosol cans.

The relationship between changing public expectations and the quality of life which technology has enabled industrialized societies to enjoy is complex and itself in a process of change. Generalizations are perilous when dealing with such social complexity, but it is clear that managers of all enterprises are going to have to cope with growing resistance among segments of the public to technology-based change. Examples from some of the other technological change cases we have researched make the point that positions such as DuPont's response that no ban should occur until the case against fluorocarbons was absolutely certain are probably becoming inappropriate means of coping with criticism.

Until recent times, manufacturers had a nearly unfettered right to introduce new technologies, products, or processes without any external social review. The first, and probably most significant break with this traditional approach was the establishment of the environmental impact statement as a required procedural step in matters covered by the 1970 National Environmental Protection Act. Whereas the traditional approach utilized potential legal liability (e.g., negligence actions) to safeguard the public from technologies or products that went awry ("act first, cope with problems later"), the environmental legislation forced the proponents of change to articulate the first and second, order impacts of their proposal and submit that statement to external review ("think first, and then act if appropriate"). Philosophically, as well as practically, the environmental impact statement has signalled a major shift in American thinking about technology. Indeed, one of the newest—but clearest—shifts in public expectations is the unwillingness of the public to endorse any business action that is taken without some forethought about the primary and secondary consequences of that action.

The examination of impacts, and the rethinking of public values and concerns that impact statements have produced over the past decade has generated numerous controversies over technology. Perhaps the greatest of these has been that surrounding nuclear power as a means of meeting future energy needs. Public opinion surveys highlight a curious, but meaningful relationship in this area. There is a substantial public sentiment that favors making some tradeoffs with respect to the physical environment in order that another energy crisis like that of 1973 should not reoccur. As in the case of fluorocarbons and refrigeration, there is the expectation that something will have to be given up in order that energy supplies be assured. Yet, when the polls focus on nuclear energy, there is an even stronger indication of public reluctance to endorse nuclear power. Is this simply a contradiction, given the power industry's broad campaign to educate the consuming public about the need for relying on nuclear power generation? Perhaps, but it can also be argued that such surveys indicate a public unwillingness to endorse a "power at any cost" philosophy. If the public simply supported the goal of more power, the industry would most likely make a straightforward commitment to nuclear generation. Fifteen or more years of environmental sensitivity, however, have probably raised the question of national priorities to a broader level of discussion than ever before. The evidence seems to suggest that the public is sending a double message to industry. First, there is a desire for more power and a willingness to sacrifice some physical environmental harm to achieve it. Secondly, however, there are tradeoffs between particular technologies and particular secondary impacts, some of which are substantially less desirable than others. Hence, strip mining of coal is probably less undesirable than are nuclear power plants, though on an absolute basis there is probably no majority in favor of strip mining per se. The point is that public discussion and awareness of technology-related tradeoffs is significantly more sophisticated today than in the past, and much of this is attributable to the kind of questioning environmental impact statements have stimulated.

There are numerous manifestations of this concern with second order impacts. The Toxic Substances Act (1976) established a mechanism by which all new chemical products could be tested, evaluated, and accepted or rejected for public introduction on the basis of their primary and secondary impacts. Concern for employees in the chemical industry, their families, and even their unborn children has produced pressure for major changes in the regulation of workplace hazards and exposure to chemical production operations. Is there a manufacturer that will publicly stand behind a statement that says that some cancer, some birth defects, some death to employees or the public is warranted by the value of a particular chemical product? There may be a firm with such a view, but if so, it represents an attitude toward public expectations of corporate performance that woefully underestimates the questioning of technology that is now under way.[32]

---

[32] E. F. Schumacher, author of *Small Is Beautiful*, is, more than any other, the prophet of the "appropriate technology" movement. One can find the principles articulated in that appropriately small book applied to countless factual settings and technology-related controversies ranging from the supersonic transport to food production in less developed countries.

Finally, rethinking the promise of technology has not been confined to cases involving solely the physical environment or manufacturing and industrial firms. The appropriateness of technological change has emerged as an issue in such service areas as medicine, where the use of body-scanning diagnostic machines and sophisticated life-prolonging technology are being questioned as to their cost, value, and appropriateness in a modern society. Two of the cases we researched which most clearly demonstrated the questioning of technological appropriateness involved service industries which have heralded specific technological innovations as the springboard for their future development. The banking industry has, since the 1960's, been preparing for the arrival of EFTS, "electronic funds transfer systems." Plastic cards and ubiquitous computer terminals were forecast to be technological foundations of a checkless banking system. By the late 1960's, banks began formulating corporate strategies on the premise that EFTS would be a reality by the mid-1970's. A National Commission on Electronic Funds Transfers was even created by the U.S. Congress in 1974 to plan the transformation from a paper dominated financial system to an electronic based system. But public skepticism of an all-electronic system, which would penalize the cash user, and which could not be guaranteed safe against invasion of individuals' financial privacy was cast into serious public question. It may be that, in time, the banking industry will successfully introduce electronic funds transfer systems over the objection of an unwilling public, but that time is not likely to be any time soon. It may be, as Sanford Rose wrote in an article for *Fortune*,[33] that it makes little sense to communicate by checks when technology is making it more feasible and economical to use electronics. But such optimism ignores the fact that technological feasibility and economic efficiency are increasingly less relevant as reasons, by themselves, for instituting large scale change in a society.

Similar to the banking industry's commitment to EFTS, the supermarket industry has embraced the technology of electronic scanners as a means of speeding checkouts, lowering labor costs, and improving inventory, cash flow, and sales records. Electronic scanners depend, however, on a common language. Specifically, the industry has spent many years and much effort in developing a "universal product code" (UPC) which is a series of printed lines of varying length and width that indicate the item, size, and price of a labelled product. The problem with the system, however, is that consumers don't know—and couldn't without some electronic device of their own—what the UPC lines mean. In a supermarket, this means a buyer wouldn't know the price of a product until it was passed over the electronic reader at the cash register. Complaints

[33] Sanford Rose, "Checkless Banking Is Bound To Come," *Fortune* (June, 1977), pp. 118–130.

about such a situation brought the early trials of such scanners in supermarkets to a screeching halt. For supermarkets, it is a waste of their resources to have both the UPC and a stamped price on each can, bottle, and package in the market. The result of this conflict between industry requirements and public expectations has been an extremely slow introduction of scanners into supermarkets. In mid-1977, less than 200 of the nation's 32,700 supermarkets were using the scanners. New adoptions were occurring at a rate of only about 100 per year, partly because each new adopting store may be required to fight the battle of consumer resistance anew. Hence, in supermarket retailing, as in banking, the technology which the industry views as holding the key to its future is a technology whose appropriateness is seriously questioned by large segments of the public.

chapter six

when public values change

INTRODUCTION

As a business is founded and grows, its success depends on its ability to meet the public expectations and values that shape the market for its products and services. Marketing, as a managerial activity, has long been concerned with consumer decisions, behavior, satisfaction, and dissatisfaction. The recent wave of concern about product safety, quality and usefulness that is known as "consumerism" is a more visible manifestation of what has always been at the heart of corporate survival: the need to meet public expectations. Changing public expectations have broad implications for the organization. In the previous chapter, the impact of changing expectations was seen in the environmental area with respect to the continued use of popular technology. Similarly, the impact of changing expectations was discussed with respect to the emerging concern for privacy (EFTS) and traditional product pricing (the Universal Product Code).

While the impact of changing public expectations and values underlies the social issues theory that is the foundation of this book, there are certain cases that stand out for special consideration because the challenge for management is almost entirely defined in terms of coping with new public values. Two specific cases are discussed in this chapter. The first deals with the television industry, which has done perhaps as much as any industry, save the automobile, to shape the way Americans live today. The particular controversy discussed deals with the manner in which networks and advertisers have responded to the controversy over increasing violence on television.

The second case deals with a conventional practice of providers of credit: discriminating between good risks and bad. In the case of home mortgages, banks have traditionally looked at the condition of a neighborhood as one factor in determining the creditworthiness of a particular building. Inevitably, sections of each city have been identified as poor risk areas because of crime, vandalism, and so forth. The practice of systematically refusing to make loans in such areas is now frequently referred to as "redlining." The fact that redlining has been a traditional practice, well established as part of the normal way of conducting the business of mortgage lending, holds no virtue with critics. The direct calling into question of redlining practices, and the assumptions which underlie them, reflects a new set of public values. For the banking industry the task is one of coping with the challenge these new values pose to their routine and established practices.

CONFLICTING VALUES: TELEVISED VIOLENCE

Resolutions

A shareholder resolution, coordinated by the Interfaith Center on Corporate Responsibility, was submitted to eight large advertisers during the spring of 1977 calling for a drastic reduction of gratuitous violence on television. The eight companies were: Proctor & Gamble; Sears Roebuck; Colgate-Palmolive; Gillette; McDonald's; Pillsbury; Eastman Kodak; and Schlitz Brewing. The resolution urged each company to adopt a policy that "shall not allow its advertisements to appear in television programs containing excessive and gratuitous violence."[1] The resolution stated that studies have shown a connection between violence on television and an

[1] *News for Investors*, Investor Responsibility Research Center (IRRC), Volume IV, No. 1, January 1977, p. 1.

adverse influence on both children and adults, who can adopt unrealistic values and attitudes about the role, amount and effects of violence. The resolution concluded, "We believe that it is not in our company's interest to have its products identified with violent programs when there are popular and highly rated programs for our sponsorship which do not rely on excessive violence for their content."[2]

The resolution was eventually withdrawn from four companies which agreed to state publicly that their corporate policy was to avoid sponsorship of programs containing unnecessarily violent material. Colgate-Palmolive, Gillette, Eastman Kodak, and Sears, Roebuck all stated that it had been company policy to avoid sponsoring such programming, and that such a policy would be continued. A specific statement of policy guidelines was provided by Eastman Kodak:

> It is the policy of the company to refrain from advertising on televised programs which include violence for its own sake, when violence plays no part in or makes no important contribution to a dramatic statement.
> It is the policy of the company to refrain from advertising on television programs which contain overly graphic displays of brutality and human suffering.
> It is the policy of the company to refrain from advertising on television programs which portray anti-social behavior which because of its nature and the manner of portrayal could easily stimulate imitation.

Colgate-Palmolive agreed to include a statement of policy in its next quarterly report to shareholders. Gillette agreed to summarize its procedures for advertising on violent programs in its annual report. Schlitz Brewing told their advertising agencies to avoid sponsoring shows depicting excessive violence, glorifying violence or other anti-social practices.

McDonald's wrote a letter to the Interfaith Center on Corporate Responsibility declining to include the resolution in the proxy statement because to do so would pre-empt a certain amount of discretion that must be retained by the management of the company. The company's management noted that there are, from time to time, certain television programs which, while containing a certain degree of violence, have such a high degree of overriding social significance as to make their sponsorship by McDonald's Corporation reasonable and in the best interest of the country, the company, and its shareholders. Examples cited were ABC's "Roots" and the NBC documentary, "Violence in America."

[2] *Ibid.*

The Pervasiveness of Television and
Television Violence in Society

In the last 30 years, television has steadily grown from a rare novelty into a social force of unprecedented pervasiveness. The Census Bureau reports that 96 percent of American homes have at least one television set, more than have refrigerators, indoor plumbing or stoves. The television set is used for an average of six hours per day, and for pre-schoolers the average is seven per day. Children normally begin watching television three to four years before they enter school. The average person watches for three hours per day. Most children now spend more time with television than any activity other than sleep, including school.

In a 1974 survey by S. C. Nielson Company, 82 percent of the sample felt that television had a positive effect on children, 9 percent rated negative. Yet, in a 1975 *TV Guide* poll, 71 percent felt there is too much violence on television; 72 percent felt the same way in an NBC poll. The NBC poll also revealed that 70 percent felt that television violence leads to anti-social behavior. The Federal Communications Commission received 2,000 letters critical of televised violence in 1972 and 25,000 in 1974. As *TV Guide* noted, it seems clear from poll results "that public dismay over televised scenes of violence is stronger than ever; that Americans in overwhelming numbers . . . are certain that a need exists for some such device to reduce the amount of violence on American television screens."[3]

Despite this public sentiment it appears that Americans have a big appetite for action and violence-packed programming. As indicated by the Nielson ratings during the fall 1976 viewing season, four out of the ten most popular shows on television rated relatively high in violence. Because the networks have discovered that violent shows do obtain high ratings, they realize that these are the shows which contribute heavily to advertising revenues. Those shows with the higher ratings are in greater demand by the sponsors.

Measures of Television Violence Content

Presently there is no precise definition on what constitutes "violence" in television. An accepted standard has not yet been developed by the industry or the National Association of Broadcasters. Those who have done studies on the effects of television violence have set their own criteria for measuring the violent content of shows. This indecisiveness has led to the various conflicting findings produced from these studies.

Three groups have measured the frequency of violent acts on network programming and/or the amount of violence, but arrived at strikingly different conclusions:

[3] *Ibid.*, p. 3.

CBS Study. The Office of Social Research conducted a study in the fall of 1975 and found that the rate of violent incidents declined from the year before by 39 percent on CBS, 32 percent, NBC and 20 percent, ABC. In 1976, a more extensive study conducted found a 36 percent decline on CBS, and an overall 24 percent reduction in prime-time programming. Violence declined not only during "family hour" (8–9 P.M. EST), but after 9 P.M. as well.

Gerbner Findings. Dr. George Gerbner, of the Annenberg School of Communications at the University of Pennsylvania, found "television violence increased sharply in all categories including 'family viewing' and children's program time on all three networks."[4] Gerbner charted an index of violent content, measuring the levels of violent action in programming for all three networks for 1967 through 1975 and then assessed the 1975–6 season in terms of the index. He found a rise in violence at all hours including children's daytime programming.

Citizens Committee Results. The National Citizens Committee for Broadcasting measured and ranked the violence content of individual prime-time programs. They also ranked the sponsors of prime-time advertising according to the violence levels on the shows they sponsored. The findings showed that the incidents of violence increased 29 percent in a six-week period in 1976 as compared to a similar period in 1975. They also found the lowest level of violence to be on the CBS network.

There is a definite controversy over the definition of violence. CBS found an average of two to three acts of violence per prime-time hour. Gerbner, using a broader definition and monitoring more periods, found an average of 9.5. CBS sees gratuitous violence on the decline, especially in its programming. Gerbner's study reveals the opposite, with eight out of 10 programs (nine out of every 10 weekend children's hour programs) still containing some violence. Both have agreed to compare data and methodology, but a mutually agreeable research method has yet to be found.

The three major networks say they are taking the necessary steps to reduce excessive violence, but do not view the problem as serious or clear cut as the critics believe. Gerbner and the NCCB feel that the violence level is high enough to rank as a major social problem.

The Effects of Televised Violence

In response to public concern, nine congressional hearings have been held on the issue of televised violence since 1952. In 1971, the Surgeon General's Scientific Advisory Committee on Television and Social

---

[4] *IRRC Analysis N,* March 21, 1977, p. N-3.

Behavior published a 2,300-page report dealing with the issue. The conclusion reached by the committee stated that television violence does have an adverse effect on certain members of society. Moreover, the causal relationship between televised violence and antisocial behavior is sufficient to warrant appropriate and immediate remedial action. The crux of this argument is that television violence is the foremost factor in converting people with potentially violent tendencies into live practitioners of violent acts. It also leads to apathy towards aggressive, violent situations. "The evidence does indicate that televised violence may lead to increased aggressive behavior in certain subgroups of children, who might constitute a small portion or a substantial proportion of the total population of young television viewers."[5] It also noted that "television is only one of the many factors which in time may precede aggressive behavior. It is exceedingly difficult to disentangle from other elements of an individual's life history."[6]

The report was subject to some criticism by violence critics because the networks had considerable influence in the composition of the committee. The critics believed the report to be biased, as five of the 12 members had some industry connection and the networks had vetoed the proposed membership of seven well-known violence critics.

Clearly, there is no consensus on the conclusion reached by the Surgeon General's Committee. Several studies have shown differing opinions on the issue. Liebert and Baron (1971) found a greater willingness by children who had seen aggressive material to hurt more frequently and for a longer period. Those children also tended to be more aggressive in a play-type situation. Stein and Friedrich (1971) concluded that television violence and aggression had no significant effect on children's later behavior, except for a mild stimulation among those who were initially high in aggressive behavior. They did however, find an increase in pro-social behavior among those children who viewed pro-social material. Seymour Feshback (1971) provided a study that suggests that violence in television action programs may actually reduce aggressive behavior.

Despite the variety of the findings there appears to be an emerging consensus that there is some type of causal relation between viewing violence on television and aggressive behavior. The social science literature is calling for more studies. However, many observers feel that there is a limit to what the social scientists can do in the resolution of this dispute. James Q. Wilson has written: "In the cases of violence and obscenity, it is unlikely that social science can either show harmful effects or prove that there are no harmful effects. . . . These are moral issues, and ultimately all judgments about the acceptability of restrictions on

[5] *News for Investors, op. cit.,* p. 5.
[6] *News for Investors, op. cit.,* p. 6.

various media will have to rest on political and philosophical considerations."[7]

Critics' Concerns

Those who actively oppose violence in television programming firmly believe that the evidence regarding the effects on children and adults more than justifies efforts to reform current programming. Albert Bandura of Stanford University has noted that, given the known capability of television to influence behavior and the known marketability of conflict, the use of brutal content is a proper matter of public concern. Others have argued that the issue is one of network irresponsibility, not public policy.

The networks depend largely on advertising for revenue and the price they charge a sponsor is directly related to the audience size of the show. Action and adventure programming has consistently been able to deliver and hold audiences. To the advertisers, violence means excitement because excitement means ratings; ratings, in turn, mean sales!

The critics argue that the networks, in aggressive pursuit of ratings, ignore evidence that televised violence leads to aggressive behavior. They allege that television is not being run like a public service as federal law has determined, but rather, as a profit-dominated economic enterprise. Senator Warren G. Magnuson (D-Wash.), Chairman of the Senate Commerce Committee, has said: "The gratuitous use of violence for the sole purpose of attracting and maintaining audience attention is a common programming practice. Violence portrayed without showing the human consequences is cheap and it degrades the viewer and the perpetrator. . . . The risks of continuing the current course of television are frightening."[8]

There are several other consequences that concern the critics. For example, there is a concern that children will not learn to appreciate non-violent conflicts and crises. Arnold Arnold's book, *Violence and Your Child* suggests: "A child addicted to action 'adventure,' in which a hero blasts his way to success, is not likely to be similarly enthralled when watching the risks taken by astronauts, scientists, artists and others engaged in less hostile pursuits. To appreciate their crises, conflicts and struggles, viewers need value judgments more subtle than those required to appreciate shooting sprees."[9]

[7] *IRRC Analysis N, op. cit.*, p. N-6.
[8] *IRRC Analysis N, op. cit.*, p. N-6.
[9] *IRRC Analysis N, op. cit.*, p. N-7.

Another important concern is that viewers may accept violence as legitimate and effective behavior in conflict situations. The 'good' guys are just as bad an influence as the 'bad' guys because they don't get punished for their crimes. Their violence is justified by the pursuit of law and order. When children identify with a hero, they see him settle differences by violence rather than by peaceful negotiation.

In his study, Gerbner has shown another consequence of viewing televised violence. After taking a sample survey of both children and adults, he found that heavy viewers, especially the uneducated and young, believe the world to be a place of personal danger and violence. They are also more likely to feel that people are untrustworthy. As a result of televised violence people believe crime in the streets to be rampant; that even walking down the street is an endangering act.

Network Responses to Criticism

The networks believe that they are being unjustly criticized. In their view, they are being blamed for persistent social ills over which they have no control. They feel that there is a wide variety of programming from which to choose and that they have already cleaned up violent programs. Parental supervision is censorship enough rather than removing programming that some viewers enjoy and that obtain the ratings.

Critics of television violence believe people can learn anti-social behavior from any type of violence, be it comedic, cartoon or dramatic violence. The networks claim this is unfair and too sweeping a definition. As Alfred R. Schneider, an ABC vice-president, testified before the House Interstate and Foreign Commerce Subcommittee on Communications on March 2, 1977, "We feel that it is improper not to make distinctions between those incidents that may cause tension, distress, or increased aggressive behavior in audiences, and those that are unlikely to do so. . . . The primary issue is whether violent sequences in entertainment programs affect behavior, rather than perceptions or attitudes or taste levels." This difference was emphasized in 1976 when NBC aired "Baa Baa Black Sheep" during the "family viewing hour."[10] When questioned about this issue, NBC-TV President Robert T. Howard simply stated that NBC didn't consider it a violent program. In contrast, the National Citizens Committee rated the show one of the most violent.

All three networks firmly believe that the use of violence in television programming is necessary and a part of American life. It has traditionally been a part of art and drama. Fredrick S. Pierce, president of ABC, has argued that throughout history the essence of some drama has been conflict, and that violence has always been one means to resolve conflict.

[10] Family viewing hour is the first hour of prime-time programming, 8–9 P.M. EST.

Finally, the networks point out that the First Amendment guarantees them and their writers freedom of speech. Attempts to censor their programming constitute a violation of this right, and putting pressure on advertisers to enforce economic censorship is also illegal in the network's view.

Family Viewing

In September, 1975, the National Association of Broadcasters and the networks agreed on an amendment to the NAB Television Code designating the first hour of prime-time programming (8–9 P.M. EST) as the "family hour." The amendment, which was also to cover the hour previous to prime-time (i.e., 7–8 P.M., EST), provided that programming would refrain from showing anything inappropriate for the general viewing public. The objective of "family hour" was to self-regulate the industry rather than to substitute for parental guidance.

However, much of the television industry, i.e. local broadcast outlets, did not agree with the idea of "family hour." The consensus argued that it was instituted under pressure in order to forestall government regulation. The networks denied this allegation, but this did not appease other elements in the industry. Indeed, guilds representing the writers, producers, and actors filed suit against the networks and the NAB charging that "family hour" is an infringement of the First Amendment.

As a result, in November, 1976, Judge Warren J. Ferguson of the U.S. District Court in Los Angeles ruled that the "family hour" was instituted because of improper influence by the FCC. He said that the NAB could not impose restriction on the content of programming as a condition of code membership. Although Judge Ferguson's decision was appealed, the NAB announced plans to replace the "family hour" with a new set of voluntary guidelines.

Advertiser's Responses to Criticism

Sponsors have an indirect impact on television programming. They have no jurisdiction over content, but by refusing to sponsor a show, companies can assure that its life will be even shorter than if the public refused to view it. The 1977 shareholder resolutions were directed at the sponsors as a means of forcing the managements of major advertisers to adopt anti-violence policy and thereby apply economic pressure to the networks.

Much of the advertising industry objects to being put in a position of exerting economic influence. Peter Allport, president of the Association of National Advertisers argued that, an individual advertiser may, and has an obligation to his stockholders and employees, select programs which are in accord with his best marketing judgment. Advertisers have a right

TABLE 6-1

1977 TARGET COMPANIES

Their expenditures on T.V. advertising in 1975 and their rank in over-all advertising expenditures:

RANK	COMPANY	TOTAL T.V. EXPENDITURES 1975 (IN THOUSANDS)	% OF 1975 AD. BUDGET IN T.V.
1	Proctor & Gamble	$261,198.7	95.1
8	Sears Roebuck	73,761.4	88.6
10	Colgate-Palmolive	67,497.4	86.0
13	Gillette	61,254.1	92.4
19	McDonald's	57,544.1	95.3
35	Pillsbury	31,362.3	91.7
58	Eastman Kodak	14,929.7	63.5

to purchase time or space according to their own criteria. The use of economic leverage to dictate what broadcasters should not present to the American public must be as strongly resisted for television, according to Allport, as it would be if advertisers were to try to dictate the editorial content of newspapers or magazines

Nevertheless, a growing number of advertising agencies and corporations who are major sponsors are taking a stand against supporting programming with excessive and gratuitous violence. To date, five out of 10 "most violent advertisers" on the National Citizens Committee for Broadcasting list have indicated a change in policy. Among the more prominent are General Motors, American Telephone and Telegraph, Union Oil and Kimberly-Clark.

A variety of advertising agencies have expressed concern with television violence and the climate it creates for advertisements. J. Walter Thompson has been the most active agency in the area and has done several studies of the issue. In one survey of 1,000 people, the agency found that:

- 47% felt programming had gotten worse, and half of them blamed violence or police/detective shows for the decline;
- 23% thought violence "extremely harmful," 17%, "very harmful" and 35%, "somewhat harmful" to the public;
- 36% said that violence on TV makes them "uncomfortable";
- 48% did not think advertisers were at all concerned with the issue of television violence;
- 1.4% said that they had avoided buying a product they saw advertised on a violent program;
- 25% approved government action to control the amount and content of television violence.

J. Walter Thompson is now working on a supplementary study to determine whether advertising during a violent program causes a loss of advertising effectiveness.

Other agencies claim that each client has a particular segment of the market they are trying to reach through their advertising. For some products, the ideal audiences are those who watch the hard action/crime shows where violence is prevalent. Nevertheless, most anticipate an overall reduction of violent programming in the future.

Outlook for Change

The resolution submitted to corporations by the Interfaith Center on Corporate Responsibility had a dual purpose: to keep the issue in the public eye and to awaken the corporations to their second order impacts on society. A media consultant for the organization explained that the resolution was deliberately filed in somewhat vague terms to encourage careful evaluation by the companies and to avoid hinting at censorship.

The networks, in attempting to appease the critics, have cut down on the amount of violent programming, but the debate over how much violence is permissible seems certain to continue. There is much uncertainty concerning what types of violence actually affect the behavior of different groups and segments of the public. Thus, the controversy over where the industry's social responsibility begins and ends is unlikely to abate.

Federal regulation is a continuing concern of the networks. The FCC has the power to deny the license renewal to any local station it believes is not operating in the public interest. Whether or not it will apply that power to violent programming remains a question. The networks steadfastly argue that any censorship will be a direct violation of the First Amendment guarantee of freedom of speech.

Those who support the reduction of violent programming seem to prefer changing public opinion as a means of changing network behavior rather than government intervention. Many of the advocates believe that audiences support excessively violent shows because they have no other viable alternatives. Therefore, they are attempting to convince broadcasters and advertisers that it is in their best self-interest to produce and sponsor less violent programming.

The recent changes in advertising policies by major corporations proves that there is a sensitivity toward the issues involved. Prospects for major changes are complicated by several factors, however: the current scarcity of available network advertising time and the resultant high prices; the difficulty of distinguishing what is actually gratuitous violence and what types are socially acceptable; and the high ratings these shows obtain without fail. What is certain, however, is that the networks, advertisers, advertising agencies, federal government, and public action groups are carefully considering the appropriate next step.

SHIFTING VALUES: REDLINE/GREENLINE

Introduction

Redlining is generally understood to be the selective withholding of mortgage funds by lending institutions based on geographical criteria. It is believed to occur when mortgage lenders discriminate against mortgage applicants solely on the basis of the location of the property involved, disregarding the financial stability of the applicant, condition of the property and the bank's actual loss experience in the area. Lending institutions are said to draw an imaginary red line around a blighted area. It is claimed by members of the community that this practice stifles the flow of funds to urban neighborhoods and therefore increases the likelihood of their decline. Lenders, however, assert that their decisions are based on sound lending policies and fiduciary responsibility. Therefore, they contend that redlining does not exist, but if it did, it would be financially justifiable. According to Grover Hanson, President of First Federal Savings and Loan Association of Chicago, "We're not even sure of what we've been accused of doing. Redlining doesn't exist. If our neighborhoods are deteriorating, that's a social problem, not a bank problem."

According to critics, redlining takes many forms, all of which operate to deny mortgage funds for property in urban neighborhoods.

(1) Requiring down payments of a higher amount than are usually required for financing comparable properties in other areas;

(2) Fixing loan interest rates in amounts higher than those set for all or most other mortgages in other areas;

(3) Fixing loan closing costs in amounts higher than those set for all or most other mortgages in other areas;

(4) Fixing loan maturities below the number of years to maturity set for all or most other mortgages in other areas;

(5) Refusing to lend on properties above a prescribed maximum number of years of age;

(6) Refusing to make loans in dollar amounts below a certain minimum figure, thus excluding many of the lower-priced properties often found in neighborhoods where redlining is practiced;

(7) Refusing to lend on the basis of presumed "economic obsolescence" no matter what the condition of an older property may be;

(8) Stalling on appraisals to discourage potential borrowers;

(9) Setting appraisals in amounts below what market value actually should be, thus making home purchase transactions more difficult to accomplish;

(10) Applying structural appraisal standards of a much more rigid nature than those applied for comparable properties in other areas;

(11) Charging discount "points" as a way of discouraging financing.

Background

In 1964, an elderly Chicago couple, Mr. and Mrs. Theodore Angelos, decided to move into a smaller home. Their two-flat, brick house was located in one of Chicago's older, working class neighborhoods. Angelos assessed his property at $40,000, but subsequent FHA appraisal determined its worth at $20,000. Although the price fell short of their expectations, the couple settled for $20,000. They then proceeded to pay a commission of 6% to a realty agent and 14% or 14 points of mortgage discount to the mortgage banker just to sell their "undesirable" home. The FHA's redlining thereby cost the Angelos more than $20,000.

Their daughter, Mrs. Gale Cincotta, viewed the entire episode with consternation. It was this experience which led her to become one of the most outspoken leaders of the anti-redlining forces in both Chicago and the nation during the 1970's. She also became a founder of the National People's Action on Housing (NPAH).

Community Action

The early anti-redlining activities were organized by people with experiences similar to Mrs. Cincotta. Their protests began as gatherings at the banks on Saturday mornings to distribute flyers and to confront bank officials with charges of redlining. This approach gave way to more effective annoyance tactics like depositing a sum of money and withdrawing a dollar at a time. The bank officers felt the pressure and more of the public began paying attention to the issues of redlining.

Neighborhood residents claimed that the financial institutions helped to promote urban deterioration. They contended the bank's refusal of conventional mortgage loans opened the way for unscrupulous individuals such as profit-hungry realtors, brokers, savings institutions, mortgage bankers and big investors to buy up property and gain control of the neighborhoods. Real estate values plummeted and taxes sky-rocketed. These fast-buck operators offered to purchase homes at a fraction of the cost, aware of the redlining procedure, and of the difficulty residents faced in attempting to sell their property on the market. Through conversion to apartments, abandoning and tearing down, as well as the entrance of transients, decay begins. Citizen groups declared that a viable neighborhood could exist only if loans for home improvement and purchasing were made accessible.

In April 1974, the Citizen's Action Program (CAP), a federation of sixty Chicago neighborhood groups under the leadership of Father Albin Ciciora, initiated a campaign to obtain pledges for the withdrawal of $40 million in deposits from institutions accused of redlining. These deposits were then placed in banks which CAP felt were making a greater contribution to the local community. This tactic was called *greenlining* and became quite successful.

Community groups also presented the results from the Bank of America's affirmative inner-city lending program. A management evaluation of the $200 million New Opportunity Home Loan Program (NOHL), begun in 1968, revealed that the program had operated at a small profit. The program had had a high rate of delinquencies and foreclosures, but since the bulk of loans were government-insured, the Bank had little in the way of actual losses. From 1968–75, the Bank loaned $181 million to 10,563 families, 70 percent of which went to those in the inner-city, the remainder to rural poverty areas.

These groups not only asked lenders to halt their redlining activities, but also tried to find out where their deposits had come from and where they had then made their loans. This knowledge would be instrumental in a consumer's decision to support with his savings deposits those institutions which were responsive to community needs. The political leverage created by such disclosure was believed to be the needed force in changing the redlining procedure.

The Banks' Position

There are two principal types of thrift institutions[11] in the United States, savings and loan associations[12] and mutual savings banks. These institutions perform two basic functions:

(1) stimulate and protect the savings of millions of individuals by offering maximum returns consistent with the safety and accessibility of deposits.

(2) channel those savings into productive investments, particularly mortgage loans (they are primarily mortgage lenders in the United States).

[11] Commercial banks tend to serve the business sector and do not engage in mortgaging as a general practice.

[12] These are also known as building and loan associations, co-operative banks, homestead associations, building associations and savings associations.

Charter K, Revised, states that the institutions' objectives "are to promote thrift by providing a convenient and safe method for people to save and invest money and to provide for the sound and economical financing of homes."

Most of the assets of thrift institutions are invested in real estate mortgage loans. At the end of 1970, mortgage loans represented 73 percent of the total assets of United States mutual savings banks and these institutions' investments were restricted by law, regulation and custom, primarily to loans secured by residential real estate and one-to-four family, owner-occupied homes. Recognizing the dangers of a restrictive, long term portfolio, some states have allowed a small percentage of assets to be invested in government securities, installment loans and in mutual savings banks, and credit card operations.

Lenders insist that inner-city conditions are not a result of the alleged redlining. The property always has to be inspected first. To make these inner-city loans was frequently in violation of sound lending principles with these criteria cited: appraisal of the property's value, the neighborhood's character and prospects, and the owner's ability and willingness to repay the loan over a period of years. "A lending institution is bound by statutory and regulatory requirements to apply sound credit standards in any real estate transaction."[13] In addition, the bank's obligation to maximize the return on the investment of the depositors and shareholders has to be considered.

Bankers have opposed disclosure of loan and deposit data mainly because of the time and expense involved and because it is felt that this information would be misinterpreted by community groups. It is believed that these organizations would not patronize any lender who did not show a certain geographical concentration in the loan portfolio.

Mutual Savings Banks

Mutual Savings Banks originated in the Northeast around 1816, when commercial banks did not accept funds from small depositors. The MSB's were started by community leaders and businessmen as cooperative organizations encouraging thrift among the working class in addition to investment. The varied, small holdings were grouped by these banks and invested in high quality bonds. As the clientele grew and changed in character, the MSB's evolved into professionally managed institutions. Throughout their history, Mutual Savings Banks compiled an excellent record for safety as a result of their conservative investment policies, enabling them to enjoy strong growth.

Since 1950, the major trend in the asset distribution of MSB's has

[13] *American Banker*, May 21, 1975, p. 4.

been toward mortgages and corporate and other securities; they now constitute 70 percent and 20 percent of total assets, respectively. There has also been a trend away from U.S. Government Securities that have been accumulated since the 1930's, especially during World War II. The accumulation of mortgages has made the MSB's almost as specialized in this investment as Savings and Loan Associations, which hold about 85 percent of their assets in mortgages.

Mutual Savings Banks operate under state charters in 18 states; 75 percent of all MSB's are located in New York, Massachusetts and Connecticut. These institutions are subject to the laws and regulations of their respective states. The significance of this regulation has been mainly in what geographical restrictions are placed on lending by MSB's and on the portfolio mix which such institutions are allowed to maintain. The larger New York and Massachusetts banks have member-owned companies to assist in mortgage acquisition and servicing, and to provide secondary liquidity. Several have access to Federal Home Loan Bank Board credit facilities as members of the Board.

The banks are managed by a board of trustees. Their earnings are funneled back to depositors in the form of higher interest rates on savings after appropriate deductions for operating expenses and additions to protective reserves have been made. Total mutual savings banks' resources now exceed $100 billion. Time deposits are the main source of funds. Most banks are also members of the FDIC.

MSB's try to maximize earnings within a safety constraint, requiring conservative policies of lending and investing. Investments are made mostly in mortgages, which are both safe and high in yield. Property inspections and appraisals are required for each loan. Other regulations, which vary by state, include:

- single-family, owner-occupied conventional loans are regulated as to loan-value ratios, maximum amounts, maturity dates, territory;
- FHA and VA loans follow FHA and VA regulation, with no territorial (in state) restrictions;
- multifamily loans are regulated as to loan-to-value ratio (66 percent to 80 percent) and term (up to 25 years).

Asset limitations are imposed on mutual savings banks, in that no greater than 70 to 75 percent of assets can be invested in conventional loans. Investments of assets differ for many reasons. For example, in Massachusetts, an increasing proportion of residents' saving in the form of deposits is invested outside the State; presumably, such opportunities are more profitable. Massachusetts banks have traditionally been "capital exporters." Hence, these institutions have a history of seeking alternative investment opportunities outside their local markets.

Appraisals and the Appraiser's Role

The major issue in lending has centered around risks and who must assume them. Bankers often assert that whatever faults traditional lending may have, it has determined market value over time. On the other hand, a market approach on uninsured loans seems to create many uncertainties as far as future liability is concerned. The acceptance of conventional appraisal standards has resulted in a "natural" curtailment of credit that has paved the way for urban blight and caused an outcry against such practices.

There have been some changes in the concept upon which traditional appraising has worked. Specifically, changing economic and social conditions and the prolonged state of inflation have created pressure to reexamine old appraisal assumptions. The key in determining what comparable values were evident in the present neighborhood is illustrated by market demand and resale value. The process of determining these "comparables" has been a sensitive undertaking for the appraiser. He might endorse a loan falling well below a consumer's expectations or might veto the loan should he have an adverse feeling about the neighborhood. Traditional considerations include:

(1) Physical appearance of a neighborhood.
(2) Social economic make-up of a neighborhood.
(3) Availability of transportation in the neighborhood.
(4) Availability of convenient shopping.
(5) Quality of school system.
(6) Availability of churches.
(7) Number of recreational and cultural facilities.
(8) Availability of utilities and other city services.
(9) Protection against "adverse" influences (e.g., "incompatible" residents, density changes, patterns where single-family structures are being converted into higher density dwellings.)

All these are subject to the appraiser's own interpretation. Too often, critics charge, suburban standards are used and if bias exists, it is subtle.

Federal Legislation

Recent activities by the National Committee Against Discrimination in Housing (NCDAH) and hearings by the Senate Banking Committee have illustrated that redlining is widespread and damaging to city neighborhoods. During the Senate hearing chaired by Senator William Proxmire, both industry and government witnesses steered away from using the term redlining, preferring to talk about disinvestment . . . The Proxmire hearings showed that disinvestment takes place under the very noses of authorities charged with implementing the fair housing and civil rights statutes: 90 percent of the mortgage loans made in the District of Columbia were made in the Maryland and Virginia suburbs, and almost one-half of loans made within the District, which is predominantly black, went to upper-middle-class white neighborhoods. Proxmire, in summary, said, 'Perfectly sound neighborhoods in every major city in America are dying prematurely for lack of mortgage credit. We are wasting our most valuable housing resource—sound existing homes.'[14]

The Home Mortgage Disclosure Act of 1975, S. 1281, proposed by Senator Proxmire, cleared the Senate Committee by a vote of 8–5 and went on to the full Senate for action. The bill required federally chartered banks and savings institutions to make public an annual list of the number and amount of mortgages and home improvement loans made by each postal zip code area in their regions. In addition to the number and dollar amounts of mortgages, the data would also have to disclose whether the loans were made to owner-occupied homes or to absentee landlords and whether they were conventional or under the federal support programs of the FHA or the VA. The information compiled would be released completing the fiscal year. Lending institutions would be required to present the material for public viewing at each office. The banking regulatory agencies and the Federal Trade Commission would enforce the provisions of the Act.

The bill was a heavily lobbied issue; on one side, banks and savings and loan associations began massive letter writing campaigns to Senators; on the other hand, big-city mayors, the AFL–CIO and several civil rights groups worked hard for the passage of the bill. Housing and city groups claimed that disclosure legislation would be a first step in solving problems of redlining. There was testimony by Gale Cincotta giving examples of three Chicago banks which drew their deposits from Chicago neighborhoods, but made their mortgage loans outside the city area.

Banking organizations opposed the bill, feeling if deposit and loan data were released, consumers would misinterpret it. John H. Perkins, speaking on behalf of the American Bankers Association, asserted that to enact legislation requiring public disclosure of only the number of loans in each section of the city without explaining both the realities of sound credit and the other contributions made by the lender in that area of the city would give the citizen a false impression. One might believe that banks and other lenders were obligated to provide mortgage financing on an equal basis throughout the city and that if they did not, such institutions would be discriminating unfairly.[15]

[14] "The Thin Red Line," *The New Republic* June 21, 1975, p. 3.
[15] "Community Groups Take Redlining Complaint Against South Chicago S & L to FHLD Parley," *American Banker*, April 4, 1974, p. 3.

Opposition was also based on the belief that disclosure would inhibit capital flows, *and that savings deposits and mortgage lending were separate and distinct banking services.*

The bill, which Proxmire labelled "mild" was greatly debated and discussed. The Senate passed the bill by a vote of 45–37, and sent it to the House. After some debate, the House also approved the legislation. President Ford signed the bill and it was enacted. This federal regulation applied to 276 Standard Metropolitan Statistical Areas (SMSA) and was pertinent to all federally chartered banks, savings and loan associations, and credit unions in those areas.

In Senator Proxmire's words,

> I have proposed a simple disclosure law that would give local citizens the right to know where their neighborhood banks and savings and loan associations issued their mortgage loans and I would expect an informed citizenry to do the rest.[16]

Beginning September 30, 1976, nearly 8,500 banks and other institutions making home loans were required to publish information showing by census tract where they were making mortgages. The law required records for the first time which showed how neighborhoods, racial groups, and income groups benefitted from lending practices.

Ninety days after the conclusion of each year, these lending agencies were required to post in "some conspicuous space" a chart illustrating the numbers of loans by category and census tracts or zip codes. There was not, however, any provision made to further analyze the data once it had been accumulated.

Massachusetts

On May 20, 1975, Massachusetts' new Commissioner of Banking, Carol S. Greenwald, spoke before the Massachusetts Banking Association and proposed a two-prong program to halt the practice of redlining.

First, she announced the issuance of a directive requiring all banks with more than $20 million deposits and operating in the Boston SMSA to furnish different types of information indicating where their depositors resided, average deposit size, where mortgage loans were given, average mortgage loan size, and the types of mortgage loan by census tract, so as to closely identify those neighborhoods hidden in data by zip code. National banks were called upon to disclose the data voluntarily.[17]

Preliminary analysis of information acquired through the disclosure act for the five largest Boston savings banks indicated that:

---

[16] *Ibid.*, p. 4.

[17] They have since been required to do so by the Proxmire-initiated bill.

- For every savings dollar deposited from a Boston address only 9 cents was returned in one-to-four family mortgages in the city of Boston.

- In suburban Boston, for every dollar deposited, 31 cents was invested in one-to-four family mortgages.

- In the rest of the state and outside of Massachusetts, 54 cents was invested in one-to-four family mortgages for each dollar deposited.

This data was to be filed with the Commissioner of Banks; it would be made available upon request to the public at all banking offices. Ms. Greenwald responded to the skeptical bankers, who feared that the data would be misinterpreted, by stating that either the Commissioner's office or a disinterested expert would analyze the data before public disclosure.

The Commissioner decreed this data important to the effectiveness of her office. Opponents of this measure claimed that where deposits came from was not highly significant and that too much time, effort, and personnel were required to compile and analyze it. The relevant issue was where the mortgage money was going and what types of mortgages were being given.

The second part of Commissioner Greenwald's program involved the creation of a Mortgage Agency, which would function as an insurance fund to reduce the risk for any individual bank making mortgage loans in marginal neighborhoods. The Massachusetts Mortgage Agency (MMA) would insure an individual bank against loss up to 100 percent of the unpaid principal on high risk mortgages. Membership in the proposed agency would be mandatory for all financial institutions operating in Massachusetts. The insurance fund would be created by pooling the members' profits. MMA would have the authority to insist that a lending institution make such an insured loan. The agency would also have the power to require every financial institution in the Commonwealth to expend up to 1 percent of its time and savings deposits for loans made under the provisions of the MMA. The bankers' reaction to this part of the Commissioner's directive was hostile. They contended that the intent of the order was "to force banks to use their depositors' funds in high risk loans" and that to do so was "fundamentally at variance with the safe investment of funds entrusted by our depositors."[18]

When Commissioner Greenwald refused to withdraw her order, 26 Massachusetts banks filed suit declaring that 1) the restrictions placed on them by the Commissioner were beyond her legal authority; 2) that they were too costly and unreasonable; and 3) that the ruling was discriminatory because only state-chartered institutions were required to comply.

[18] "26 Mass Mutuals, Co-op Banks File Suit Against Greenwald to Halt Redlining Rules," *American Banker*, June 17, 1975, p. 1.

The banks argued that the Banking Commission's responsibility was to supervise the banks to insure that sound, prudent principles of investment were practices; her role was not to require that depositors' funds be used as tools of social policy!

Compromise was reached later in August, 1975. Under the agreement, state-chartered financial institutions in the Boston SMSA were required to report their mortgage and deposit information by census tract for particular areas of the city, and by zip code elsewhere. In addition, Greenwald agreed to withhold the deposit information and release it only in five-bank totals.

The Bankers Respond

In September, 1975, John E. Wilkinson, President of the Charlestown Savings Bank, at the annual convention of the Savings Bank Association of Massachusetts, presented the banking community's response to Commissioner Carol Greenwald's proposal to form the Massachusetts Mortgage Agency. He announced that Boston's seven largest savings banks had elected to form a Review Board which would study rejected mortgage applications for residential urban property and decide whether such loans were viable. The board was composed of bankers and community group representatives as voting members, and the Commissioner of Banking and a representative of the Mayor's office as participating, nonvoting members. If the Review Board found that the applicant met appropriate standards and his property was found viable, the loan would be assigned to one of the participating banks.

Commissioner Greenwald commended the bankers' plan and sought to build upon it by introducing legislation which would require financial institutions to invest specified amounts of funds in home mortgages. Accordingly, she stipulated that the Board would have to be in operation before the opening of the 1976 legislative session.

John Wilkinson stated that due to legal problems, the banks would be forced to delay immediate implementation of the Review Board. He cited three areas needing discussion:

- the intricacy of getting a group of banks together on an allocation program without risking violation of the anti-trust laws;
- the selection of appropriate people for the board;
- the possibility of illegality if any bank's board of investment decided to accept an MRB-allocated loan which had already been denied as unsound.

The shortlived rapport between the bankers and the Commissioner was severed. Greenwald claimed that the banks were stalling. On November 16, she proposed legislation making it illegal to discriminate against any mortgage loan application as a result of the property's location. She declared that if voluntary action to create the Review Board was further delayed, she would introduce law to create her previously proposed Massachusetts Mortgage Agency.

Boston Banks

Boston and its lending institutions have served as a prime example of a limited number of large thrift organizations dominating the financial market. One-half of the savings banks in Boston have held more than 90 percent of the entire combined assets of all Boston savings banks. They continue to hold approximately 26 percent of the assets held by the 171 savings banks in Massachusetts. The circumstances of the cooperative banks were similar, with 12 of the 23 banks in Boston controlling about 85 percent of the total assets of all Boston based cooperative institutions. The federal savings and loans in the city operated in the same manner, with one-half of the banks controlling 86 percent of the outstanding mortgage loans.

Of the 16 Boston savings banks, the largest eight hold 67 percent of the combined real estate mortgages controlled by the city's savings banks, cooperatives and federal savings and loans. Only 48 percent of these bank's assets, however, are held in in-state mortgages.

It became apparent that these banks' methods of action decidedly influenced the supply of mortgage resources in Boston. As a bank's investment program developed, it determined a greater part of the economic growth. Since 1965, banks have directed their expansion into liquid investments rather than long-term conventional mortgages. Financial institutions began to diverge from the mortgage market, buying and selling mortgages like any other kind of liquid asset.

There evolved a certain fund-drain; money that was deposited in Boston was channeled into supplying mortgages in other cities or states, often hurting city residents. Supporting the financing of land acquisitions, development and new communities has become the banks' major interest. These loans are considered to be "safe" loans.

> It is senseless to chide mortgage lenders for their aversion to inner-city lending. . . . (It) is a weak choice compared with other investment alternatives. The extra costs of inner-city lending are quite real. The personal supervision needed for mortgage origination and servicing in the inner-city requires special skills on the part of the lender. The property and the area in which it is located also warrant an extra measure of lender attention. The very marginal nature of inner-city

lending increases the chance of default and foreclosure. This is undoubtedly the greatest cost of inner-city lending.[19]

The Banker's Perspective

Bankers' primary complaint regarding urban lending has revolved around the fact that outsiders are quick to criticize lending policies but few offer positive, feasible solutions. Critics' allegations that urban lending is correlated to urban housing have successfully pressed bankers into a defensive position. They have frequently stated that simply providing money does not solve housing problems; indeed, it occasionally causes greater problems. Not only do loan underwriters need to consider a consumer's financial background, but the party's "ability to own and *maintain* one of these properties."

Bankers in general believe that lenders in the urban area should play an active part in community development, both through loans and through direct neighborhood involvement. Some believe this can be accomplished through community leadership, assistance to community groups in dealing with political bodies, and through financial and investment aid.

But many also believe that the time has come to stand up for traditional banking values and practices. Some feel their role as repositories of community trust and faith has been undercut and their actions wrongly attacked.

Robert Spiller, President of the Boston Five Cents Savings Bank stated,

> There are many participants and factors in urban lending, and I would like to discuss their responsibilities. First, all of the intermediaries must be brought together so that all views can be aired and understood. Second, lenders must make a commitment to provide mortgage funds to buyers of homes in the neighborhoods. Third, local government must upgrade and equalize the support services to insure the liveability of a neighborhood. . . . I wonder how many savings bankers have spoken forcefully to public officials about the quality of these services when they are accused of not lending in a given neighborhood! . . . (Fourth), Local residents must indicate by deeds, not just words, their desire to protect and upgrade their neighborhood! . . . Fifth, real estate brokers play a critical role, and must travel a most judicious highway. The dangers of racial steering, blockbusting, overselling are always present and with the real estate

[19] H. David Raper, Jr. published in *Forum I,* a report on the Federal National Mortgage Association's conference to develop new solutions to residential finance problems in the inner city.

broker as the agent between buyer and seller, his improper actions could destroy all of the efforts of the other participants. Finally, there is the role of real estate appraiser which largely has been unrecognized. There is no doubt that the absence of a voice from the appraisal . profession has contributed to the controversies of the past several years. Perhaps their experience and knowledge of neighborhoods could well have done much to bring the complexities of neighborhood survival into full focus at a much earlier date.[20]

Herbert Grey, President of Suffolk Franklin Savings Bank, has adamantly maintained that mutual thrift institutions have not turned their backs on the city.

We are all a part of the city, we depend on the city for our future, and we have not turned our backs on it. Quite the contrary, we are actively involved in the affairs of the city and the problems of urban growth.[21]

BUSINESS ASSUMPTIONS
AND PUBLIC VALUES

At the outset of this chapter, the point was made that an organization's continued prosperity depends on its ability to meet changing public expectations. The two cases presented above suggest the extent to which public expectations and organizational legitimacy are linked. Yet, in both cases there seems to have existed great resistance to making the adaptations that would narrow this expectations/performance gap. We should ask why.

Certainly, there is a degree of complexity in both situations that makes simplification a great hazard. But there is one point that is clear in both cases. Namely, the enterprises involved in these social conflicts have been built on a set of assumptions about the public and the relationship of their industries to the public. In the television industry, this assumption is often expressed in the form of programming developed on "the least common denominator" dimension. If programming must be geared toward mass audiences, and if the least common denominator is a sub-high school diploma level of education, is it any wonder that violence characterizes programming from cartoons to serious drama? For all the proposals to limit televised violence, one must wonder whether the organizational responses will ever be satisfactory if the management is unable to seriously examine their fundamental operating assumptions.

The banking industry is little different than the television networks

---

[20] Quoted in *Savings Banker*, April, 1977.
[21] Herbert W. Grey, *Boston Globe*, May 7, 1977.

in regard to assumptions. There is no evidence in either the presentation above, or any other research on redlining, that bankers are willing to question assumption that loans are made on individual properties and that risks to those properties are environmental as well as specific to the property. On several occasions, critics have raised the possibility of establishing a separate fund for inner-city investments that would be operated in much the way assigned risk automobile insurance pools operate—that is, with a guarantee to the public that anyone could get such a loan. Such a plan might be called the most extreme form of "Greenlining," but unfailingly, such plans have drawn banking industry opposition. Why? Beneath the specific objections to particulars of such plans, there seems to flow a deep current of objection to the idea that any segment of the public, much less the entire public, should be entitled or guaranteed access to mortgage money. The critical assumption that bankers make in their lending operations is that no one—individual person, organization, or municipality—has a *right* to a loan. To the extent a guaranteed mortgage pool would subvert that principle, it must be opposed as the unholy precedent that could eventually undo the banking system.

Thus, we are brought full circle to the question posed at the outset of this chapter. How can a management cope with new public values when those emerging values seem to undermine the very foundations of the industry? Coping with change is not easy when the change seems to threaten the very existence of the industry! Yet, as we shall see again, this is exactly the situation in which the need is greatest for imaginative managerial responses.

part
three

proactive patterns
of response

chapter seven

creating environmental change

ALTERING THE EXTERNAL ENVIRONMENT

The corporate responses to change discussed in the preceding chapters each involved a measure of reaction to changes in the firm's external environment. The adaptive pattern of corporate behavior is characterized by this essentially reactive approach, one which emphasizes the organization's efforts to respond to the environment *after* it has changed. Those examples do not adequately describe all corporate actions with respect to external actors and influences.

An entirely different approach to the external world is frequently manifested by corporate behavior designed to produce change in the environment. These actions reflect different management views of external influences, ranging from a tactical concept of "defuse the issue by acting first" to a strategic conception such as "the world is our oyster, and we can shape it to serve our interests." While attitudes vary widely among managers, firms, and industries, there are ample numbers of instances in which such actions occur to demonstrate the existence of these approaches. Indeed, in recent years, the great volume of publicity and literature surrounding corporate misconduct has highlighted the extent to which managers in some organizations, especially large corporations, have developed such a concept of appropriate behavior toward other actors and society itself.

ITT may have provided the most dramatic example of the proactive approach toward the environment, and Harold Geneen has been its most arrogant spokesman. In the 1970's, ITT was the central actor in two of the most publicly offensive and outrageous examples of manipulative behavior. The company, which had grown to ninth in size on Fortune's list of the top 500 industrials in 1970 had done so by acquiring other companies at a dizzying pace. In the space of a decade (1961-1971), ITT acquired more than 250 separate entities. Moreover, the insatiable thirst for growth was whipped up by Geneen's corporate vision: 15 percent growth in sales, profits, and return on investment.[1] Over the course of a decade, then, this institutional purpose generated an average of 50 mergers per year, or the equivalent of a major new acquisition every two weeks for ten years! Little wonder that most observers of professional management believe that Geneen will go down in history as one of the most remarkable managers of twentieth century capitalism.

Geneen's success was not without its obstacles, however. A 15 percent growth goal, maintained over a period of years, inevitably means that new acquisitions have to become increasingly large. As the sales and asset bases of the parent became larger each year, it became increasingly difficult to acquire the following year's 15 percent growth. Because accomplishment of that goal was ITT's shibboleth, however, it was unthinkable to Geneen that the goal could not—much less *should* not—be achieved. The answer to this problem lay in the acquisition of increasingly larger companies. By 1972, ITT had acquired such giants as Levitt Homes, Continental Baking, Sheraton Hotels, Canteen Corporation (vending machines), Grinnell Corp. (fire prevention equipment), and Hartford Fire Insurance Company. Each was among the largest companies in its industry and each had enough assets independently to have qualified for a position in Fortune's 1972 listing of the top 500 corporations.

Predictably, antitrust objections were raised to ITT's continuing acquisition program. In 1970, despite indications from the Antitrust Division of the Justice Department that the acquisition was unacceptable, ITT went

---

[1] Anthony Sampson, *The Sovereign State of ITT* (New York: Stein and Day, 1973).

forward and acquired Hartford Fire Company, the largest United States fire insurance company, with its $1.98 billion in consolidated assets in 1969 and huge excess cash reserves ($400 million). As the Antitrust Division continued to move against ITT, the company acted to change the legal and political environment. Through its Sheraton Hotel subsidiary, ITT committed $400,000 to the Republican National Committee for the 1972 convention expenses. Through its lobbyists, including the famous Dita Beard, the company contacted Attorney General John Mitchell, his successor, Richard Kleindienst, and according to some accounts, President Richard Nixon, in an effort to remove the antitrust obstacles. On July 31, 1971, after months of refusing to compromise or settle the case without ITT's divestiture of Hartford Fire, Antitrust chief Richard McLaren announced a settlement of the case which permitted ITT to keep Hartford Fire. The settlement was widely branded a "sellout." On August 5, 1971, the Sheraton pledge was announced. Shortly thereafter, McLaren was named a Federal court judge in Illinois by President Nixon.

The public outrage at ITT's manipulation of the Justice Department through its high level political contacts in the Nixon White House was great, but was to be outdone by the disclosure of the company's activities in Chile. In the corporate version of the "Ugly American," ITT became a synonym for the "Ugly Multinational" because of its behavior in Chile. In 1970, socialist candidate Salvadore Allende mounted the most successful campaign by a socialist candidate in Chilean history. Part of his platform was the nationalization of critical industries, including the communications business which ITT operated under a Chilean charter. As the election drew near, ITT's Chilean operatives predicted an Allende victory over two more conservative candidates. At best, Allende might be stopped without a clear majority, in which case the election would be decided by the Chilean Congress. To force this result, ITT pumped in money, attempted to discredit Allende, and sought to draw other multinational companies into similar activities, all in violation of Chilean law.

When Allende failed to get a majority, and the election went to the Congress, ITT intensified its efforts, even making a pledge of $1 million to the American Central Intelligence Agency to finance a covert campaign to prevent Allende's election. Finally, ITT even participated in a series of actions designed to disrupt the Chilean economy to an extent that a military coup would occur before Allende could assume office. When all of these actions were eventually disclosed before a U.S. Senate Subcommittee on Multinational Corporations, ITT Senior Vice President, Edward Gerrity, commented: "What's wrong with taking care of number one?"[2]

[2] U.S. Congress, Senate, Report to the Committee on Foreign Relations by the Subcommittee on Multinational Corporations, *The International Telephone and Telegraph Company and Chile, 1970–1971*, June 21, 1973, p. 17.

ITT's behavior in both instances raised issues at the heart of the relationship between corporations and society. Are there consequences to corporate size that are inevitable and beyond the power of public control? If a corporation acquires political influence and political access as a normal consequence of its wealth and profits, and uses that influence to shape an environment that further favors its own profit oriented interests, can the public interest be safeguarded? That is a public policy issue, to be sure, but it is one that is raised by a concept of the corporation/society relationship which assumes the legitimacy of any action to change the environment if it serves the corporate interest.

Action to create external change need not and usually does not reach extremes suggested by the ITT examples. Yet, as an approach to dealing with the environment, *proaction* is a normal and frequently applied management concept. The two cases discussed below illustrate proactive responses to economic problems in the environment. The first case discusses the problems facing fire insurance companies which insured property in inner city locations. The underwriting losses they suffered presented a major difficulty, but one which was not susceptible of easy resolution. When the riots of 1967 occurred, however, an opportunity developed which allowed the fire insurers to change the political realities surrounding their business and create a political solution to their economic problem. The case strongly suggests that industries, or major segments thereof, can pursue a coordinated strategy designed to change the economic and/or political environment.

The second case discusses a short term effort to change public opinion about the desirability and impact of legislation to ban disposable beverage containers. The "bottle bill" campaigns of 1976 were a concerted effort by proponents of such a ban to enact legislation, directly or through public referenda, that would curb throwaway containers. Our case discusses the efforts of a coalition of interested corporate actors to change public opinion in one state where such a referendum was being held.

CHANGING POLITICAL REALITIES:
THE INNER CITY FIRE INSURANCE CRISIS

Fire insurance has generally been considered a social necessity since the 1700's. During the 1960's, two severe problems developed in the fire insurance business which directly stemmed from the necessary character of such insurance. The first related to the underwriting pressures on insurers to withdraw from the fire insurance business on inner city markets because of increasing hazards to insured property; the second related to the catastrophic losses occasioned by the urban riots and civil disorder which occurred during the summer of 1967. Together, they constituted a market problem of such serious consequence to fire insurers that complete abandonment of the inner city became a frequently discussed form of insurer response.

The Inner City Market

Like many other insurance problems of the 1960's, that of providing insurance to the inner city involved a basic dilemma between the availability of insurance coverage and price of such coverage. Fire insurance and crime insurance in particular, were considered necessities by inner city property owners and businessmen but were either unavailable from insurers or available only at a price that was not affordable.

Some of the dimensions of the inner city insurance problems are illustrated by data discovered after the 1967 riots. Following those riots, President Lyndon B. Johnson appointed the National Advisory Commission on Civil Disorders to investigate the origins of the riots and to recommend measures for preventing or containing them in the future. The Commission in turn, recognized that there were special problems associated with insurance and, on August 10, 1967, appointed the National Advisory Panel on Insurance in Riot-Affected Areas. This panel undertook to investigate inner city insurance needs, industry capacity to meet those needs, and alternative means of closing any gap between needs and capacity.

As part of its investigation, the Panel surveyed 1500 homeowners and 1500 businessmen in the inner city areas of Boston, Cleveland, Detroit, Newark, Oakland, and St. Louis. According to the survey results, which were reported in January, 1968, over 40 percent of businesses and 30 percent of homeowners had serious property insurance problems.[3] Specifically, 20 percent of businessmen and 6 percent of the homeowners surveyed were without fire insurance coverage, and in Detroit, over 12 percent of the homeowners were without it. Of the uninsured, 35 percent of the businessmen and 50 percent of the homeowners said that insurance was simply unavailable; nearly 30 percent of both groups claimed that whatever insurance was available was excessive in cost. In addition, 50 percent of the businessmen surveyed had no burglary and theft insurance, 30 percent said it was too costly and 25 percent said it was unavailable at any price.[4]

The problems of availability and cost of coverage were an understood, but unquantified matter before the mid-1960's. Insurers had with-

[3] President's National Advisory Panel on Insurance in Riot-Affected Areas, *Meeting the Insurance Crisis of Our Cities*, (Washington, D.C.: U.S. Government Printing Office, 1968) p. 2.
[4] All data derived from President's National Advisory Panel, *Ibid.*, pp. 115–160.

drawn from the market on an individual company basis, not en masse, and although the cost of available insurance had been increasing for many years, no concerted effort to remedy the situation had been attempted. The Watts riots in Los Angeles during the summer of 1965 focused public attention on the conditions existing in the inner city areas of some large cities, however, and some attempts were made to improve availability. But on the whole, public concern was latent and governmental responses limited until the 1967 riots. The number of deaths, the extent of the carnage, and the duration of those disorders riveted public attention on the inner city and convincingly suggested that the "long hot summer" of 1967 could, and might well be repeated in 1968.[5]

The relationship between an industry and society varies with scope of involvements, the importance of specific issues, and the duration of the relationship. In the case of fire and other casualty and property insurance coverages, the general need for such coverage by property owners made the scope of the interpenetration between the industry and society quite broad and the long standing history of this relationship magnified the problems involved in limiting availability. But it was the salience of the inner city insurance problem to both inner city residents and property owners and to the insurers that most precisely identified the importance of the matter. Insurers, as well as property owners, had a large stake in resolving the inner city insurance dilemma.

The stake of the insurers is reflected in several ways. In 1966, for ex-

TABLE 7-1.
STOCK AND MUTUAL COMPANY PREMIUMS
WRITTEN BY SELECTED LINES, 1966

| | PERCENT OF TOTAL PREMIUM VOLUME | |
	STOCK CO'S	MUTUAL CO'S
Fire Insurance	8.69	4.91
Extended coverage	2.59	1.46
Other allied lines	0.87	1.13
Burglary & theft	0.64	0.21
Plate glass	0.24	0.11
Total premium volume	$15,197,000,000	$5,788,000,000

Source: Best's Aggregates and Averages, 1967.

[5] See National Advisory Commission on Civil Disorders, *Report of the National Advisory Commission on Civil Disorders* ("The Kerner Commission Report") (Washington, D.C.: U.S. Government Printing Office, 1968).

TABLE 7–2.

COMBINED LOSS AND EXPENSE RATIOS
FOR STOCK AND MUTUAL PROPERTY-LIABILITY INSURERS,
SELECTED LINES OF INSURANCE 1957–1966 AVERAGE

	STOCK CO'S	MUTUAL CO'S
Fire insurance	102.0	85.3
Extended coverage	103.9	91.4
Other allied lines	90.8	88.3
Burglary and theft	101.8	99.5
Plate glass	103.1	98.5

1966

	STOCK CO'S	MUTUAL CO'S
Fire insurance	100.4	86.2
Extended coverage	89.3	81.5
Other allied lines	89.6	79.4
Burglary and theft	105.3	110.0
Plate glass	101.1	101.0

Source: Best's Aggregates and Averages, 1967

ample, the property-liability (nonlife) insurance industry had assets of about $41 billion and annual premium income of $22 billion. Among the relevant property lines of coverage in considering the inner city, fire insurance produced the largest volume of premium ($1.6 billion in 1966) for the industry, which represented 8.69 percent of the stock companies' overall premium income volume and 4.91 percent of the mutual companies' in 1966. Among nearly all relevant coverages involved in the inner city dilemma, stock insurers' involvement was larger than that of mutual companies.

Testimony presented before the President's Panel indicated that stock insurers were writing over 80 percent of all fire and extended coverage (wind, smoke, riot, vehicle, and hail occasioned losses) between 1957 and 1966. Thus, during the riots, it was the stock companies which stood to suffer the largest numbers and dollar volume of claims. Equally important, however, was the fact that stock insurers had been operating in these basic lines of insurance for nearly a decade with a combined loss and expense ratio that was higher than that of the mutual companies.

To combat these high loss ratios, insurers had been imposing special requirements of properties within redlined urban areas such as direct underwriting inspections, coverage restrictions, and a variety of surcharge, deductible, and coinsurance clauses. On an underwriting basis alone, abandonment of the inner city market was becoming a rational economic response. The stock companies were being tempted, in effect, to follow the lead of the mutual companies and lower their loss ratios by insuring only the most preferred urban properties.

According to the Advisory Panel, the constricted market for fire and property insurance for inner city markets was attributable to standard insurer underwriting practices. "The basic factor underlying the shortage of insurance in urban core areas is that insurance companies generally regard any business in those areas as relatively unprofitable. Instead of basing their decisions to insure solely on the merits of individual properties, many companies consider the application of an inner city homeowner or businessman on the basis of the neighborhood where his property is located."[6] The result had been the development of a variety of technical devices for limiting the receipt of such applications through underwriting standards and the identification of "redline" districts within which business ought not be written by agents. Such a course of behavior was, of course, quite consistent with the standard approach of seeking to create an underwriting profit on each piece of insured property. But this course of action had generally been failing for insurers before 1967.

Into the bleak underwriting picture of the inner city, the riots injected a second major loss element: the catastrophic loss. As the insurance commissioner of Michigan commented during the Advisory Panel hearings, the riots "introduce yet another uncertainty into the very markets with which insurers, acting individually, had been unable to cope prior to the riots."[7] For insurance companies, especially stock insurers, the prospect of continued civil disorder was especially disturbing. In the aftermath of the 1967 riots over $75 million of claims had been filed.[8] As Seymour E. Smith, an Executive Vice President of the Travelers Insurance Companies, characterized the matter in this manner during the Advisory Panel's 1967 hearings: "We are basically sales oriented. We want to write every risk we can on which we think we can make a profit. We are geared to viewing those risks, to the hazards inherent within the risk itself. It is the external environmental hazard that we are not able to cope with nor to control, and the only one that seriously concerns us is this riot potential."[9] Although the companies had the capacity to sustain another loss of such magnitude, the pertinent question was whether the inability to estimate probabilities of further disorders would lead companies to prudently withdraw all coverage from the inner city as a means of minimizing future

---

[6] President's National Advisory Panel, *op. cit.*, pp. 5–6.

[7] *Ibid.*, p. 72.

[8] This was considerably less than the $715 million loss sustained by insurers from Hurricane Betsy in 1965, but did amount to about 13 percent of the entire industry's 1966 underwriting profit.

[9] President's National Advisory Panel, *op. cit.*, p. 223.

losses. Such a course of action would operate to place the burden of any losses squarely with the public, either directly on property owners or indirectly through some government-sponsored program.

Industry Responses

There were three major facets of the inner city insurance problem for the individual companies involved. First, there was an organizational aspect to the problem. The technical and managerial subsystems within an insurance firm had the information and factual basis to support a course of action that involved not writing any further insurance on inner city property, and indeed, for cancelling that which was already in force. In many firms, this coalition was sufficient to sway the institutional subsystem into approving such a market withdrawal. For firms which had not withdrawn, the 1967 riots provided further evidence of the absence of a feasible market strategy other than abandonment.

The organizational dynamics resulted from the second, or economic, aspects of the problem. If risks were judged on an individual property basis, the premium charged an insured had to be commensurate with the probability of the risk of loss. Underwriters argued that the estimated probability of a loss depended, only in part, on the insured property itself. Another element in the equation had to be the nature of the nearby properties and the general neighborhood. As an area deteriorated, even an exceptionally well-preserved property in the area acquired a higher probability of loss. If one judged risks on a neighborhood or community standards basis, rather than an individual basis, whole districts were evaluated for insurability on the basis of aggregate characteristics. During the early 1960's various insurers used combinations of the individual property and community standards rating schemes to appraise the insurability of properties. Irrespective of the rating system, however, by the mid-1960's the inner city areas of many metropolitan communities were unacceptable risks. The economics of insuring the inner city had simply become too unattractive to insurers.

The third facet of the inner city insurance dilemma for the firms was political in nature. Great concern was manifested in industry councils about the effect of a complete withdrawal of insurance coverage. Urban areas, and the inner city in particular, had become politically volatile topics during the mid-1960's at both the state and federal levels of government. Whatever the rationale presented by the technical and managerial subsystems of the insurers in favor of abandonment, that course of action was deemed certain to provoke serious public consequences. Whatever the arguments favoring a strategy of abandonment, the issue of private insurer legitimacy would surely be raised should a major movement develop among the companies (especially the stock companies) to withdraw from the inner city.

The alternatives to withdrawal were limited in number, but some had received industry attention during the early part of the 1960's. In some cities, the industry had voluntarily established "Urban Area Plans" which were programs to induce greater insuring of urban core properties. The critical feature of these plans was that the insurers agreed that they would not refuse to insure a piece of property without first taking into account the inspection report prepared by a designated private or government agency. In this way, all properties in a redlined district, for example, received an individual and independent evaluation of their insurability.

Another response that received considerable attention during the mid-1960's involved development of a pool of insurer resources which were used to underwrite risks otherwise unacceptable to individual insurers. Although the industry had historically not favored pooling arrangements for risks which could not be individually written, the arrangement received much publicity when such a program was established in California in 1965 to provide insurance to businessmen in the Watts area of Los Angeles. Although the Watts pool was voluntary in nature, insurers were leery of the legislative temptation to make such pooling compulsory.[10] Indeed, during the spring of 1967, several months before the riots, a number of cities and states had begun to implement various combinations of voluntary and involuntary pooling arrangements.

The tendency of state legislatures to think in terms of compelling insurers to accept virtually all properties for coverage and to provide a risk pool to cover the marginally unacceptable properties was not viewed with enthusiasm by the industry. Nonlife companies had experience with pools in the automobile insurance area and had found them to be costly. Moreover, pools for providing insurance to the inner city were designed to cover "normal" fire and casualty losses. The catastrophic losses caused by the riots were a dimension of the inner city problem for which existing pools provided no answer.

As indicated above, insurer losses from the 1967 riots amounted to about $75 million, an amount which the President's Advisory Panel concluded the industry was well able to sustain. Nevertheless, the climate of public opinion and the formalization of a presidential inquiry into the causes of civil disorder, as well as the establishment of a special presidential panel to examine the relevant insurance questions, provided a unique opportunity for the industry to cast its underwriting and profit problems directly into the public policy process for resolution. As the transcript of the hearings held before the Advisory Panel makes clear, the insurance in-

[10] *Ibid.*, Chapter 3 of the final report, pp. 55–85.

dustry sought to achieve through public policy what it could not do through the market—safeguard the primacy of the private insurance industry while receiving a guarantee that they would not be unduly injured by catastrophic losses arising as a result of the riots.

The basic device sought by the industry was a "back up" arrangement whereby either the states and/or the federal government would guarantee that private insurers would not have to bear the full cost of a catastrophic loss. Given such an arrangement, the insurers then seemed prepared to discuss alternative means of guaranteeing a market for necessary fire and casualty coverages including Urban Area Plans and voluntary, as well as involuntary pooling arrangements.

Michigan's Commissioner of Insurance, David J. Dykhouse, clarified the policy questions involved when he commented:

> If one believes as I do, number one, that property insurance on a continuously available basis is a social necessity, two, that the socially acceptable minimum coverage for property is basic fire and extended coverage . . . and three, that the private insurance industry should be the fundamental force in providing this insurance, then two basic issues must be met head on and resolved. . . . First, who will determine what property is eligible for basic property insurance? And second, if the eligibility for such insurance remains solely an industry decision, should a financial subsidy in some form be provided the industry by government?[11]

As to the first question, testimony from industry representatives indicated a preference for a system involving only the insurers or an insurer-dominated rating bureau. As to the second, it was either discreetly avoided or claimed that since riots were a sociological phenomenon, society as a whole ought to bear the consequences.

The testimony of the Executive Vice President of the Travelers Insurance Companies is illustrative. "I find it irresistible, sir, if I may, . . . to respond to the question that you asked the previous witness as to the differentiation between catastrophes from natural rather than those resulting from social change.

"While the precise timing and location of hurricanes and other acts of God or aberrations of nature are not precisely predictable, there is a body of knowledge that is available. We have access to meteorological studies, predictable patterns. In addition, there is a large premium base to support these aberrations.

"We do not have as an industry any depth of technical knowledge as to sociology.

[11] President's National Advisory Panel, *Hearings before the President's National Advisory Panel on Insurance in Riot-Affected Areas* (Washington D.C.: U.S. Government Printing Office, 1968), p. 67.

"Furthermore, I doubt if there is any individual in this room that really knows or has a strong ability to completely predict what is going to happen in the nature of social change. It is the completely unknown that is staggering our industry.

"The magnitude of what has happened in the past is now what we are talking about. It is what conceivably could happen, and as long as this cloud hangs over us, of completely unknown dimensions, in which we have no expertise, we have no background of knowledge, no reasonable degrees of protection or predictability, that we find ourselves in this position."

The manner in which industry representatives testified before the Panel on the compelling need for a governmental backup arrangement suggested unanimity of thinking, if not a more structured agreement. Others perceived a note of industry coercion on the matter. The Insurance Commissioner of California, Richard Roddis, commented for example:

> . . . As far as the public of California is concerned, it seems to me anything is satisfactory which in fact provides a stable and continuous market for all necessary coverages.

But Roddis was also quick to note the complex political aspects of the situation.

> There is a piece of brinksmanship involved in all of this . . . We have the leadership of a very substantial number of the major companies in this country—in fact, the companies which really are the principal commercial market in these urban areas—who have in effect said, as I understand their presentations to this Panel and partially to Congress, that if they are not effectively relieved of at least the more extreme forms of the riot hazard, they cannot really continue to stay in these markets.
>
> . . .
>
> In other words, they say, "We need the backup," and the implication is that if they don't get the backup, they are going to be pretty disenchanted with urban area plans, voluntary pools, just about anything else, and in fact they may have to cut back. Now, we face a summer that, in the first place, will be an election year. It could be a summer that is a powder keg. What happens come June if they haven't got the backup, and if they mean what they say, they may have to start backing out. It seems to me that many of the state legislatures, particularly the big urban states, are in fact going to find themselves in a position where they are going to have to move in the direction of compulsory pools simply to be able to conserve the market. That, though not economically sound, is apt to be the de facto political result.[12]

---

[12] *Ibid.*, p. 59.

Commissioner Dykhouse also took note of the political aspects of the insurers' call for government participation.

> There has been such a determined drive lately, however, on the part of many insurers, notably the AIA companies to seek federally subsidized reinsurance for riot and crime connected losses, that some discussion of this is necessary. Now, the industry may well be using the social problem of riots, in combination with the horrors of insurance shortages, as a lever to force federal reinsurance for riot (coverage) at subsidized rates, which if exposures in urban areas are not increased could result in a better financial and underwriting result for the companies and reattract investment capital. Some critics have made this charge and there may be some truth to it.[13]

Moreover, according to Dykhouse, however useful such reinsurance proposals might be for the insurers, such a plan would not solve the basic problem of actually providing insurance to the inner city. Reinsurance is the sale of a part of a given risk to another company. According to Dykhouse, there was no reason to believe that just because the insurers could purchase reinsurance from the government that they would deliberately go into the inner city and write additional amounts of coverage. The primary insurers would still have to assume some portion of the risk associated with the inner city property and reinsurance would not change that.

The stock insurance companies were united by organizational, economic, and political interests. They were the foremost suppliers of fire insurance coverage to the inner city, they had suffered the largest losses, and they had a large stake in whatever plans resulted. Because of these common interests, stock insurers had long been active in supporting the existence and efforts of the American Insurance Association (AIA), a stock insurer trade association. During the 1967 hearings, the AIA was the primary stock insurer spokesman.

The program developed by the stock companies and presented by the AIA at the hearing consisted of five main points:

(1) That a government reinsurance program was an essential ingredient of any plan and that this reinsurance might initially be funded by the federal government, thereafter by the states.

(2) That an urban areas inspection plan would include mercantile and residential properties.

(3) That a pool, if required at all, be voluntary in nature and administered on a national basis.

[13] *Ibid.*, p. 72.

(4) That such a pool reinsure fire and extended coverage risks not written under the urban areas inspection plan, and, in addition, that burglary risks also be eligible for pooling.

(5) That all riot and civil disorder losses, wherever located, would be reinsured by the government above a certain percentage of earned premiums.[14]

The various points of the program were expanded upon, in greater detail by representatives of AIA member companies. William O. Bailey, Vice President of Aetna Life & Casualty, and in charge of the property and casualty underwriting department, emphasized the mechanics of a federal backup system in his presentation.[15] Bailey's testimony related the company's prior participation in urban area plans, in the Watts pool, and Aetna's preparedness "to support the extension of the urban areas concept to additional geographic areas and to commercial properties just as soon as necessary catastrophe protection against the riot peril is indicated."[16] It also touched on the other industry goals of a voluntary pool arrangement, the primacy of individual insurer judgment about insurability, and the need for a bureau-operated inspection service. Bailey added:

> While in general, we do not favor pooling as a means of spreading coverage among insurance companies, my company would support the concept of a voluntary pool to afford needed fire and extended coverage protection for those insurable properties which cannot find an individual company market because of acute environmental factors which cannot be removed and which are beyond the control of the insured. If such a pool were developed, it should operate as a reinsurance facility for the subscribing companies and be available only after the urban areas inspection procedure has been applied.[17]

In short, convincing federal and state governmental authorities of the need for a government supported backup system was an intensely political act. The stock insurers recognized this and pursued a common strategy of political action through the AIA.

The industry's arguments prevailed and in 1968 Congress enacted a federal reinsurance program for riot occasioned losses. That legislation

[14] Statement of Lawrence Jones, President of AIA in *Hearings*, pp. 185–194.

[15] Seymour E. Smith, Senior Vice President of the Travelers Insurance Companies, emphasized the need for a federal backup system; he was followed by Bailey; H. Clay Johnson, President of the Royal-Globe Insurance Companies described the role of pools in the program; Louis W. Niggeman, President of Fireman's Fund American Insurance Companies, concentrated on the importance and implications of insurer solvency.

[16] William O. Bailey, testimony before the President's National Advisory Panel, *Hearings*, p. 226.

[17] *Ibid.*, p. 227.

stands as a monument to the concentrated efforts of the industry, and the stock companies in particular, to remove the obstinate insurance problems of the inner city market to the public policy process for disposition. That transfer was accomplished at a time when the industry's bargaining leverage was impressive. The riots had provided an occasion for the stock insurers, through the AIA, to press federal and state governments for relief from a market problem that the companies alone had been unable to resolve in their operating environment. Raising rates and/or reducing available coverage were traditional market responses; both were limited alternatives for insurers because of public pressures. A government sponsored reinsurance plan surfaced as an alternative that would preserve both insurer profitability and insurer legitimacy by providing subsidized coverage to the inner city at affordable rates. Not surprisingly, the new plan was described as a fine example of private sector–public sector cooperation in the public interest.

In retrospect, the 1967 riots appear to have not been the change that prompted the insurers to respond so much as the occasion which allowed the stock companies to shape the operating environment in their own best interest. In this regard, the action of the stock insurers in support of a federal reinsurance plan was more manipulative than adaptive in character.

In January, 1968, the President's National Advisory Panel on Insurance in Riot-Affected Areas submitted its report and called for the establishment of a voluntary participation plan whereby insurers would assure every property owner an individual inspection of the property, written notice of improvements necessary to make it insurable, and guaranteed insurance if the property was maintained according to reasonable insurance standards. These were the so-called FAIR Plans, an acronym for "fair access to insurance requirements." The FAIR plans were to be supplemented by state pools which would guarantee insurance to qualified property even when the property was subject to an environmental hazard. Lastly, the Panel recommended creation of a National Insurance Development Corporation to provide reinsurance to member companies who participated in the FAIR Plans.

Within the year, Congress enacted legislation to implement the Panel's recommendations. The federal government agreed to serve as the "backup" or reinsurer for the state insurance pools in which insurers could voluntarily participate. In brief, federal participation constituted the "carrot" of riot reinsurance protection; in return for it, participating insurers promised to meet the inner city's insurance needs either directly, or most likely, through the state pools. State legislatures had to implement the FAIR Plan legislation by creating the pools, either directly or through their state insurance commission. By mid-1969, 27 states had done so; these states represented 75 percent of the property insurance premiums collected in the United States.[18] Yet at the same time, riot-occasioned losses in the first half of 1969 had declined to $15 million, a decrease which some feared might reduce the attractiveness of the federal reinsurance coverage and lead insurers to withdraw from FAIR Plan participation. Since then, the FAIR Plans have continued to function but have regularly faced the twin problems of insurer "dumping" (i.e., placing most inner city risks in the pools) and the threatened withdrawal of companies from the underwriting pools.

During the Panel's hearing, California Insurance Commissioner Roddis observed that "The business responsibilities of the insurance underwriter and the cry of the ghetto for succor and social justice are not readily reconcilable."[19] The insurance needs of the inner city, however, were, in fact, a matter which the industry—and the stock insurers especially—could not ignore. The interpenetration between the insurance industry and society made the provision of fire insurance a highly salient matter to insurers and the inner city alike. The problem was the inability of the market to resolve the problem to the satisfaction of both the industry and the relevant publics. By removing the issue to the public policy process, the industry attempted to both resolve the issue and stabilize its operating environment.

CHANGING PUBLIC OPINION: THE BOTTLE BILL CAMPAIGN

Protection of the physical environment has become an increasingly major item on the national public policy agenda. Since the early 1960's, public concern with, and expectations about, business efforts to clean up past industrial pollution, minimize current pollution, and eliminate future adverse environmental effects have increased dramatically. One effect of this change has been expansion of its impact from such "dirty" industries as steel and mining to less polluting businesses such as packaging. Beginning with the first "Earth Day" celebration in 1970, public awareness of the environmental impact of such consumer oriented products as plastic bottles, tin cans, and disposable packaging grew rapidly.

Since these early consciousness-raising efforts, major steps have been taken by public action groups to educate consumers about the environmental impact associated with normal patterns of goods consumption, and programs have been undertaken to force industries, through pressure and legislation, to change their involvement in the promotion of a "throwaway society." "Bottle bills" are legislative manifestations of the

---

[18] Alfred M. Best, Inc., *Best's Aggregates and Averages*, 1970.
[19] Richard Roddis, testimony before the President's National Advisory Panel, *Hearings*, p. 49.

effort to attack what has been called the "disposable culture." By requiring that all beverage containers, including cans and bottles, carry deposits with mandatory refunds to encourage refilling and recycling, proponents seek to eliminate one-way containers as a major source of environmental damage. If adopted, however, such legislation would also attack the foundations of several industries which have evolved with, and because of the throwaway revolution.

The Massachusetts Bottle Bill

On November 2, 1976, voters in Massachusetts went to the polls both to elect officials and to decide the fate of a number of issues for which public referenda were being held. Question #6 on the referendum ballot posed the question of whether or not the Massachusetts legislature should enact a "bottle bill."[20] The bottle bill question was the result of an initiative petition sponsored by the Committee For A Massachusetts Bottle Bill, which was self-described as an "umbrella organization supported by hundreds of individuals and public interest groups." Active participants in the organization included consumer groups and well known environmental action organizations such as the Sierra Club, Wildlife Federation, and Audubon Society. The Committee was originally formed in the summer of 1975 by ten individuals who submitted their first initiative petition seeking bottle bill legislation. In September, 1975, concerned citizens began the process of collecting the 60,000 signatures required by law. By December of that year, more than 100,000 signatures had been collected and filed with the Secretary of State. The bill was then scheduled for consideration by the Massachusetts legislature in the spring of 1976. Following considerable lobbying on the part of proponents and opponents, the legislature failed to enact a bottle bill or any compromise legislature by its deadline of early May. That failure prompted the Committee to announce "phase II" in its campaign: a drive to gain more signatures and force the question to be placed on the ballot in November. On July 7, 1976, the Secretary of State announced that more than 25,000 additional signatures had been filed with his office and that the bottle bill would be on the November ballot.

The Massachusetts bottle bill would place a minimum five cent deposit on all containers used to sell beer or carbonated soft drinks in the state (10¢ on containers with a capacity of 32 or more ounces) and would prohibit the sale of metal beverage containers with flip-tops. The proposed legislation would not apply to containers for dairy products or natural fruit juices, nor to biodegradable containers. The Secretary of En-

---

[20] Other referendum questions included such volatile issues as a ban on handguns, equal rights for women, changes in the state income tax, and elimination of the Sunday Blue Laws.

vironmental Affairs would be authorized to certify the containers as reusable or recyclable. A dealer could refuse to accept any empty beverage container which contains materials foreign to its normal contents. The bill further stated that the Attorney General would enforce the provisions, and that violations shall be subject to civil penalty for each violation of not more than $1,000. The proposed legislation would be effective February 1, 1977.

Federal Reserve Report

Certain economic effects of a mandatory deposit law in Massachusetts were suggested. In the March, 1976, issue of the *New England Economic Indicators*, published by the Federal Reserve Bank of Boston, a study by one of the Bank's economists concluded that:

(1) the requirement of a minimum deposit on beverage containers would increase employment opportunities in Massachusetts, although payrolls would decline in certain industries, and

(2) there is very little likelihood that the proposal would produce a noticeable increase in retail beverage prices; in fact, some prices might fall.

Proponents argued that passage would result in a net increase of jobs, between 97–1,380 full-time positions, not including the positive secondary employment influences in the construction and machine tooling industries. Possible employment increases resulting from the development of regional breweries and/or a recycling center were also believed likely.

The report stated that wholesale prices of soft drinks would probably drop at least 20 cents per case for 7- to 12-ounce bottles and 25 cents per case for 12-ounce cans. Similarly, the wholesale prices for beer would decrease at least 39 cents per case for bottles and 32 cents per case for cans.

Two additional recommendations were made in the report. First, to avoid some of the potential adverse economic effects, any mandatory deposit law should be enacted with an effective date of at least one or two years after the legislation is passed. Secondly, the small size of the New England states exacerbates border problems associated with differential legislation. Uniform legislation for all New England States, if not for the entire United States, would make compliance easier and would increase the benefits of the legislation.

The Campaign

In comparison to industry lobbying against the Massachusetts bottle bill, support for the bill appeared to be low-key. Both major newspapers, the *Boston Globe* and the *Boston Herald,* favored passage of Question No. 6 in their editorial columns. However, the news reports tended to be mixed. More columns were "pro" Question No. 6 in the *Globe* than were "con," but many of the "pro" articles were concerned with the possible loss of jobs.

An examination of the Committee for a Massachusetts Bottle Bill, the major proponent, also shows the low-key nature of the proponent's campaign. This group was headquartered at the offices of the Massachusetts Public Interest Research Group (PIRG) and was self-described as "an independent, university-based student action group working for political and social change." Norman Stein, a former PIRG student who devoted his full time through the summer and fall to the bottle bill campaign, appeared to be the leader of the Committee's efforts in Eastern Massachusetts. The majority of the expenditures for the Committee, which totalled $10,900 were paid as salary to Mr. Stein. (In contrast, the two campaign directors for the opponents earned $20,900 and $8,200.) The rest of the help was largely volunteer involving contacting people on street corners, writing letters, or leading discussion groups to persuade voters to approve Question No. 6.

The campaign was low-key more because of insufficient funds than from a decision that this would be the best way to proceed. The Committee did have some money to fund media advertising, but not nearly enough to combat opponents. In addition, polls showed a majority of the public in favor of a bottle bill and the proponents were very sensitive to not "turning people off" by overselling their position.

The Opponents

In Massachusetts alone, the industry lobby was credited with assembling a "war chest" of approximately $667,000 with which to work.[21] As of September 15, 1976, the State Campaign and Political Finance Office reported that the lobby had spent $462,843.63 to oppose the bill. The 39 corporate contributors to the "Committee to Protect Jobs and the Use of Convenience Containers in Massachusetts," the name used by the industry lobby in Massachusetts, included:

Can Manufacturers Institute, Washington, D.C.	$150,000
Various Coca-Cola Bottlers from across the U.S.	102,385
Pepsi-Cola Bottlers	43,000
Anheuser-Busch	33,300
Glass Container Corporation	62,000
Adolph Coors, Colorado	11,160
Owens Illinois of Toledo, Ohio	25,000
American Iron & Steel Institute, Washington, D.C.	17,833

[21] "Emotions Overshadow Substance in Debate Over Bottle Bill," *Boston Sunday Globe,* October 3, 1976, p. 32.

Results

Despite the efforts of the Committee for a Massachusetts Bottle Bill, and due to the overt efforts of the Committee to Protect Jobs and the Use of Convenience Containers in Massachusetts, the bottle bill was defeated on November 2, 1976, by a vote of 1,220,722 against, 1,201,579 for,[22] or a defeat by .8% of the votes from figures representing 99 percent of the precincts. The Committee for a Massachusetts Bottle Bill collected the required additional 1,000 signatures to petition for a recount if it was allowable. However, according to Massachusetts law, on a referendum question, the results must be less than .5 percent apart to allow a recount. Therefore no recount was ever taken. State Representative Lois G. Pines, one of the prime sponsors of the bill in the legislature, said after the election that she intended to introduce the same legislation early in the 1977 session of the legislature.

Previous Bottle Bill Legislation

Prior to the time bottle bill legislation was proposed in Massachusetts, three states had enacted similar legislation: Oregon in 1972, revised in 1973; Vermont in 1973, revised in 1975; and South Dakota, effective July 1, 1976. Three other states voted on the issue at the same time Massachusetts did: Maine, Colorado, and Michigan, where efforts to pass a bill had occurred for 10 years.

Oregon passed the first mandatory deposit legislation in June 1971, effective October 1, 1972. The major difference between its law and the bill proposed in Massachusetts was that in Oregon, only a minimum two-cent deposit is required on "certified" containers—that is, containers that are used by, and will be accepted for reuse by, more than one manufacturer. A five-cent deposit is required on all other beverage containers.

Vermont law was enacted on April 10, 1972, effective September 1, 1973. It differed from the proposed Massachusetts legislation in that a handling charge of 20 percent of the deposit is to be paid by the manufacturer or distributor to the retailer. The Vermont law did not ban flip-top cans, but effective January 1, 1977, Vermont extended its legislation to ban nonrefillable glass containers, the use of "flip-top" cans, and non-biodegradable carriers (i.e., the plastic ring holders).

According to Donald Webster, director of Vermont's Agency of Environmental Conservation, beverage container highway litter by volume decreased 76.1 percent in one year. As a result, litter from other sources dropped 4.9 percent, total litter volume down by 32.9 percent. In Oregon, total litter by volume declined 39 percent, including 83 percent for all

---

[22] *Boston Globe*, November 3, 1976.

containers (96 percent if nonreturnables purchased out of state or before the effective dates are discounted).[23]

In Oregon, one year after the bottle bill was enacted, refillable soft drink containers were being returned at a rate of 96 percent, and refillable beer containers at an 80–95 percent rate.[24] In Vermont, the beverage container return rate in 1974 was 89 percent, in 1975, 95 percent.[25] The Environmental Protection Agency has estimated that if in 1973, 90 percent of all bottles had been refilled, and 80 percent of all cans had been recycled, between 5 and 6 million tons of raw materials would have been saved that year. This represents a savings of about four million tons of glass, one million tons of steel, and 300,000 to 350,000 tons of aluminum.[26]

Beverage Industry

A mandatory deposit law would affect two major groups: soft-drink bottlers and brewers. Collectively, they are referred to as beveragers. The beveragers use four basic types of containers: 1) aluminum cans, 2) steel cans, 3) glass bottles and 4) plastic bottles.

On a deposit-returnable container, the deposit is imposed as an increased price by the bottler or brewer. Thus, just as the increased price for the deposit is carried forward through the distribution system, the container should go back through the distribution system to the beverager. For each beverage produced, the beverager may get to keep the deposit, or have to pay back the deposit to a distributor or consumer in return for any container of the type which the beverager has produced in the past few months.

Broken glass bottles are not returnable, but most cans are. The consumer or distributor is more certain of receiving a refund from a can in the future (it's hard to break); but the can is less valuable to the beverager than a bottle, since it is not directly refillable. Because of this, some observers feel beveragers will increase the proportion of beverages sold in glass if a mandatory bottle bill is passed. Many others dispute this conclusion. They cite consumer demand for cans. Of the 82 billion cans produced in 1975, 42.6 billion (52 percent) were soft drink and beer cans. Of the 42.6 billion, 26.1 billion (61 percent) were beer and 16.5 billion (39 percent) were soft drink cans.[27]

---

[23] "Mandatory Deposit Legislation," *Environment News,* USEPA, New England Regional Office, Boston, Massachusetts, July, 1976, p. 13.

[24] *Ibid.*

[25] Webster, Donald, Director, Vermont Agency of Environmental Conservation, letter, September 24, 1976, E.P.A. Boston.

[26] "Resource and Environmental Profile Analysis of Nine Beverage Container Alternatives," EPA Report, 1975.

[27] *Modern Packaging,* "A Face-Off in Metals," June, 1976, p. 22.

Aluminum recycling is highly economical. Prices for recycled materials were rising toward the end of 1975 and the first quarter of 1976. Reynolds entered into can recycling ten years ago, and in 1976 Reynolds and other aluminum producers paid 15 cents per pound for cans returned to 2,000 collection centers in the United States. Some 25 percent of all aluminum sold for can bodies now comes from recycled material.[28] According to one can company executive,[29] roughly 65 percent of beverage cans are made of steel and 35 percent of aluminum.

Can Industry

Dramatic changes have been occurring in the can industry for at least 15 years. The industry as a whole has struggled with many problems caused by overcapacity, price competition, and the emergence of plastic containers. The National Can Corporation depends on can profits more heavily than do its two biggest competitors, American Can Corporation and Continental Group, which have adopted strategies of business diversification.

Reynolds Metals Company and Kaiser Aluminum and Chemical Corporation became major success stories in the 1960's when they began producing aluminum cans. Today, Reynolds is generally believed to be the price setter for cans.[30] This may not continue since can makers have now developed the technology for two-piece steel cans which are considerably cheaper than three-piece steel or two-piece aluminum cans. Two-piece steel cans made initial inroads in the beer market because the high concentration in the brewing industry allows brewers to run long decorating runs without label changes, which are costly in multipiece production.

To further complicate matters, a price war has occurred in the industry. Aluminum lids are used on two-piece beverage cans of both steel and aluminum. For the past three years, Alcoa has initiated price hikes up to 70 percent on lid stock while the price of its can body stock (made from an ingot carrying the same price) rose only a fraction of that amount. "The aluminum companies have been subsidizing their can body sheet with higher prices on end stock. That's a trick as old as business itself."[31]

The steel can and aluminum can producers are usually different firms, and require quite different technologies. Yet, all processors require large capital investments to achieve economies of scale, and investment advisers believe the winner will be the corporation or industry which most

[28] *Business Week,* "New Threats to the $6 Billion Can Industry," November 22, 1976, p. 79.
[29] *Modern Packaging, op. cit.*
[30] *Modern Packaging, op. cit.,* p. 20.
[31] *Business Week, op. cit.*

accurately predicts and prepares for future demands. Bottle bill legislation introduces a great uncertainty into this intensely competitive environment.

Glass Industry

As with cans, the largest users of bottles are the beverage industries. Soft drink and beer packers use approximately 50 percent of the 281 million gross shipped in 1975. In addition, total shipments to these users increased by approximately 37 percent in 1975.[32]

The glass industry has been aggressively trying to drive down its costs and keep its prices competitive with cans. Brockway Glass Company, the second-largest glass container maker in the United States, has planned to market a high-speed bottlefilling machine that, it claims, will surpass the speed of the most efficient can-filling line and cut the number of workers needed to man it. The glass industry does not have the capacity or the capital to assume all growth in the container business. Ironically, bottle bill legislation would seriously reduce the industry's growth potential. Thus, glass bottle manufacturers, through their trade association, have launched a $3 million marketing campaign that stresses the recyclability of glass and the abundance of raw materials—limestone, sand, and soda ash—from which it is made.[33]

The glass industry would feel two major effects if a mandatory deposit law were enacted: (a) the number of bottles manufactured would be reduced, since bottles would be refilled several times; (b) new capital investment would be required since one-way bottles and returnable bottles are manufactured differently.

Plastic Industry

In 1974, 62 percent of the estimated 32 gallons of soft drinks consumed per capita in the United States were sold in containers of 28 ounces or larger.[34] Plastic bottles have the greatest advantage in the large, family-size beverage bottles of 32 ounces or more. The difference in weight, in shipping costs, and ease of handling by consumers, counts the most. For retailers, the thinner walls of plastic containers can reduce overall shelf space requirements by 15 percent.[35]

[32] *Modern Packaging*, "Glass Presses Its Advantage," June, 1976, p. 24.
[33] *Business Week*, op. cit.
[34] *Chemical Marketing Reports*, "Plastic Bottles Seen Capturing Soft Drink Market," February 23, 1976.
[35] *Industry Week*, "Plastic and Glass Impact Upon Metal Beverage Containers," October 13, 1975, p. 54.

For all the advantages of plastic containers, there are several problems associated with them. They are more expensive and have a limited shelf life as the bottle expands under pressure causing the fill level to lower. Plastic containers cannot be used for beers that are pasteurized. Environmentalists cite several faults also. They tend to increase litter by increasing the use of throwaway containers. Plastic can produce harmful gases and is capable of contaminating ground water when disposed of in municipal incinerators and open dumps.[36] Finally, the United States is suffering from an impending petroleum shortage and plastics require a great deal of this resource in their manufacture.

Bottlers

Bottling plants tend to be more numerous than breweries (about 2500 currently) because the operations for diluting syrup are very simple. It has been cheaper to ship the concentrated syrup to small regional bottlers where it is diluted to the appropriate concentration, then packaged and transported to nearby retailers. However, bottlers may soon follow the regionalization trend of the brewers. Between 1970 and 1974, 7,900 workers lost their jobs in the soft drink industry. Coca Cola has announced plans to phase out 900 franchised bottling plants by 1980, and replace them with 78 centralized plants.[37] A bottle bill would seriously affffect the capital facilities planning which now assumes the filling of one-way containers.

Brewers

It had been suggested that because a bottle bill will give competitive advantage to brewers located close to the consumer, it may have a significant effect in reversing the industry trend toward concentration.[38] Since 1935, the number of U.S. breweries has been reduced from 765[39] to 98.[40] These 98 are owned by 49 companies, five of which control 69 percent of the market.[41] It is contended by proponents of bottle legislation that this type of centralization would not be possible under a returnable, refillable system—that such centralization is totally dependent on one-way con-

[36] *Seventh Annual Report of the Council of Environmental Quality,* September, 1976, p. 64.

[37] *Environmental Action Foundation,* "Bottles and Sense," 724 DuPont Circle Building, Washington, D.C., 20036.

[38] Kopcke, Richard, "The Economic Effects of Requiring Deposits of Beverage Containers," Federal Reserve Bank, Boston, p. 3.

[39] *Environmental Action,* "State Bottle Bills: Taking the Initiative," July 17, 1976, p. 9.

[40] Vlantes, Stanley, Editor, *Modern Brewery Age Blue Book,* 1976, p. 6–8.

[41] *Business Week,* "Turmoil Among the Brewers—Miller's Fast Growth Upsets the Beer Industry," November 8, 1976, p. 59.

tainers and that if throwaways are banned, the national firms would be forced to localize their production.

The giants are obviously worried. Modern technology has already eliminated many jobs in the industry and will continue to be the main source of job reduction. A massive addition to capacity by the nation's largest brewers is currently planned, which will serve to push more regional breweries out of the industry, causing a loss of jobs for their employees. *Business Week* magazine concluded that such overcapacity and heated competition would reduce the number of brewers from 49 to 15 by 1980, putting almost 90 percent of the market into the hands of just five companies—Anheuser-Busch, Miller, Schlitz, Pabst, and Coors. Between 1971 and 1976, these five have squeezed the regional brewers by expanding their collective share of the market from 53 percent to 69 percent.[42]

The impact of containers on the cost of beer is immense. Three of the largest brewers, all heavily into non-returnable cans and bottles, claim that containers constitute 56 percent of their average manufacturing expenses. This is almost three times the amount spent on labor and nearly four times the cost of the beer's agricultural ingredients.[43] Cost savings in this area can have a significant effect on profits. In addition, new, light-weight metal, one-way containers can be shipped 1,000 miles or more, enabling the majors to invade the local markets of smaller rivals from large centralized breweries.

The issue of non-returnable cans and bottles is a costly one for industry. Brewers insist that threatened federal and state legislation would force them to spend $3 billion to convert their packaging lines from the aluminum can to the returnable bottle.[44]

However, a clue to the adaptability of this industry to legislative changes came in Vermont after it strenghtened the law, requiring that all bottles be refillable by January 1, 1977. "Within one week, Schlitz flooded the market with refillable bottles and advertising that said, 'Save money with money-saver refillable bottles.' "[45]

Growth in usage of non-returnable beverage containers from 42 percent of beer containers in 1958[46] to 83 percent in 1974 can best be understood by explanation of elements which contributed to this trend. First, during the 1960's there was a general rise in the level of disposable personal and discretionary income, as well as a corresponding increase in lei-

[42] *Business Week*, "Turmoil Among the Brewers, *op. cit.*

[43] Selby, Earl and Miriam, "Can This Law Stop the Trashing of America," *Reader's Digest*, March, 1976, p. 4.

[44] *Business Week*, "Turmoil Among the Brewers, *op. cit.*

[45] *Sports Illustrated*, "The Point of No Returns," August 2, 1976, p. 42.

[46] Murphy, Pat., "A Cost/Benefit Analysis of the Oregon 'Bottle Bill,' " *New Marketing for Social and Economic Progress and Marketing's Contribution to the Firm and Society*, American Marketing Association Publication, Combined Proceedings Series #36, 1974, p. 347.

sure time. An outgrowth of this phenomenon was a demand for convenience. One example of the demand for convenience was an increasing popularity of beer packaged in no-deposit and no-return containers, even though they cost more. The increased number of different kinds of containers, used once and disposed of, caused the price of beer to rise, but the consumer was willing to pay. The containers were employed as a marketing device to differentiate the product, since the product itself was basically homogeneous. Therefore, the marketing mix elements were enhanced by non-returnables.

One factor affecting United States breweries is the way beer is marketed. Market segmentation, new-product proliferation and heavy advertising are now replacing production efficiency and price promotion as the keys to growth in brewing. In addition, there is a slowdown in the growth rate. Beer consumption grew by 48 percent in the United States between 1966–76 partly because the number of people in the 18–34 age bracket grew by 37 percent, far faster than the total population. This group is the traditional beer-drinking group, consuming more than 50 percent of all beer sold. However, the group will become middle-aged in the 1980's and the growth in the beer-drinking age group will probably flatten out.[47]

The secret to growth of national brewers has been the market share they took from regionals by building more sophisticated production facilities. Now the planned expansion will wipe out other major breweries, not just the small regionals. The only brewer with a "built-in safety valve" is Coors.[48] Since they sell in only 20 percent of the United States (about 12 states), all they need to do is expand their market in order to increase sales.

Coors has converted its entire operation to refillable bottles and recycled cans. Paying a bounty for the return of its bottles and for aluminum cans, the brewery has experienced high return rates and has found the process to be economically advantageous.[49] Most significantly, Coors has favored a national mandatory deposit regulation, but is opposed to state-by-state deposit laws. One Coors spokesman stated, "Our industry cannot live with a proliferation of state laws, each uniquely different in its requirements. Coors believes that some kind of deposit law is imminent and unavoidable." However, "(we) would prefer a uniform deposit law on beverage containers administered federally."[50]

As a whole, breweries have enjoyed non-returnable containers since both shipping and handling costs have been reduced and profits improved. The availability of more package types helped increase sales, as

[47] *Business Week,* "Turmoil Among the Brewers," *op. cit.*
[48] *Ibid.*
[49] *Ibid.*
[50] *Fortune,* "While the Big Brewers Quaff, the Little Ones Thirst," November, 1972, p. 105.

lighter-weight throwaways can go everywhere conveniently and can be disposed of anywhere. Satisfying consumer demand has proved profitable for the brewers and they leave no doubt that they are prepared to fight to keep it that way.

Wholesalers and Retailers

A mandatory deposit bill would have a serious effect on both wholesalers and retailers. The principal burden for retailers involves the additional space necessary to store returned bottles, with some additional labor expenses also likely. Retailers are quick to point out that modern stores are not designed with large storage areas, thereby making it likely that storage will either be on a makeshift basis or will come at the expense of actual shelf space. Makeshift arrangements are also likely to cause problems with health department officials; loss of shelf space will force prices higher and reduce consumer choices on other products. Wholesalers have similar problems, primarily that of redesigning a delivery and return system that can accommodate large numbers of returnables. Stockpiling of returnable bottles and cans will require space that many wholesalers do not presently have available. This, they argue, will force them to raise the prices they charge for beer and soft drinks. Ultimately, retailers and wholesalers both claim, the consumer will pay an increased price for the inconvenience of a clumsy, two-way returnable system.

The Industry Campaign

The singular objective of the industry lobby has been to defeat local bottle bill legislation and to ultimately minimize the likelihood of national legislation. The strategy for achieving this objective is two-fold. First, industry dollars flow from throughout the United States into the "bottle bill" area. Secondly, they attempt to divert public attention away from the bottle bill as an answer to litter problems towards more suitable industry alternatives. In Massachusetts alone, the lobby spent approximately one million dollars to defeat the 1976 referendum. More than half of the funds came from outside the State.[51]

Industry argues that mandatory deposit legislation is discriminatory, focusing on only a fraction of "total" litter. They believe direct results will be higher prices, inconvenience, loss of jobs and higher taxes, all without reducing litter. As alternatives, they argue for tougher litter laws and better education programs to change consumer behavior patterns. Therefore, through the years industry has developed a variety of schemes to promote their alternatives.

[51] *Boston Globe*, October 2, 1976, p. 5.

In 1953, Keep America Beautiful (KAB) was created and bankrolled by the industry lobby. KAB contends that litter is a "social problem" because only people litter. They call for more public education on the evils of littering, urge stricter enforcement of the anti-litter laws, more litter baskets and more litter pick-up. They do not advocate any cutbacks in litter producing items. [52] Over the years, industry has contributed millions of dollars to KAB.

In 1968 and 1969, KAB financed a roadside-litter survey, designed by North Carolina's Research Triangle Institute. According to the results of the survey, beverage containers are less than 20 percent of roadside litter. Several studies of the experiences in Oregon and Vermont refute this claim. In addition, the results of the KAB study are questionable since it involved litter counts on the first two miles of main highways in each of only 29 states. It did not look at road or recreation areas and the counts were not taken in summer when litter is at its peak. It also did not include the millions of flip-top openers littered from beverage cans. [53]

In 1971, the Anheuser Busch Company commissioned the Management and Behavioral Science Center, a part of the University of Pennsylvania's Wharton School of Finance and Commerce, to look at some of KAB's work. The Center's report concluded that KAB programs and other anti-litter efforts by industry had neither significantly reduced litter nor shown promise of doing so. Said the report: "Most of these efforts have been directed more toward presenting or delaying restrictive legislation action or taxes than toward reduction of litter." [54]

The KAB initiated a litter-control law in Washington State in 1970. The law established a litter tax not only on beverages and containers, but also on food, tobacco, household paper products, newspapers, magazines and soap. The voters were impressed, shelved an impending bottle bill and passed the litter law in 1971. In 1974, the container industry paid $24,-094, less than 3 percent of the total tax collection of $902,111. A full 52 percent of the tax came from wholesale and retail food establishments, which naturally passed it on to consumers. The state claimed a 60–70 percent litter reduction, but nearly seven out of every 10 Washingtonians polled still saw a need for a bottle bill in their state. [55]

Another industry attempt to waylay bottle bill legislation has been the promotion of "resource recovery." They have even established a National Center for Resource Recovery. Resource recovery is, however, inherently more expensive than source reduction (e.g., returnable containers) and has proven to be more complicated in practice than the-

---

[52] Selby, Earl and Miriam, "The Whys Behind a Bottle Bill," *Reader's Digest*, July, 1976, p. 170.
[53] *Ibid.*, p. 171.
[54] *Ibid.*
[55] *Ibid.*, p. 172.

ory.[56] Some of the problems inherent in broad scale resource recovery are (1) for every 100 tons of garbage, there may be no more than 13 or 14 tons of recoverable, salable metals and glass; (2) except for aluminum, scrap brings low prices; (3) meager economic rewards provide little incentive for consumers to return non-returnable glass bottles or steel cans; and (4) markets for scrap are not always available.[57] As a result of the impact of these factors, many recycling centers have been closed, and those remaining open make little dent in reducing the volume of containers entering the solid waste stream.[58]

The Massachusetts Campaign

The industry lobby has fought the battle of the bottle bill in other states and local communities. Their machinery for waging a campaign is well-oiled and has an admirable record of success. Hence, when it became clear that the referendum question would appear on the November ballot, the lobby was well-prepared.

The first step in a campaign is the establishment of a committee that appears non-partisan and public spirited in challenging the idea of a bottle bill. In Massachusetts, the committee was known as the "Committee to Protect Jobs and the Use of Convenience Containers in Massachusetts." Other misleading names that have been used by industry-supported groups have included Citizens Committee Against Initiative 256 in Washington state; in Eau Claire, Wisconsin, the Eau Claire Consumer Information Committee; and in Florida, the Dade (County) Consumer Information Committee.[59] The Committees are the mechanism which provides public speakers and statements about the bottle bill, places advertising and coordinates the media campaign against the bottle bill, and serves as a conduit for contributions to, and expenses for, running the campaign.

In the early months of the referendum campaign, the industry's committee focused its efforts on disputing the truth of such assertions as those contained in the Federal Reserve Bank's report on the favorable impact of the bottle bill. By early September (the last 60 days), the industry took the offensive in trying to change public opinion. In the early summer, various public opinion polls estimated that as much as 65 percent of the voters favored a bottle bill. According to one industry official, this was a normal plurality for the proponents at that time. The plan was to shave

---

[56] "Fact Sheet on Question #6," Publication of the Committee for a Massachusetts Bottle Bill, September, 1976, p. 2.

[57] Selby, July, 1976, op. cit., p. 172.

[58] Murphy, Pat, op. cit., p. 349.

[59] Selby, Earl and Miriam, "The Lobby That Battles the Bottle Bills," Reader's Digest, May, 1976, p. 241.

away at that plurality throughout the summer and wage a full media campaign during the final 45 days.

The media campaign in Massachusetts eventually zeroed in on an Environmental Protection Agency study of the Vermont bottle bill as the source of its keynote theme: "If the Bottle Bill Passes, It Could Cost Your Family Over $100* A Year." The asterisk refers to a note which stated "$100 per year for the average family based on consumption of 8 oz. cans of soft drink . . . ; consumption of beer based on 12 oz. cans . . . ; additional total cost per unit/case based on Vermont Study (U.S. Environmental Protection Agency)." In the advertising displaying this message, the asterisk was bright red and the reference to the U.S. Environmental Protection Agency was circled in bright red. There was no doubt that the advertising was designed to suggest that it was the EPA that created the $100 estimate, not the industry. In fact, just the opposite was true.

On October 8, 1976, the EPA issued an official news release protesting the advertisement as misleading and distorted. In part, that release stated:

> "The main thrust of the massive advertising campaign is that if the bottle bill passes, it could cost each family over $100. This is followed by a reference to a Vermont study by the U.S. Environmental Protection Agency. The E.P.A. reference is circled in red and marked with red asterisks in order to bring it to the attention of the reader. It is clear that the purpose of this tactic is to imply that E.P.A. predicts that the bottle bill will cost Massachusetts families over $100 a year. This is totally false. The Agency strongly objects to the implication and the misuse of an E.P.A. report in reaching an unfound conclusion. . . . It is clear to us that the Committee's claim is based on very faulty analysis. For example: It first assumes that the Massachusetts citizens will throw away 57% of deposit containers and forfeit the deposit. This assumption alone accounts for nearly 55% of the claimed price increase. Experience in the States of Oregon and Vermont . . . shows that over 90% of the deposit containers are returned for refund. National return rates for refillable beer and soft drink bottles are closer to 95%.
>
> "In addition to misrepresenting the price data presented in the Vermont report, it selects the extreme upper limits of the Vermont price increases and inflates these numbers by 4% annually.
>
> "It neglects any shift to refillable bottles and the price reductions that would occur from such a shift. Numerous price surveys conducted by the E.P.A. and others have found that beer and soft drinks sold in refillable bottles are much lower priced to the consumer than beverages in the throwaway bottles and cans."[60]

[60] U.S. Environmental Protection Agency, Statement, October 8, 1976, Region 1, J. F. Kennedy Building, Boston.

The industry's campaign to use the Vermont figure and misstate EPA's role in making the $100 estimate was not limited to one advertisement. It appeared repeatedly in newspaper advertising, billboards, and radio messages. As the final pre-election days passed, the messages bombarded the public. *"The Bottle Bill Is Full Of Empty Promises,"* read one full-page newspaper ad. *"If a $50 Fine Doesn't Stop A Slob, 5¢ A Can Won't"* read another. The impact of a bottle bill on consumer prices, and the inconvenience of carrying heavy bags of bottles back to the store were constantly emphasized.

The campaign to change public opinion and sway voter preferences touched on more than costs and convenience, however. Public health hazards were cited on several occasions as a serious aspect of the bottle bill legislation. According to the Committee's fact sheet, "most health experts oppose the returnable system because the total effect of all those unwashed bottles in homes, stores, cars, and garages would create vexing if not unmanageable sanitational problems."[61] In fact, the Massachusetts bottle bill specifically stated that the retailers "may refuse to accept any empty beverage container which is in an unsanitary condition and contains materials which are foreign to the normal contents of the beverage container."[62] Officials in Oregon and Vermont indicated in writing that the returnable bottle laws enacted in those states had created no health problems; neither state had cited any store as a health hazard for having empty beverage containers. In addition, the United States had long used returnable bottles without significant sanitation problems.

The lobby also appealed to the voters' sense of consumer sovereignty. It claimed that the bill restricts the purchaser's freedom of choice by: 1) virtually wiping out throwaways so that the consumer cannot buy them if he/she chooses, and 2) driving the smaller, private label beer and soft drink brands out of the competitive market. The industry also cited the inconvenience of washing, storing, and returning empties, and the added burden on the elderly "who find one trip to market taxing enough as it is."[63] Similarly, the lobby repeatedly argued that beer and soft drink makers adopted throwaways because the consumer wanted them.

Throughout the bottle bill campaign, the industry's operatives showed great concern for countering proponents' arguments with point-by-point confrontation and refutation. There was a direct and deliberate effort to show that over time, the industry's "truth squads" would convince the electorate and eat away at the pro-bottle bill plurality. By late September, the industry was claiming success as a *Boston Globe* survey

---

[61] "Fact Sheet," *op. cit.*, p. 3.

[62] House Bill #3544, Commonwealth of Massachusetts, "An Act of Controlling Environmental Pollution by Littered Containers," Section 316 (e).

[63] "Fact Sheet," *op. cit.*, p. 3.

seemed to show increasing anti-bottle bill sentiment. The *Globe,* with the largest circulation in New England, regularly presented a "Forum" column which asked readers to express their opinions on particular public issues. The bottle bill was the subject of the "Forum" on September 20, 1976. Readers using the newspaper ballots which accompanied the article apparently favored the bottle bill by a 3-to-1 margin, with approximately 1,-200 votes in favor and 400 against. However, facsimile ballots had also been submitted, with only about 80 in favor of the bill and *over 1,700 against!* Total votes in favor, 1,280; against, 2,100.

According to an article explaining the overall plurality against the bottle bill, the newspaper noted that many of the facsimile ballots had been submitted by employees of the bottle and can companies, as well as the retail and wholesale distributors, dealers, and their friends. Employees of such firms as National Can Company, Owens-Illinois, and Coca-Cola Bottling told *Globe* reporters that facsimile ballots were distributed at their places of work. At least three persons whose names appeared on the facsimile ballots said they had not responded to the "Forum," and two said they never even heard of the bottle bill. Curiously, the facsimile ballots had all been photocopied and addressed by machine. The bottle bill's proponents assailed the industry for its "Watergate-style dirty tricks."

Dirty tricks or not, the industry's campaign against the bottle bill eventually succeeded. In the final weeks before Election Day, the economic impact of the bottle bill was repeatedly driven home by the industry. The returnable bottle bill attacks jobs, not slobs, claimed the lobby. It was said that nearly 1,000 jobs would be jeopardized at the state's two glass bottle manufacturing plants, four can manufacturing facilities, and two corrugated box plants. Their combined payroll was $14.8 million annually, most of which was paid to "head of the household" employees. These gloomy industry estimates contrasted sharply with the Federal Reserve Bank's study, which forecasted creation of between 97 and 1,380 new jobs, and a net increase in payrolls of between one and ten million dollars. The industry's estimates cast great doubt on the Bank's forecast, and in a state that had been experiencing severe unemployment problems for several years, even the threat of a loss of jobs was telling. Not surprisingly, an uncertain public is likely to value 1,000 existing jobs to a nebulous 1,300. Doubt and uncertainty about the future is a powerful weapon in the battle for retaining the status quo. On November 2, 1976, a majority—albeit a razor-thin majority—voted against the Massachusetts bottle bill. The industry had won its battle for public opinion.

chapter
eight

impeding
external change

USING AND MISUSING
THE LEGAL SYSTEM

The corporation has numerous ways of buffering itself against the impact of changing public expectations. One of the most frequently used means for doing so is the legal and administrative process. The American legal system is a remarkably resilient mechanism for adjusting conflicts between individuals, institutions, and social purposes. It is an evolutionary system, one which changes more slowly than many would wish, but probably faster than the most established social interests desire. It is a force for change, however, and one which has served as an extremely effective means for implementing public policy goals and objectives.

One of the virtues of a legal system that changes, but not too fast, is that the actors in a society—institutions and individuals—can comprehend and shape their actions according to a set of rules which abide over long periods of time. To take a simple example, a multi-year employment contract would be worthless if the parties to that contract could not assume that its terms would be enforced by the courts over its lifespan. Planning, whether by individuals or institutions, is an essential act in a complex industrialized society, and a relatively stable legal system permits that planning to be accomplished with some degree of certainty. For that reason alone, managers often look to the prevailing rules of the game as a baseline for future corporate activity. The law changes more slowly than public expectations, is easier to monitor for changes, and is less given to rapid shifts in direction. In an uncertain management environment, the law offers a measure of certainty and predictability to which managers and corporations often cling with great resolution. In such a context, it is easy to understand why many managers endorse the idea of waiting until the law changes before acting to meet new public expectations of corporate performance.

Out of the desire for certainty, and the ability of the legal system to ensure a degree of certainty greater than public opinion alone can provide, comes a managerial willingness to resort to the legal process to *defend* the institution against change. In extreme cases, this can even extend to using the legal process as a means of altering a public environment which supports new kinds of corporate behavior. Such an extreme is discussed here with respect to the enforcement of pollution abatement regulations in Minnesota in the case of Reserve Mining. The company's steadfast adherence to legal procedure and its lawyers' ability to continuously find new bases for delaying the implementation of a ban on direct dumping of taconite tailings (an iron ore byproduct believed to be cancer-producing to humans) is an extreme example of proactive behavior to impede the accomplishment of new public goals. By deliberately altering the legal environment surrounding the dumping issue, Reserve Mining has successfully created a situation in which it is free to dump its taconite waste into Lake Superior regardless of consequences to public health.

STONEWALLING IT AT RESERVE[1]

Background

The Reserve Mining Company is located in Silver Bay, Minnesota, and is the wholly-owned subsidiary of the Armco and Republic Steel corporations. It mines low-grade taconite rock, which is pulverized in order

[1] The most thorough discussion of the complex technical, scientific, and regulatory problems surrounding this case is by Frank D. Schaumburg, *Judgment Reserved: A Landmark Environmental Case* (Reston, Va: Reston Publishing Co., 1976).

to magnetically extract concentrations of high grade iron ore. These are then formed into pellets which are used by the parent companies for their smelting. The waste product results in "tailings," approximately two-thirds of the original taconite rock.

The iron ore deposits in the basin of Lake Superior have long been the basis for industrialization in the area. But, as with most natural resources, there comes a point when the source is depleted. In the 1950's the iron ore mining industry was faced with two alternatives for survival—to import the iron ore or to create a substitute process delivering the necessary product. The solution devised in the late 1940's was the mining of taconite, a lower grade iron ore which enabled the mining companies to both continue and expand. The taconite beneficiating process had not yet been adapted to large scale production, but Reserve was willing to take the risk. As it turned out, the process was able to immediately pick up the slack facing the U.S. iron industry, thereby also revitalizing the stifled economy of northern Minnesota. The citizens of the area were in favor of bringing in the new taconite process and fought the restrictive tax laws which had hindered capital investment.

Reserve initially proposed to create a plant which could produce five million long tons of concentrated pellets per year. This process would yield 10 million tons of solid residue for disposal. The company required 130,000 gallons of water per minute to operate the beneficiating and power plants. This is comparable to the amount of water consumed per minute by a city with one million inhabitants.

With the influx of new production, Reserve gave employment to over 3,000 people. In addition, it built the town of Silver Bay, a community of private homes for employees and their families. Silver Bay was professionally designed and developed. Initially, the company provided secondary sewage treatment and water filtration facilities, something new to North Shore communities.

In choosing a workable site for Reserve, many options were discussed. Although the Babbitt Mine[2] area seemed the most likely, further study revealed that this site lacked a reliable supply of water and the necessary land for on-land tailings disposal. The location of Silver Bay proved optimum for these reasons. Further explanation was given by H.S. Taylor, the mines manager affiliated with Reserve in 1947:

> "We have shown one of the primary reasons why we are going to Lake Superior is to try to reduce our costs so that we can compete with direct shipping (high-grade) ores. . . ."[3]

[2] Babbitt Mine, Babbitt, Minnesota, located on the eastern end of the Mesabi Range.
[3] Transcript, 2nd public hearing on applications of Reserve Mining Co., June 17, 1947, St. Paul, Minn., p. 35.

Following the formation of Reserve in 1947, eight years of engineering, investigation, and planning were to take place before the application for permits could be pursued. Reserve first had to obtain a permit from the Minnesota Department of Conservation to appropriate the required water from the lake for the ore processing and power plant operations. The second required permit was from the Minnesota Pollution Control Agency (MPCA) to discharge process waste and cooling water back into the lake. A third permit had to be obtained from the U.S. Army Corps of Engineers to ensure safety for lake navigation. Reserve needed to construct both a dock and harbor to facilitate transport of the finished pellets.

The last necessary step was to organize public hearings for those individuals and groups who wished to voice their interests and concerns as required by state law. Because of the importance of the issues and preservation of natural resources, a total of nine hearings would eventually be held. The first hearing was held June 5, 1947, the ninth, on November 4, 1974.

Reserve hired two leading engineers as consultants, Dr. Lorenz Straub, the Director of University of Minnesota St. Anthony Falls Hydraulics Laboratory and Dr. Adolph Meyer, a prominent hydraulics engineer. It was determined that the success of the operation hinged on two factors:

1) The presumed effectiveness of the heavy density current phenomenon. (Reserve's discharge resulted in a fluid slightly more dense than lake water. The tailings would hence flow undisturbed to the bottom.)[4]

2) The existence of a 900-ft. deep trough in Lake Superior.

The Chairman of Hearings, Chester A. Wilson, was convinced that the tailings would not affect the water quality past one mile of the planned site and that they would not affect fish life, water supply, or navigation. Dr. Mario Fischer, Director of Public Health for the city of Duluth, expressed his concern as a result of lack of research regarding deep currents in the lake.[5] Dr. John Moyle, aquatic biologist with the Minnesota Department of Conservation, claimed that the fish spawning grounds would not be disturbed. He noted that only the fish near shore would be influenced by the high turbidity.

Dr. Samuel Eddy, Professor Emeritus of Zoology at the University of Minnesota insisted that the tailings would reduce spawning areas located

---

[4] Until 1968, little contradictory evidence existed to prove that the heavy density current didn't act as predicted.

[5] Although this study was deemed desirable, one was not conducted until several years later when tailings were discovered in water supplies.

close to the plant, and would probably upset the balance of the fish population in a 10–15 sq. mile area near the plant. Fear developed that commercial fishing would be wiped out. Fishermen have chronically complained that other uses of the lake negatively affect the fishing industry. Records show, however, that overzealous fishermen and overfishing have been their own worst enemy.[6] Interestingly, in later years, Reserve built a pond entirely from taconite tailings and stocked it with lake trout to demonstrate the apparent safety of the effluent.

Concern was aired about the quality and composition of the water. It was pointed out that some problems are inherent in any efficient mixing zone. Thus, water quality in a mixing or discharging zone is generally not required to meet the rigorous standards of purity.

Other opponents debated the addition of large amounts of silica deposits into the lake water. This could cause silicosis, a disease of the lungs produced by long-term inhalation of silica dust, or otherwise prove harmful when ingested. Dr. Fischer asserted that although inhalation might prove dangerous, there was little evidence that direct ingestion was any cause for alarm.

In December, 1947, the Minnesota Water Pollution Control Commission (MWPCC) issued its permit. The Department of Conservation published its findings and appropriated 130,000 gallons per minute of lake water. Then in April, 1948, the U.S. Army Corps of Engineers authorized the go-ahead for construction.

These conditions were established:

(1) The tailings, including power plant return water, were not to include any material quantities of water-soluble matter, organic matter, oil, sewage or other waste except taconite residue.

(2) The tailings were to be discharged into a designated 9 sq. mile zone of discharge.

(3) The tailings were not to result in material clouding or discoloration of the water at the surface outside of the discharge zone except as caused by natural phenomena, including storms.

(4) The tailings were not to exert any material effects on fish life or public water supplies.

(5) The tailings were not to result in any material interference with navigation or in any public nuisance outside of the discharge zone.

Eventually, the question of semantics would make these conditions unenforceable; the lack of clarity in the conditions left them open to the varying interpretations of many interested groups.

[6] USDI-FWPCA, An Appraisal of Water Pollution in the Lake Superior Basin, April 1968, p. 18.

Between 1947 and 1960 there were relatively few complications in establishing the operation disposing of the taconite tailings. In 1960, Reserve applied for and received a permit from the Army Corps to increase dumping for a 10-year period. This was eventually altered to permit increased dumping for an indefinite time. Reserve, in keeping with its reputation as an "ideal" company for the North Shore area, invested in a lake monitoring program. No state or federal agency conducted any scientific studies of the lake between 1947 and 1960. The prevailing attitude seemed to be one of rejuvenation, growth, and optimism for the industry. Appreciation and conservation of the ecology had been more philosophy than practice. That state of affairs would not continue however.

A Turning Point

Positive public sentiment about the industry began to dissipate as concern for the environment and natural resources grew. In 1965, the Federal Water Quality Act was passed and the Minnesota State Legislature established the Minnesota Pollution Control Agency (MPCA) in 1967 to develop water pollution standards and enforce regulations. Concurrently, there developed a lengthy set of legal inquiries into governmental interference, corporate privileges, and intrastate pollution in the state of Minnesota. In Minnesota, it appeared the governor could virtually prevent any legal action against a company unless the pollution produced a public health hazard.

Between 1966–68, under the authorization of President Lyndon B. Johnson, the Secretary of the Interior carried out studies of principal water sources. Upon analyzing the composition of Lake Superior's water supply, the government charged that Reserve's effluent was polluting the lake. Lake Superior had long been valued because its pure, crystal blue water served as a multifunctional resource for transportation, water supply, residence disposal, commercial fishing and recreation.

Since a relatively small amount of fresh water actually enters the lakes, a long hydraulic residence time is inevitable. A droplet of water entering Lake Superior may not be flushed from the lake for 500 years or more. Any water quality management plan had to take this into consideration. Currents tend to mix the water fairly well, except during the summer when certain areas of the lake stagnate.

In 1968, the Taconite Study Group was formed, with Charles Stoddard, Regional Coordinator for the Secretary of Interior, as chairman. It was comprised of representatives from the Bureau of Sport Fisheries and Wildlife, the Federal Department of Water Quality, the Bureau of Commercial Fisheries, the Bureau of Mines and the Geological Survey. State regulatory agencies from Minnesota, Michigan and Wisconsin were also invited to participate. Their report was critical of Reserve's dumping.

The "Stoddard Report," as it was called, was never officially released; it was classified as an internal staff report. In 1969, it was leaked to the press in Washington, D.C., and these findings were made public:

- · Reserve emptied more discharge than did all U.S. tributary systems into the lake in one year;
- · A considerable portion of solids escaped the density current;
- · The lake's currents were sufficient to carry particles long distances;
- · A permit was violated due to discoloration of the lake;
- · The turbidity was much too great;
- · The federal and state water quality standards were violated in the overabundance of iron, lead, copper, zinc and cadmium;
- · Sufficient phosphorous to stimulate algae growth was found;
- · Tailings had displaced or covered bottom fauna;
- · The actual discharge was responsible for some changes in the fish population.

The Report proposed an alternative of on-land disposal.

Litigation

A "Conference in the Matter of Pollution of the Interstate Waters of Lake Superior and its Tributary Basin—Minnesota, Wisconsin, Michigan" was initiated by the Secretary of the Interior and held on May 13, 1969. Although Reserve Mining's activity was the primary focal point, the general intention of the conference was of an exploratory, fact-finding nature. As before, many different conclusions surfaced. The FWPCA recommended continued surveillance while the Stoddard constituents demanded a limited three-year extension with definite alternatives studied.

Edward Furness, Reserve's president, presented the industry's case which emphasized the positive impact of the company on Minnesota's economy. He insisted that the use of Lake Superior resulted in "no waste of water, no injury to water, and it incorporates harmless, permanent, deepwater deposition of inert tailings."[7] He went on to say ". . . In all our operations we have followed good conservation practices. We pledge to continue."[8] Wisconsin's representative from the State Department of Natural Resources concurred and stated that there was no indication that the tailings were responsible for interstate pollution.

When conservation groups were called on to testify, they did not produce sufficient data to corroborate their pleas and accusations. Charles Stoddard took the stand, not in his official capacity, but as a concerned citizen. Chairman David Dominick refused to consider Stoddard's report as evidence.

[7] Proceedings of "Federal Enforcement Conference," first session, pp. 375–8.
[8] *Ibid*, p. 380.

The general recommendation from the hearing was that the Reserve should attempt to locate alternatives. But the company had already done so, it claimed, by hiring the firm of Trygve Hoff and Associates of Cleveland as consultants. They had determined that an on-land disposal site meant that within 22 years it would become absolutely imperative to dump water and waste into the Beaver River, which flows back into Lake Superior. Hence, it was a limited option and one that also entailed exhorbitant operating costs.

Dominick more or less summed up the intricacy of the situation by asking,

> "Can our complex legal and administrative machinery really enforce pollution control laws in the face of heavy economic and political pressures to study, to postpone, to discredit; and yes, even to use improper influence not to act?"[9]

On the second and final day of the executive session, the conferees delivered their recommendations for future action. Of the 21 recommendations, the following were aimed most specifically at Reserve:

> 1. "The FWPCA and the States keep the discharge of taconite tailings to Lake Superior from the Reserve Mining Company, E. W. Davis Works, under continual surveillance and report to the conferees at six-month intervals on any findings that interstate pollution is occurring or is likely to occur and the state of Minnesota is urged to take such regulatory actions as necessary to control the intrastate pollution resulting from these discharges, if any."[10]

> 2. "Reserve Mining Company be requested to undertake further engineering and economic studies relating to possible ways or means of reducing (to) the maximum practicable extent the discharge of tailings into Lake Superior and submit a report on progress to the Minnesota Pollution Control Agency and the conferees within six months of the date of issuance of the Summary of Conference by the Secretary of the Interior."[11]

An optimistic note was sounded by a conference member at the closing of the session:

"I really think we have achieved a breakthrough. We really have developed something in the very difficult field of Federal-State relations. Also we are dealing with the kind of resource where our responsibility is so great that we can't permit ourselves a serious mistake."[12]

[9] Ibid., p. 667.
[10] Ibid., p. 172.
[11] Ibid., pp. 179–80.
[12] Ibid., p. 248.

On December 24, 1969, Reserve filed suit against the MPCA contesting the validity of certain provisions of the federal-state water quality control standards as they applied to the company. On February 13, 1970, the state denied Reserve's charges and counterclaimed that the company was, in fact, polluting Lake Superior, thereby violating Minnesota's statutes Chapter 115 and Regulation WPC 15. The court was requested to schedule a deadline for Reserve's operation to adopt the legal provisions.

A short time later, Judge C. Luther Eckman issued a restraining order against Reserve, and explained the restraining order in these terms:

> This court feels that the time has come to brush aside all legal technicalities and procedures that may impede a resolution of these questions without further delay by taking the problem out of the public and political arena and into the court for a full and comprehensive judicial review, where the interests of both the public and industry can be fully explored and protected.[13]

The court found that (1) there was no substantial evidence that the discharge of tailings had "rendered the waters unclear or noxious or impure" as required by law to establish pollution, (2) After 15 years of operations and discharge, there were no measurable adverse or deleterious effects on water quality or use of Lake Superior insofar as its drinking water quality (or) any condition affecting health, affecting fish life or their reproduction or interference with navigation. However, the discharge did effect the aesthetic enjoyment as a result of the "green water" and accounted for a decrease in the presence of Pontoporcia (scud)[14] in the vicinity of discharge zone.

Judge Eckman refused to rule on the problem of pollution as raised by the MPCA's counterclaim. Although Reserve could not be legally charged, the court concluded that the present method of the tailing's discharge must be altered. Eckman ordered Reserve and the MPCA to arrive at a mutually acceptable plan of operation. On May 15, 1971, Reserve was required to submit new plans to the MPCA, with a two-year installation time limit. Although this decision appeared to be the most practical, the state was dissatisfied and moved to appeal the case in the Minnesota Supreme Court.

Seven months after the close of the first federal-state enforcement conference, the conferees reconvened. On August 12, 1970, the participants met again to consider basic pollution-related issues. This time the

---

[13] "Order for Temporary Injunction and Stay of Proceedings" issued by Judge C. L. Eckman on April 30, 1970 in Minnesota Lake County District Court.

[14] Food eaten by smelt. This only resulted in minimal effect on fish population as a whole.

conferees were more concerned with the health aspect and the focus was turned to all lakeshore industries, not solely Reserve. By the time of a second meeting in January, 1971, the controversy revolved around the impact on-shore dumping was having on both aquatic and terrestrial ecology. Reserve's management indicated that a study of plausible alternatives was in process. The conferees agreed to form an ad hoc committee to report back to the delegates in 45 days.

At the third session, April 22, 1971, Reserve's modified discharge system was presented and rejected. The company, with Edward Fride as spokesman and counsel, responded that critics of the plan were being unfair to the company and that Reserve had complied in good faith with Eckman's decision. Chairman Dominick concluded on the second day that William D. Ruckelshaus, Administrator of the Environmental Protection Agency, should bring suit against Reserve Mining Co. under section 10(c) (5) of the Federal Water Pollution Control Act.[15] Reserve was subsequently ordered to develop a pollution abatement plan acceptable to EPA within 180 days or be subject to suit by the U.S.

On February 2, 1972, EPA filed suit in the U.S. District Court, District of Minnesota, against Reserve Mining Co., with Judge Miles W. Lord presiding. Reserve was charged with violating the laws and regulations of WPC 15, the Refuse Act of WPC 15, the Refuse Act of 1899 and federal common law nuisance standards. Forty-eight specific charges were filed.[16] Pretrial actions continued throughout the year.

The Asbestos Concern

The year 1973 was monumental in the proceedings against Reserve. Newspaper headlines[17] announced findings of asbestos fibers in the drinking water, a likely cancer threat. Both the fibers in the smokestacks' emissions and the tailings' discharge were identical to asbestos-form fibers. The story set off new shock waves. Immediately, U.S. Senator Robert Griffin (R-Mich.) and U.S. Representative David Obey (D-Wisc.) sought injunctions to end Reserve's operation. The Environmental Defense Fund joined as a plaintiff in the suit for an injunction. Ralph Nader told newsmen that this discovery presented "the most demonstrable eco-catastrophe in the country's history."[18]

The asbestos findings cast the controversy in a new light. The actual amount of tailings and discharged dust was no longer the principal concern. Now it was the composition of the discharge, its biological effects

---

[15] Proceedings of "Federal Enforcement Conference," third session, p. 442.

[16] *St. Paul Dispatch*, June 15, 1973.

[17] *Duluth News Tribune*, August 11, 1973.

[18] *New York Times*, January 7, 1976, p. 6.

and its final destination that were at issue. Reserve continued to emphatically insist that the tailings largely settled to the Lake's bottom.

The legal activity continued at a dizzying pace when Reserve filed a counterclaim and sought damages for undue interference on the basis that they did maintain legal permits. Damages were sought for compensation for impairment of their contractural rights in violation of the constitution of Minnesota and the United States.

On January 4, 1974, Judge Lord ordered that Armco and Republic, Reserve's parent companies, be joined as co-defendants. Reserve appealed the decision, and the court demanded that company officials and documents be subpoenaed. Reserve's lawyers had long argued that no onland disposal system had ever been planned. The subpoenaed documents proved that several options had, in fact, been explored. Judge Lord ordered more documents subpoenaed and examined. The trial became increasingly complex. Judge Lord was outraged at evidence that showed political contributions by the company, schemes to undermine regulatory efforts, and slanderous notations. On March 29, 1974, the parent companies were ordered to rejoin the proceedings as co-defendants.

Armco's president publicly accepted responsibility for the concealment and for Reserve's submission of misleading evidence designed to prolong the trial. Commenting on the profitability of such delay, even in light of a major health hazard, Lord noted: "The people of Duluth had that unwelcome addition to their diet for five months while you (Reserve) made $5 million profit." Ironically, the Armco annual report for 1973 shows it had also established a Committee on Corporate Responsibility.

The Trial

On April 28, 1971, EPA administrator Ruckelhaus alerted Reserve of its violation of federal water quality standards based upon the recommendation of the Federal Enforcement Conference and pursuant to Section 10 (c) of the Federal Water Pollution Control Act. The company was given 180 days to meet these standards or be subject to suit by the federal government. On February 2, 1972, the EPA brought action against Reserve in U.S. District Court, Judge Miles Lord presiding, as a result of the company's unsatisfactory compliance. The federal government charged Reserve with violation of WPC 15 (the Federal-State Water Quality Standards), the Refuse Act of 1899 and Federal Common Law Nuisance Standards. In total, there existed 48 specific charges.

As a result of the potential impact of the case, Wisconsin and Michigan joined as plaintiffs, as did the Minnesota Environmental Law Institute, Northern Environmental Council, Save Lake Superior Association and Michigan Environmental Confederation. Eventually, several organizations came to intervene on Reserve's behalf, claiming specific economic interest in the future of the company. These groups include the villages of Babbitt, Silver Bay and Beaver Bay, Silver Bay Chamber of Commerce, Range League Municipalities and Civic Associations, Northeastern Minnesota Development Association, Duluth Area Chamber of Commerce, St. Louis and Lake Counties and Lax Lake Property Owners Association.

There were three major questions to be considered at the trial.

(1)   The quantity, composition and fate of the taconite tailings discharged into Lake Superior;

(2)   The public health impact and significance of the tailings' air emissions from the Reserve plant; and

(3)   The effect of the tailings on the ecology, appearance and overall quality of Lake Superior.

Over 100 witnesses were called to testify on the technical aspects of these questions during the trial. Witnesses were called by Reserve, by the plaintiffs and by the court itself.

The plaintiffs based their claim for an injunction banning dumping on five separate bases:

(1)   Reserve's discharge was subject to abatement because the discharge of taconite tailings reduced the quality of Lake Superior's below the water quality standards established under the Federal Water Protection Control Act.

(2)   Reserve's discharge constituted interstate pollution which endangered the health and welfare of persons in the states of Michigan and Wisconsin.

(3)   Reserve's discharge violated the Refuse Act, which provides that it shall be unlawful to discharge refuse matter of any kind or description whatever other than that flowing from streets and sewers and passing therefrom in a liquid state . . . unless a permit is first obtained.

(4)   A common law nuisance existed in that the discharge of tailings contains substantial quantities of amphible fibers, many of which are identical or similar to known asbestos fibers, and which constitute a public health hazard to persons depending upon the lake for drinking water. It was further alleged that the discharge stimulated the growth of algae and bacteria, created substantial increases in turbidity, impaired the ecological balance of the lake, accelerated the eutrophication of the lake, caused the green water phenomenon, and substantially detracted from the natural scenic beauty and aesthetic enjoyment and use of Lake Superior.

(5)   A common law nuisance existed as a result of the substantial quantities of amphibole fibers released in the air which endan-

gered the health of all those people who breathed the conta-
minated air.

Reserve's legal strategy was to dispute the precise nature of the discharge, its biological effects, and the eventual destination of the discharged tailings. The company denied the existence of a serious health
threat, asserting that the commingtonite—grunerite did not have a fibrous
form and was otherwise distinguishable from amosite asbestos, the known
human carcinogen. Reserve claimed that the tailings largely settled to the
bottom of the Lake in the Great Trough close to the plant.

Reserve also counterclaimed, and sought damages on the basis that
since the company had valid permits and licenses, any restriction, limitation or termination of its rights would effect the taking of defendant's
property without just compensation in violation of the Fifth Amendment.
In addition, Reserve also asked compensation for impairment of its con-
tractual rights in violation of the constitutions of the United States and
Minnesota. Each action added months to the trial.

On April 20, 1974 Lord finally ordered Reserve to stop dumping
tailings into Lake Superior and cease all air emissions. He issued the following findings of fact:

(1) Reserve Mining Company is set up and run for the sole benefit
of its owners, Armco Steel Corporation (Armco) and Republic
Steel Corporation (Republic), and acts as a mere instrumentality or agent of its parent corporations. Reserve is run in such a
manner as to pass all its profits to the parents.

(2) Reserve, acting as an instrumentality and agent for Armco and
Republic, discharges large amounts of minute amphibole
fibers into Lake Superior and into the air of Silver Bay daily.

(3) The particles, when deposited into the water, are dispersed
throughout Lake Superior and into Wisconsin and Michigan.

(4) The currents in the lake, which are largely influenced by the
discharge, carry many of the fibers in a southwesterly direction toward Duluth and are found in substantial quantities
in the Duluth drinking water.

(5) Many of these fibers are morphologically and chemically
identical to amosite asbestos and an even larger number are
similar.

(6) Exposure to these fibers can produce asbestosis, mesothe-
lioma, and cancer of the lung, gastrointestinal tract, and
larynx.

(7) Most of the studies dealing with this problem are concerned
with the inhalation of fibers; however, the available evidence
indicates that the fibers pose a risk when ingested as well as
when inhaled.

(8) The fibers emitted by the defendant into Lake Superior have the potential for causing great harm to the health of those exposed to them.

(9) The discharge into the air substantially endangers the health of the people of Silver Bay and surrounding communities as far away as the eastern shore of Wisconsin.

(10) The discharge into the water substantially endangers the health of the people who procure their drinking water from the western arm of Lake Superior including the communities of Beaver Bay, Two Harbors, Cloquet, Duluth, and Superior, Wisconsin.

(11) The present and future industrial standard for a safe level of asbestos fibers in the air is based on the experience related to asbestosis and not to cancer. In addition, its formulation was influenced more by technological limitations than health considerations.

(12) The exposure of a non-worker populace cannot be equated with industrial exposure if for no other reason than the environmental exposure, as contrasted to a working exposure, is for every hour of every day.

(13) While there is a dose-response relationship associated with the adverse effects of asbestos exposure and may be therefore a threshold exposure value below which no increase in cancer would be found, this exposure threshold is not now known.

The judge also found that as a matter of law, Reserve was in violation of the Minnesota Pollution Control and Air Emission statutes. The court concluded that since Reserve's discharge polluted the "waters of Lake Superior as to endanger the health and welfare of persons in Minnesota, Wisconsin, and Michigan . . . the discharge is subject to abatement" pursuant to the Federal Water Pollution Control Act.

The court found that a common law nuisance was created under federal and state common law and the applicable state laws of nuisance. In addition, the court also indicated that a condition in Reserve's original permit indicated that the terms of the license "shall not be construed as estopping or limiting any legal claims against the permittee . . . for any damage or injury to any person or property or to any public water supply resulting from such operations." Thus, the state permits were not a defense to the claims brought against Reserve. Furthermore, the terms of the permits had been violated.

Judge Lord included a discussion of the economic and technological feasibility of abatement by studying what modification could be made, the expense and Reserve's ability to cover the expenditures. Moreover, he charged Reserve with acting in bad faith in misrepresenting facts, producing biased studies and reports, and intentionally evading the submission of its fully engineered plans for alternative means of tailings disposal.

In the last analysis, the Judge found that the "company can afford to abate the health threat, has the technological ability to abate the health threat, yet refuses to do so. . . ." The court realized that the work force at Reserve would suffer immensely if the plant were shut down, but believed that Reserve was using the workforce as "hostages" to continue its present mode of operations. Finally, Lord concluded, "this Court cannot honor profit over human life and therefore has no other choice but abate the discharge."

Reserve Appeals

Judge Lord issued his injunction halting the Silver Bay taconite operation on April 20, 1974. Within hours, Reserve had convinced a three-judge panel of U.S. Circuit Court of Appeals (8th Circuit) to hear the company's emergency appeal. After presentation of arguments from both sides' counsel and review of Lord's opinion, the panel ordered a stay of injunction pending a hearing on May 15. On April 22, Reserve reopened and resumed its operations.

On May 15, after hearing arguments on the appeal, the court extended the stay of Lord's injunction for another 20 days, subject to certain conditions. On the question of public health, the court was unsure that adequate evidence was available to determine proof of a "substantial health hazard" as charged by Lord. The court questioned how to precisely determine what the lower level of exposure was, and whether that level, once established, was safe.

The inability to answer such questions was of crucial legal importance. In a court of law, governed by rules of evidence, unknowns may not be substituted for actual evidence. The Court of Appeals concluded that Judge Lord, "carried his analysis one step beyond the evidence."

The court did not respond to the issue of pollution as it had with the health problem. The court described the discharge as a "monumental environmental mistake" and issued a three-part ruling:

(1) Reserve's plans for onland disposal and control of air remissions had to be submitted for review and recommendations within 25 days of the order;

(2) The state was given an additional 20 days to file comments on such plan;

(3) The district court (Judge Lord) was to consider Reserve's plans and accompanying recommendations, and then report its recommendations to the Court of Appeals within 15 days.

Upon reconvening, Judge Lord rejected the new plans, a modification of the original Palisades Plan which he and the MPCA had turned down previously. Lord also informed the Court of Appeals that several issues remained unresolved and under advisement. A conference was deemed necessary by the Appellate Judges Bright and Ross (and eventually Webster) on August 9. During this time, the Court of Appeals requested the state to locate a suitable onland disposal area, which they designated as the Lax Lake site. Total cost was estimated at $252 million, which would make the facility the most costly expenditure for pollution control by a single company in United States history.

On August 16, the Court of Appeals remanded the case back to district court with orders to "expedite the disposition of the unresolved issues."

Lord rendered his decision on these matters on October 18, 1974, in which he discussed a lengthy list of Reserve's violations of state and federal statutes and regulations. Finally, on March 14, 1975, the Court of Appeals handed down its final order on Reserve's appeal of Judge Lord's original decision. The Court of Appeals found that:

(1)	The United States and other plaintiffs established that Reserve's discharges into the air and water gave rise to a potential threat to public health. The risk to public health was of sufficient gravity to be legally cognizable and called for an abatement order on reasonable terms.

(2)	The United States and Minnesota have shown that Reserve's discharges violated federal and state laws and state pollution control regulations, also justifying injunctive relief on reasonable grounds.

(3)	No harm to the public has been shown to have occurred to this date and the danger to health is not imminent. The evidence calls for preventative and precautionary steps. No reason existed which required that Reserve terminate its operations at once.

(4)	Reserve, with its parent companies Armco Steel and Republic Steel, was entitled to a reasonable opportunity and a reasonable time period to convert its Minnesota taconite operations to onland disposal of taconite tailings and to restrict air emissions at its Silver Bay plant, or to close its existing Minnesota taconite-pelletizing operations. The parties were required to expedite consideration and resolution of these alternatives.

(5)	The evidence suggested that the threat to public health from the air emissions was more significant than that from the water discharge. Consequently, Reserve was required to take reasonable immediate steps to reduce its air emissions.

On March 31, 1975, Minnesota, Wisconsin, Michigan, and several environmental groups lost an appeal to the U.S. Supreme Court of the Court of Appeals order staying the immediate halting of Reserve's dumping operations. The Court of Appeals' ruling in favor of "Abatement on Reasonable Terms" would stand. The request for a maximum two-year limit on dumping was also rejected.

Aftermath

On January 6, 1976, the U.S. Court of Appeals ordered that Judge Miles Lord be removed from the case, citing "gross bias" and "deliberate denial of due process." Lord was accused of abandoning his impartiality and taking on the responsibilities of an advocate. He stated, "I have done my best to provide for the maximum protection of the public health consistent with due process to all concerned. As of today I can do no more." Chief U.S. District Court Judge Edward Devitt was assigned to preside over the case.

The Army Corps of Engineers requested and was granted an emergency appropriation of $5.7 million to deliver asbestos-free drinking water to Duluth and other north shore communities, a distribution sufficient for fifteen months. Meanwhile, the Minnesota Pollution Control Agency voted 8 to 0 that new health evidence did not justify an order to close Reserve. If additional information on the health hazards of asbestos became apparent, a closing order could be obtained.

On May 5, 1976, Reserve's luck changed when the federal court imposed fines of more than $1 million against Armco and Republic. $837,500 was for Silver Bay, Minnesota, because of the company's violation of state water discharge permits from May 20, 1973 to April 20, 1974. A $200,000 additional fine was imposed on Reserve for "violating court rules and orders as to discovery" of background information in the lawsuit. $22,920 was to reimburse Duluth for "furnishing interim clean-water facilities and supplies to its residents."

Later that month, another proposal for on-land disposal was rejected by a state hearing examiner. A site proposed by Reserve was rejected in favor of another which more successfully met environmental regulations. Reserve and its parent companies protested that any other site would not be economically feasible. The state accepted the examiner's recommendation nonetheless. The MPCA voted 6-3 to accept the hearing officer's suggestion and on July 7, Federal District Judge Devitt ordered Reserve to halt discharge of all ore wastes at midnight. If upheld on appeal, it would force the company to shut down as a result of its inability to agree with the state on an on-land dumping site.

Reserve and its parent owners, Republic and Armco, said that they would appeal that decision!

THE CONCEPT OF "OPERATIVE POLICY"

The Reserve Mining case shows, to an almost unprecedented extent, the ability of a corporation to distort the legal and administrative processes to a point where a clear public policy mandate is ignored in favor of corporate interests. To be sure, there were the residents of Silver Bay, Reserve's "company town," who strenuously objected to any state or federal efforts to limit Reserve's dumping. Their linkage to Reserve through an economic umbilical cord certainly shaded their view of the controversy and led them to support Reserve's efforts to continue operations. But Reserve's corporate interests still dominated their approach to this entire matter. At the time of the trial in Judge Lord's court, Reserve was netting $1 million profit per month from the Silver Bay operation. To keep that operation alive, nearly any action was deemed acceptable. Indeed, this extended to a series of statements by Reserve's managers under oath that alternative on-land site proposals had not been made when in fact they had. Even the apology from William Verity, Armco's chairman, to Judge Lord, acknowledged the profit factor at work. Ironically, 1973 was the same year Armco had established a director's committee on corporate responsibility!

The Reserve case raises to the foreground the concept of "operative policy." Too often, corporate policy statements are written and publicized as though they were intended for mostly public relations purposes. Such stated policy, as reflected in Armco's Corporate Responsibility Committee, is a sham when considered in light of the real, or operative policy of the corporation. Objective evidence—such as Reserve's stonewalling—is the basis for understanding the operative policy of the corporation. Its behavior bespeaks the true policy. Stated policy, in such circumstances, is worth little more than the paper on which it is written.

Finally, Reserve Mining raises the issue of management by lawyers. Depending on one's view, Reserve's management either abandoned its management decisionmaking role to the lawyers over an extended period of time, or it deliberately intended to stay open as long as possible and used a strategy of legal delay to keep the regulatory authorities at bay while the company continued its processing operations. If the latter is true, management chose the goal and told the lawyers to find a way to do it! In either case, Reserve's management has probably served the company's short-term profit interests well and its long-term economic interests poorly. Reserve's credibility—and that of its parent companies, Armco and Republic—has been irreparably injured in the environmental area and its public credibility damaged in other areas as well.

chapter nine

creating political stability

MANAGING UNDER POLITICAL UNCERTAINTY

As we saw in earlier chapters, the political system often presents major uncertainties as managers attempt to plan present and future actions. Two conventional approaches seem to have dominated management thinking about the ways to cope with such uncertainty. One alternative is to wait until the political change occurs, then change the organization's internal systems and structure to cope with the new reality. This adaptive pattern is essentially reactive in nature, and has characterized most managerial responses to such recent political topics in the United States as pollution, equal employment opportunities of minorities, and pension reform. The conventional alternative to such reaction has been to view the political system as an environmental element that can

185

be changed, altered, and manipulated to serve the organization's own needs and goals. In this view proactive management activity can influence key actors in government to deter political action that would be unhelpful or harmful to the organization or to undertake action that would be of assistance to the firm or industry.

It should be noted that a proactive approach toward political uncertainty is not necessarily reprehensible or illegal. For every instance such as ITT's contact with the Attorney General in an effort to deter the antitrust prosecution, or with the CIA to alter the political environment in Chile, there are countless instances in which managed organizations approach political actors to secure information or provide information about the changing political climate. Of course, the rules of each national political system differ in this respect, with the degree of openness and public access varying greatly among nations. Hence, in some political situations the quotient of political uncertainty is likely to be substantially greater than in others. In this chapter, we examine the experience of the Gulf Oil Corporation in coping with political uncertainty in several different nations. The disclosures of Gulf Oil's payments to domestic and foreign political figures was a topic of public interest and media attention in the 1975–76 period. Little discussed, however, was the underlying question of what considerations prompted Gulf to undertake such a pattern of activity. This question should be kept clearly in mind in the following case.

Business operations, including production, distribution, and marketing normally function best when there is a high degree of certainty in the environment. Uncertainty can spring from competitive forces, from changing public values, or from political influences. Whatever their source, these uncertainties jeopardize the *assumptions* upon which business plans have been made, capital investments committed, and distribution and marketing networks established. When the stakes are substantial, it ought not to surprise us that organizations will act to alter and change the environment to a more stable, and predictable state.

BUYING POLITICAL STABILITY: GULF OIL CORPORATION

On December 30, 1975, Joseph E. Bounds, former vice president of the Gulf Oil Corporation, reported to a Special Committee of Gulf's Board of Directors that in 1960 a fund had been created by William K. Whiteford, former Gulf Oil chairman, to "help Gulf maintain a political atmosphere conducive to its foreign expansion plans." At the time of this disclosure, the majority of Gulf's oil was being imported. In 1974, for example, the company produced about 400,000 barrels of crude oil and condensate daily in the United States, but received over one million barrels from

Kuwait, over 500,000 from West Africa and over 226,000 from Venezuela and Ecuador.

Background

Between 1960 and 1973, the Gulf Oil Corporation drew from this fund for political contributions at home and abroad. The fund was established by transferring approximately $12.3 million in fraudulent "capital investments" to Gulf's subsidiary in the Bahamas. Within a 14-year period, over $5.4 million from the fund was converted to cash and distributed in the United States as payments. The remainder was disbursed overseas, as contributions to the political parties of President Park Chung Hee of South Korea and President Barrientos of Bolivia, as political payments in Italy, and to a propagandist educational program created by the Arab countries.

In the early months of 1971, Claude Wild, Jr., the director of Gulf's Washington office, was visited by Lee Nunn, who requested a contribution for an independent Committee To Reelect the President (CREEP). Confirming the validity of the organization with Attorney General John Mitchell, Wild obtained $50,000 from William Viglia, comptroller of the Bahamas Exploration Co. and delivered the cash. It became customary for Viglia to withdraw about $25,000 every three weeks for Mr. Wild.

In January, 1972, Mr. Wild was once again approached by Nunn, who asked for an additional $50,000. This money was approved, obtained, and given to Maurice Stans, chief fund-raiser for President Nixon.

Also in 1972, Wild met with Senator Henry Jackson (D-Wash.) to discuss Gulf's role in helping him raise money for a presidential bid. In another meeting, a close mutual friend of Wild and Representative Wilbur Mills (D-Ark.) asked for financial support for Mills' presidential campaign. Mr. Wild secured the money in the "usual manner" and delivered $10,000 to Jackson and $15,000 to Mills.

Gulf and Watergate

In July, 1973, when a lawsuit was filed by Common Cause to force the White House to release campaign contributions, Gulf decided to voluntarily report information about its contributions to the Watergate Special Prosecutor. The $100,000 contribution to the presidential campaign was refunded to Gulf and the Bahamas Exploration Co. was formally dissolved three days before Gulf's exposure.

Gulf and Claude Wild pleaded guilty in federal court to misdemeanor charges on November 14, 1973, for payments to CREEP totalling $125,000. Testimony on file showed that a Gulf employee had made 20 trips between 1961 and 1972 to deliver sealed envelopes to U.S. Senators and Representatives, campaign aides and Gulf officials.[1] These were discreetly passed out in places like an Indianapolis motel washroom and behind a barn in New Mexico. Prosecutors began to investigate where responsibilities for these actions rested. It was brought to light that Wild had operated a "government relations" committee, employing a staff of between 40–45 people, 25 in Washington, D.C., and operated with a budget of $2 million a year exclusive of the slush fund. The "Good Government Fund" channeled contributions from individuals at Gulf to political candidates. Any indications of contributions made from this fund were destroyed immediately afterwards—from cancelled checks to airline tickets. Gulf and Wild were fined $5,000 and $1,000 respectively.

Mr. Henry, a Gulf executive, admitted signing notes for transfers to the original slush fund but claimed that someone had instructed him to do so, although he did not remember who it was. He had paid a "thank you" present of $10,000 to a New Jersey Turnpike Authority official for information about the routing of a pipeline and had given $25,000 to $29,000 from the fund to Republicans in Allegheny County (Pa.). Members of the Texas Railroad Commission, who regulated oil and gas in the state, received payments as well.

In April, 1974, the Project on Corporate Responsibility, Joseph and Charlotte Kyle, and the Council for Christian Social Action, holders of a total 37 shares in Gulf stock, filed a derivative action suit against Gulf, Mr. Wild and seven directors. The suit sought recovery of all fines, costs and expenditures incurred by Gulf as a result of the illegal activities.

The Project on Corporate Responsibility not only sought to recover costs but asked the federal court to order past and present Gulf officers and directors to pay the company more than $600,000.

In the spring of 1975, four other suits by shareholders were filed against Gulf.

Gulf, The SEC and The IRS

At this same time, the Securities and Exchange Commission filed suit against Gulf and Wild, Judge John Sirica presiding over the case. But an out of court settlement involving Gulf and the shareholders' suits was fi-

[1] United States Senators receiving funds included Hugh Scott (R-Pa.), Hubert Humphrey (D-Minn.), Russell Long (D-La.), William Brock (R-Tenn.), Mark Hatfield (R-Ore.), Howard Cannon (D-Nev.). In the House, Representatives John Heinz III (R-Pa.), Joe Evins (D-Tenn.), William Moorhead (D-Pa.), Jack Brooks (D-Tex.), James Burke (D-Mass.), Herman Schneebel (R-Pa.), Melvin Price (D-Ill.) received payments. Governor Milton Shapp of Pennsylvania and former Senators Allen Ellender (La.), Wallace Bennett (Utah), Marlow Cook (Ky.), Edwin Mechem (N.M.) and former Congressmen Richard Roudebush (Ind.), William Cramer (Fla.), Craig Hosmer (Calif.), Chet Holifield (Calif.), and Hale Boggs (La.) had also received payments. Lyndon Johnson had also received $50,000 as a U.S. Senator.

All these were asked to return the money. Letters didn't set deadlines nor did Gulf comment on what action it would take if the funds were not returned.

nally reached, the individual cases having been consolidated into one class action. Six former officers were required to pay the Gulf corporation "several millions of dollars" in stock, stock options, and cash in order to settle.

Gulf simultaneously agreed to a federal court order prohibiting any further violations and requiring the establishment of a Special Review Committee to investigate the use of corporate funds for political activity. This committee was headed by prominent New York lawyer, John J. McCloy, and included two of Gulf's outside directors.

During this time, the IRS informed Gulf of their potential tax fraud. Gulf claimed that it had acted legally because it had channeled funds to the "Bahamas Ex" as "capital investments" therefore, these were not improper reductions.

Gulf proclaimed that it would enforce stricter controls and procedures to ensure that corporate funds would never again be used for illegal political purposes. The corporate policy and budget manual were revised. The audit committee of the Board of Directors decided to meet periodically to review fiscal controls and commitments of corporate funds.

The Special Review Committee

On December 30, 1975, the report of the Special Review Committee was made public. The Committee had been established on approval of the SEC to investigate Gulf's use of corporate funds for contributions, gifts, entertainment, and any other expenses that might be involved in political activities.

The Committee found that the development of the off-the-books–fund began in 1960 by the late William K. Whiteford. Whiteford felt that Gulf needed more government support in connection with its overseas expansion interests. The company initiated a political program to voice its opinions in government circles and to develop some political strength. Written records of the funds would not be maintained and knowledge of the fund would be withheld from the Mellon family, formerly the largest holders of Gulf stock, and from the future chairmen and executive officers, Dorsey and Brockett.

Funds were transferred to an account in a bank in Nassau under the name of Bahamas Exploration Company, Ltd., an inactive subsidiary originally organized to hold exploration and drilling licenses. The arrangements were designed to protect confidentiality and avoid revelation of the nature and use of the funds. No records were kept, cancelled checks and statements were destroyed. Transferred funds were recorded in the books as deferred charges, not cash transfers, and these were written off on a monthly basis. Cash was withdrawn from the account periodically and placed in a personal safe deposit box in Nassau and then delivered to Wild.

Wild personally took charge of domestic contributions and was assisted by colleagues either employed by or associated with Gulf. He did not recall informing those involved in the disbursement that corporate funds were being used. However, cash not checks, was always distributed. Wild told the Committee that payments were distributed "mostly by requests from the recipients" though occasionally he had volunteered them himself.

It was discovered that Senator Hugh Scott of Pennsylvania, Senate Minority Leader, had been involved in some of the questionable payments. Scott indignantly denied any wrongdoing and refused to answer any pointed questions. From testimony by Thomas D. Wright, attorney for Gulf Oil, and Royce Savage, Gulf's former General Counsel, it appeared that until the early 1960's, Gulf had retained the Philadelphia law firm of Obmeyer, Rebmann, Maxwell, and Hippel, with which Scott was associated. In 1962, Savage acted to terminate the company's retainer of $20,000 because so little work needed to be done by the law firm.

At this point Scott visited the company's headquarters and urged them to continue or to reduce only slightly the retainer. Thereafter, the practice was initiated of giving Scott a gift of $5,000 every spring and fall. He reportedly asked for this money until 1973. Scott denied any knowledge that any improper campaign contributions came from Gulf. He refused to comment on whether Gulf had paid him for legal services rendered or whether the payments were "gifts."

This dual role of lawyer and senator invited scandal and the media publicized the Scott-Gulf relationship. Nevertheless, the Senate Ethics Committee concluded that any investigation in the absence of additional evidence would be premature and unwarranted.[2]

Foreign Political Contributions

South Korea. Gulf's largest foreign political contributions from Bahamas Ex were made in South Korea, where Gulf had invested close to $350 million in an oil refinery, a fertilizer plant and in petrochemical and shipbuilding ventures. Gulf gave a total of $4 million to the political party of Korean President Park in 1966 and 1971. Gulf later discovered that such contributions were illegal under Korean law.

In 1966, a contribution of $1 million was made at the request of the leading political party to help meet campaign costs. In 1970–71, $10 million more was demanded by the same party and a compromise amount of $3 million was actually given. The pressures on Gulf to make these contributions were regarded by Gulf as "an ignoble act to comply with foreign political demands." Dorsey believed the payments were made with Gulf's best intent in mind. "We were expanding and were faced with a

---

[2] *Wall Street Journal*, January 23, 1976.

myriad of problems which often confront American corporations in foreign countries." Dorsey also testified that the pressures were "even more intense than those which many American corporations were subjected to in the traumatic, scarring 1972 American presidential election." He said, expressing regret, "the responsibility is mine and I accept it." He added that the decision had brought anguish to the many people whom Gulf employs and with whom Gulf does business around the world.

With Gulf's help, President Park narrowly won reelection in 1971 and proclaimed martial law in 1972. He then barred all internal dissent. As a result, South Korean newspapers did not report Dorsey's testimony nor Gulf's public disclosures.

Doing business "Korean style" involved payment of gratitudes and gift-giving, expensive entertainment of public officials, and high level political influence in business affairs. All of these were essential for obtaining access to government agencies and decision-makers. Hence payments were required for securing permits and otherwise expediting Gulf's government business through a highly-controlled foreign bureaucracy.

During 1972–75, the "Gray Fund" was maintained as part of the off–the–books fund in Korea. It was derived from additional interest on bank deposits and rebates on insurance premiums. Approximately $33,-000 was used to provide gratuities and presents to the President's and Prime Minister's staffs, the Minister of Commerce and Industry and the Korean Central Intelligence Agency.

There was little evidence to conclude that these commercial or business payments were perceived in fact as political contributions by either Gulf or the Koreans. Acknowledging this, the Committee set out to analyze the political contacts between government and business in two specific instances.

(1) One circumstance involved Gulf's purchase of 25 percent additional stock interest in a fuel-oil distributing company for a generous $2 million. This was secured from a prominent Korean businessman who was said to have close associations with the Korean President. Two hundred thousand dollars of this amount was eventually traced to the possession of political figures. However, Gulf asserted that the price was paid only for the purpose of acquiring working control, and not for political purposes.

(2) In other cases, Gulf was involved with politically well-connected Korean nationals through its tanker sales and chartering arrangements. Even though the actual transactions proved favorable and profitable for the Koreans, the Special Review Committee concluded that there was no evidence that this

money went to political figures who aided Gulf in maintaining and controlling an efficient shipping program in its Korean business operations. The Committee found that claims that Gulf gave rebates to the Korean Ministry of National Defense on products used for national defense purposes were unfounded. Further, no evidence could link these rebates to a scheme of political payments.

According to Dorsey, Gulf "never asked for nor received anything in return for the contributions except, perhaps, the unfettered right to continue business in South Korea."

Italy. Political contributions by corporations have been a well recognized practice in Italian politics. Corporate political contributions in Italy during the time in question were considered legal only if the stockholders were informed of them.

In 1962, under the authorization of Gulf's chief executive officer, a special account, which was not recorded in the books, was created. Its purpose was to serve as a confidential receptacle for off-the-books rebates on bank deposits in derogation of fixed interest rates agreed upon by the banks. By the time the account was terminated in January, 1974, approximately $422,000 had been disbursed over a twelve-year period.[3]

In March 1968, Gulf paid $1,200,000 to obtain rights to pump crude oil into a pipeline owned by the Italian state oil company. The money was paid in Switzerland to the state company's pipeline subsidiary. While questionable in nature, the Special Review Committee concluded that no political or improper use of funds occurred.

The Special Review Committee found that from 1969 through 1972, approximately $627,000 was paid from corporate funds to three Italian publications or publishing firms. These payments were considered, in effect, to be political contributions because the publications were either owned or controlled by various political parties.

[3] Payments from the Special Account are summarized as follows:

political contributions or payments	$235,886
payments for consulting services, professional fees, etc.	$ 60,959
payments in connection with gasoline station marketing development	$ 23,538
payments for services rendered to Gulf in prosecuting certain tax claims	$ 38,462
payments to newspapers and journalists	$ 10,815
payments to two local communities affected by Gulf's Milan refinery	$15,385
payments to consulting firms for gasoline marketing studies	$ 9,076
business gifts	$ 8,545
charitable or good will contributions	$ 4,333
payment with respect to union or dealer association problems	$ 2,308
merit bonus to Gulf employee bank fees	$ 1,474

In October 1972, Gulf made a questionable $60,765 payment to a Lichtenstein organization in connection with Gulf's attempts to obtain certain off-shore drilling rights to southern Sicily. Again, the Special Review Committee found no indication of illegal or politically improper contributions on the part of Gulf Oil.

In 1973, Gulf paid $868,653 in order to expand a refinery in Milan. The payment was made to a public relations and financial consulting firm whose president was a large petroleum jobber and the head of the Italian Jobbers Association. Gulf records gave no indication as to why the payment was made; the recipient, however, assured the Special Review Committee that no illegal or improper payments were made to government officials or political parties.

Bolivia. As a result of the criminal proceedings against Dorsey and his testimony to the Senate subcommittee, certain Gulf payments in Bolivia were revealed which received particularly close attention. No evidence was found that Dorsey or the accused Bolivian national previously employed by Gulf had any knowledge of, or participation in, the Bolivian payments, however.

In 1966, when General Rene Barrientos was campaigning for the Bolivian presidency, Gulf had furnished him with a helicopter at a cost of $107,925. The Bahamas Ex account supplied the funds and the transaction was treated confidentially by those involved. When Barrientos won the presidency, he donated the helicopter to the Bolivian Air Force, refusing to return it to Gulf. The Special Review Committee concluded that the giving of the helicopter did not serve to induce any favorable political action by Barrientos. However, its use during the campaign constituted a violation of the Bolivian election law.

In 1969 and 1970, Gulf made payments to two Bolivian nationals totalling $250,000, most of which was paid in connection with an internal transport pipeline. Although no final judgment could be made by the Committee due to a lack of information, the payments most likely constituted a violation of the Bolivian Penal Code which prohibits bribes to public officials.

Another questionable payment occurred when Claude Wild made a charitable cash gift to the Bolivian Ambassador in Washington, supposedly to finance a field hospital. There was some discrepancy as to the amount paid, although testimony indicates that it was approximately $10,-000. There was no evidence that such a payment violated either Bolivian or United States law.

Mideast. Another questionable payment involving the financing of an Arab publicity campaign in conjunction with the boycott of Israel. The

Special Review Committee Report made no mention of whether or not the payment was made on the company's initiative or under duress. Dorsey explained that "it appeared that the amount was made available through the First National Bank, Beirut, Lebanon, for the purpose of helping to defray the expenses of a public education program endeavoring to bring about a better understanding in America of the Arab-Israel conflict." It was not stated why the Arabs could not finance their own campaign.

In Kuwait, Gulf and its overseas partner provided Sheik Abdulla, the ruler, with the use of an aircraft and also paid more than $2 million to build the Fahaheel Sea Club for public use.

Gulf Contributions in the U.S.

It is evident that a company's interests can be secured or advanced in the United States by purchasing political influence and utilizing the political process. But this strategy had resulted in a disastrous effect for only the Gulf Company, not the politicians. Following the Special Review Committee's report, Gulf claimed that "such conduct shall never again occur. . . ." John McCloy, chairman of the Committee, asserted that the Board of Director's action in adopting this policy had "set a higher level of corporate responsibility." But McCloy also questioned whether it was right to prohibit corporate political contributions. The failure of the United States government to prosecute or condemn the politicians involved was both "unfair and hypocritical" according to McCloy. Most of the politicians involved had argued that they didn't realize that the money came from illegal sources, yet they admitted that they knew some funds had come in sealed envelopes.

Gulf reaffirmed the privilege of the company and its employees to participate in the political process. But it emphasized that this participation "must be in full accord with the regulations, laws, and generally accepted practice of the jurisdiction involved."

At the conclusion of the investigation into Gulf's domestic and foreign political activities, the McCloy Committee made several suggestions and recommendations. "The pattern and nature of this use of corporate funds, in large part not recorded on the books at the company, has raised serious questions as to the policy and management of the company in regard to this matter," the Committee stated. Eleven executives knew of the covert transfer of corporate funds, but three were deceased and six had retired. Both the senior and executive vice presidents denied any knowledge of the contributions.

Concerning Gulf's outside auditors, Price Waterhouse and Co., the Committee found that they knew nothing of the transfer of funds. Gulf had more than 400 subsidiaries, and it had been regarded as impractical to conduct outside audits to review all of their activities. Between 1960 and

1967, Price Waterhouse's office in the Bahamas did audit the Bahamas Ex, but in view of the elaborate measures taken by Gulf officials to cover up the illicit activities, the Special Review Committee concluded it was unlikely that a normal audit process would have revealed the necessary facts. Although one Price Waterhouse partner did know of the $1 million payment in Korea in 1966, it was unascertainable whether the company itself questioned the destination of use of that payment.

No internal audits were done within the Bahamas Ex. In one instance, approval for an auditor's trip to Nassau was denied and in another, the internal auditor was instructed not to audit the subsidiary. The Committee concluded that Gulf must improve and upgrade its internal auditing department.

The Committee also analyzed the investigation by Eckert, Seamans, Cherin and Mellott, Gulf's legal counsel. It agreed with the firm's conclusion that there was "no evidence that any officer, director or employee personally profited or benefited by reason of the use of corporate funds for contributions or payments related to political activity." The motives were considered to have been acted upon in the best interest of Gulf and its shareholders. However, it was concluded that there had been "no meaningful accounting for the amount of money spent."

The Committee decided that Brockett and Dorsey should be denied participation in "any action by the board which may be deemed appropriate to implement the report." The Report went on to say that "the Committee, given all the circumstances, concludes that Dorsey was not sufficiently alert and should have known that Wild was involved in making political contributions from an unknown source. If Dorsey did not know of the nature and extent of Wild's unlawful activities, he perhaps chose to shut his eyes to what was going on. Had he been more alert to the problem, he was in a ready position to inquire about and put an end to it." The report concluded: ". . . The reality is that the long-continued practice of illegal corporate contributions or political payments by Gulf is effectively at an end."

The Aftermath

The Special Review Committee said of its own investigation:

"The Committee believes the investigation it has conducted will have been worthwhile and productive if there emerges from the trauma of the disclosures a sense of confidence that the basic facts have now been unfolded in their entirety, so that the investor and the public can look to the future with confidence that no such illegal practices, so far as Gulf is concerned, will ever recur."

The impact of the probe was felt in several ways. During the time of the Committee's investigations, Gulf Oil Corporation:

· was forced to conclude an agreement in which the government of Kuwait took over the remaining 40% of Gulf's oil fields there, effectively stripping Gulf of ownership of its most important source of crude oil;

· suspended operations in Angola because of its civil war;

· publicly apologized to the Anti-Defamation League of B'nai B'rith for the $50,000 contribution in Beirut which was used for the Arab propagandist campaign.

On January 12, 1976, Gulf's Board of Directors gathered together to discuss the Special Review Committee's report and the suggestion that Dorsey and Brockett remove themselves from the company. The Mellon family, which owned 15–18 percent of the corporation stock, led the push for a corporate housecleaning. Their embarrassment stirred up dissent within the company. Gulf director James Mellon Walton accused top management officials of not keeping him well informed. They countered that he had been told of various payments and the ensuing complications.[4]

The directors met for two days. Dorsey and three others—William Henry, president of Gulf's real estate subsidiary; Fred Deering, the Senior Vice President; and Herbert Manning, Vice President and Secretary—were asked to resign. It was originally thought that since Dorsey was only two years away from the mandatory retirement age, he might be eased out through some face-saving procedure. But the pressure for his ouster was strong. Although he was not personally regarded of poor character, and evidence fell short of proving Dorsey's awareness in the matter, there remained no doubt that he could have found out what had been taking place. The board believed that the top management had to be held accountable for what had happened.

Gulf's Board of Directors' condemnation of the "unethical and illegal" practices, and its determination that "such conduct shall never again occur within Gulf" was given much public and media notice. The sorting of evidence and cleaning up in the firm was only the first part of the board's action. Its next step was to select another capable individual to assume the chief executive's position.

The Successor

The search to find an "unsullied" man, one who had not been involved in Gulf's questionable activities and one who could improve the company's public image, was a long, drawn out process. The decision to overlook President James Lee led directors to search elsewhere for an untainted candidate.

Jerry McAfee was chosen to carry out this prescription. As president

[4] *Wall Street Journal*, January 13, 1976

of Gulf's Canadian affiliate, Gulf Oil Canada Ltd., the 59-year-old successor had guided the company through a period of rapid growth. He was praised by insiders as a strong and respected executive who could probably "calm shareholders' nerves." Another executive described him as "enthusiastic with a conservative air."

McAfee inherited a host of problems from his predecessors. The federal grand jury continued to investigate the political contributions operation and the Internal Revenue Service still probed the tax consequences of the slush fund.

But McAfee was anxious to leave the past behind and rebuild the shaken morale of Gulf's employees. His first step was to send out letters to the U.S. politicians asking them to return any illegal contributions from the firm. He then sent out letters within the company detailing a statement of principles and ethics which he hoped to implement. In the board meetings and public releases, McAfee stressed the need for credability and a "bridge of understanding" with members of government.

A year later, McAfee believed that "substantial progress" had been achieved in preventing any further illegalities and restoring confidence in the company. During that time, the following developments had occurred:

> Neither the publicity about questionable payments nor the company's efforts to halt the practice hindered Gulf from making profits. In the first nine months of 1976, profits increased 12.8 per cent, though substantially less than the industry's 35.5 percent average.
>
> Top management's support for stricter rules on conduct and a requirement that all transactions "be conducted in a manner that we would be proud to have the full facts disclosed" led to auditing of all suspicious transactions.
>
> Employees closed ranks, defending all but the "people at the top" who were involved in the payments.
>
> The new chairman and directors made efforts to be more open about company operations.

"Little odds and ends"[5] such as shareholders suits, resolutions, and publicity continue to haunt Gulf. Despite allegations and occasional headlines, Gulf has attempted to clear its name, heeding the conclusion of the McCloy report that "the tone and attitude of top management" could be the most important factor in eliminating past distasteful practices.

OPERATIVE POLICY

Gulf's behavior in dealing with political uncertainty in the United States, South Korea, and other foreign nations raises the concept of *operative policy*

[5] *Wall Street Journal*, January 24, 1976.

to the foreground once again. In Chapter 2, we pointed out that three terms—tactics, strategy, and policy—were critical to an understanding of the patterns of corporate response to change. Gulf's behavior illustrates all three concepts and the relationship among them.

Tactics are the actions of an organization in response to an immediate stimulus. They are usually short term in nature and focused on the present circumstances of the organization. Gulf's actions in responding to political pressures in South Korea are illustrative of the concept. The bargaining which followed the original request for $10 million was tactical in nature, its purpose being to lower the price of political stability for Gulf's business operations. The entire job of coping with "business, Korean style" was a series of tactical actions by local Gulf managers, each designed to eliminate the immediate pressure of the political system. In time, the stimulus-response pattern began to fail Gulf. Their operations in South Korea did not thrive, and the hoped-for benefits of political stability evaporated.

This pattern of tactical payments, designed to remove immediate political obstacles also prevailed in Bolivia, Italy, and Kuwait. Interestingly, Gulf's provision of the helicopter to Bolivian President Barrientos had an ironic, albeit poetic result. Once elected, Barrientos refused to return the helicopter to Gulf, while "donating" it instead to the Bolivian Air Force. Six months later, while flying in the helicopter, it crashed and Barrientos was killed.

The pattern of Gulf's actions in the United States was substantially different from that in South Korea and Bolivia. In the U.S., Gulf set out in the 1960's to create and maintain a political atmosphere conducive to its foreign expansion plans. Foreign expansion was a central part of Gulf's business strategy; political stability and/or support in the United States for such a course of action was a necessary part of that strategy. Thus, unlike the stimulus-response pattern in South Korea, Gulf's payments in the United States were part of a conscious and deliberate *strategy* designed to manipulate and shape the domestic political environment. Here, too, there is an irony, for the disclosure of Gulf's domestic political contributions helped set off a wave of public recrimination and criticism that even threatened to produce a breakup of the vertically integrated oil firms. Nevertheless, the irony did not occur for nearly fifteen years during which time the company, its managers, and a large number of public officials prospered from this proactive pattern of behavior.

Patterns of conduct which reflect the type of corporate strategy just discussed bring to full view the concept of *operative policy*. During the 1960's and 1970's, Gulf Oil published numerous statements of policy about its intention to comply with the law, adhere to the spirit and the letter of campaign contribution regulations, and meet public expectations. Taken at face value, such policy statements manifest a corporate concern with the institution's legitimacy and public good will. In fact, they are little more than the most suspect form of public relations nonsense. Gulf's true policy—its operative policy—was really manifested by its core interests and the behavior which served those interests. The operative policy was to buy friends and acquire political influence.

One final irony makes the point that Gulf's operative policy really was policy, imbued throughout the organization. Jerry McAfee was selected as Gulf's new chairman and chief executive after a search to find "an unsullied man." Approximately a year after his selection, first disclosures were made about Gulf's participation in a uranium cartel engineered by the Canadian government. Following months of disclosure, the story that finally emerged indicated that Gulf had not been the reluctant participant that it had officially asserted. Indeed, according to testimony of government and competitors' officials, Gulf actually urged the Canadian government to allow it to join and participate in the cartel, despite its illegality under American law. Ironically, this action supposedly occurred at the very time Jerry McAfee was responsible for Gulf's Canadian operations.

chapter ten

creating business stability

INTRODUCTION

The most familiar type of uncertainty with which business corporations have traditionally had to deal is competitive uncertainty. As organizations have become larger, and their business activities more complex, competitors have sought to find comparable methods for developing intelligence about one another. Every industry has peculiar conditions and circumstances that influence the ability of firms to learn about one another's actions. Aircraft manufacturing is peculiar in the extent to which it relies upon government contracts as its principal source of funds. The commercial airline business once abounded with competitors. In recent decades, considerable concentration has occurred, and many nations have established a single "national airline." This has served to create further pressure on aircraft manufacturers to enter contracts with governments in the supplying of both commercial and military aircraft. Because government contracting is conducted on a bid basis in many nations, aircraft manufacturers are especially sensitive to the need for reducing the uncertainty inherent in such competition. The Lockheed Aircraft case, presented here, focuses on the operative policy which that company adopted in dealing with environmental forces in the international aircraft business.

LOCKHEED AIRCRAFT COMPANY

Canada's Announcement

During the spring of 1976, negotiation of a $1 billion contract for Lockheed Aircraft Corporation to provide 18 P3 Orion planes to the Canadian government fell through with a potential loss of $750 million to the corporation. The collapse in negotiations was a result of the deadlock reached in determining ways to finance the project's start up costs.

The trouble began in February, 1976, after publicity of Lockheed's overseas bribes. It was discovered that between 1970 and 1975, Lockheed paid kickbacks or bribes totaling $22 million to government officials and political groups in 15 foreign countries to advance its overseas sales. Robert Haack, the interim chairman of the corporation, noted that "the environment at the moment obviously poses a problem for Canadian government officials who have an obligation to ascertain that Lockheed is and will continue to be a viable and financially sound company." During a meeting with several Canadian ministers, including those from defense, finance and supply, and services, Canadian Defense Department spokesman Brig. Gen. Lloyd Morrison said that he "wouldn't like to give the impression" that the contract was totally discarded, but that the purchase was under scrutiny because of the questionable payments and financial position of the company.

On February 29, the Ministry of National Defense had announced Canada would go ahead with the purchase of the patrol planes. Further negotiations would have to take place in order to determine the financial details such as the timing of the payments. The contract was originally set at $950 million, and $560 million of this sum was to remain in Canada for the manufacture of various components of the planes in that country.

As more details of the payoffs came to light, however, Canadian officials became increasingly apprehensive, and withdrew from the negotiations. As of May 19, Lockheed had only slight hopes that the Canadian pact could still be finalized. According to a Lockheed spokesman, "We are visiting with various government offices to reassess whether there is any basis for a program." The Canadian government and the ten chartered

Canadian banks still refused to provide part of the financing for the P3 Orion contract.

Shortly thereafter, Lockheed reported that its 24 lending banks had requested the company to estimate the impact of the loss or delay of Canada's proposal on its future business position in relation to the new financial restructuring program. Talk of a Lockheed financial collapse intensified in the press.

While a completion to the financial restructuring agreements was forecast for the "near term" by company spokesmen, doubts persisted. Lockheed's efforts continued to design a proposal allowing the Canadian government to secure the purchase of the P3 Orion planes for completion of its long-range patrol requirements. Not the least of the obstacles was Canadian wariness as to when, or whether, new announcements of Lockheed bribes would be disclosed.

Lockheed's Business Position

Lockheed's financial difficulties began in 1971 in the building and distribution of a wide-bodied jet transport, the L-1011 Jumbo Jet. The troubles were attributed to technical difficulties with the Rolls Royce engines and Rolls Royce's sudden bankruptcy. Rolls' RB-211 engine program was salvaged by Congress, when a guarantee was approved by just one vote in the Senate and three in the House. The government agreed to guarantee up to $250 million in bank loans to Lockheed, enabling it to purchase the engines. Those sitting on the loan board were the Treasury Secretary, the Chairman of the Federal Reserve Board and the Chairman of the SEC. At the time, the guarantee covered $195 million that Lockheed owed to 24 banks, out of its total outstanding borrowings of $600 million.

In August, 1975, following disclosure of bribes and questionable payments, the loan board ordered "that Lockheed not make any future improper payments, directly or indirectly, to foreign government officials or political organizations; including any such payments presently committed." The board said that Lockheed would jeopardize the government's loan guarantees if it failed to comply with this ruling. Treasury Secretary William Simon informed the banking community that he "does not, and will not, condone illegal or unethical activities by American business, here or abroad . . . Practices such as bribes made to secure foreign business can only increase the distrust and suspicion that is straining our national institutions."

The large airline recession during the period 1974–76 had dried up sales of the L-1011. Production was down to nine Jumbo Jets a year and the assembly line was faced with a possible shutdown.

The Tristar, a new longer range version of the L-1011, presented the best prospect for Lockheed. Many commercial airlines were being forced to consider replacement of their first generation jets. Competition in sales was keen, with the Boeing 747 and DC-10 Jumbos ranking first and second in sales. Lockheed did not have a plane to compete with these jets, but one had been designed. It could be produced with another $50–60 million of development funds, in addition to the other financing already provided by the banks.

Banks, however, were more than hesitant to provide the financing in view of the sweeping bribery charges and their extended effect on the company's business outlook. A new management at Lockheed represented some hope that the money could be acquired. Whether or not it could be obtained in time for the corporation to enter into any successful competition was unclear.

Although Lockheed had not received official rejection of the Canadian order for P3 Orion anti-submarine planes, an order considered very important by U.S. military officials, they had encountered threats from other nations to cancel military orders. President Ford's consideration of a proposal to disqualify companies who participated in the illegal dealings abroad from bidding on federal contracts presented another complication for Lockheed.

In February, 1976, Simon testified that Lockheed was behind schedule in repayment of its loans, but that a new plan called for meeting the original 1978 deadline, with $150 million to be paid off by 1977 and the remaining $45 million in 1978. The General Accounting Office warned that the corporation might not be able to meet its deadlines. The concensus of the financial community was that had it not been for the bribery scandal and its effects, there would be no problem in repaying the loans on time. In his appearance before the Banking Committee, Mr. Haack claimed that Lockheed's new policy against bribes or any sort of questionable payments was hurting the company and that Lockheed had lost a "considerable" amount of orders as competitors "have made the accommodations that Lockheed isn't willing to make."

Lockheed in Japan

In February, 1976, the Senate Subcommittee on Multinational Corporations discovered that payoffs had gone to Yoshio Kodama, a prominent leader of the ultraright-wing militarist political faction in Japan. Kodama was paid to promote sales of Lockheed's L-1011 Tristar commercial jetliners (All-Nippon had purchased six Tristars for $130 million in 1972), and Lockheed was presumed to have been used to further support proponents of Japanese rearmament. The money paid to Kodama amounted to about $7 million and was sometimes delivered in yen-filled packing crates.

Kodama was a highly controversial figure. He had spent three years in prison after World War II as a war criminal, where he developed his later political ties. He was reputed to have strong ties to the Tokyo underworld as well as being an important influence in the Japanese political sphere. Kodama was credited with helping to finance the ruling Liberal Democratic Party, personally picking several prime ministers and mediating political and business disputes for nearly 25 years.

William Findley, a partner in Arthur Young & Co., testified to having been told of Kodama's lobbying skills. Findley believed that the Lockheed-Kodama arrangement originated in 1958 and that Kodama helped the company sell F-104 Starfighters to the Japanese Air Force in the 1960's, winning in competition against Grumman Aircraft. At the time, Grumman had been looking for a buyer for its refurbished F-11F because the U.S. Navy had decided not to purchase the F-11F. The Japanese test team came to the United States to try out the plane, and returned to Japan with favorable recommendations. Negotiations ensued and Grumman's prospects looked bright. But the National Defense Council suddenly ordered a new study, and Kodama brought in Lockheed, reportedly pressing Prime Minister Kishi into a decision in favor of the F-104 Starfighter.

Most of the Kodama payments occurred in 1972–3 and were delivered by John Clutter, director of marketing development for Lockheed Aircraft Corporation International. It was during this time that the Lockheed Tristar also won out over Douglas' DC-10 for a large contract, while Kukeo Tanaka was Prime Minister. The next large distribution of payments was in 1973–75, when Lockheed channeled $2,150,000 through an agent in Tokyo named I-D Corporation to several prominent officials in the Japanese government and airlines industry for public relations purposes.

Upon disclosure of these charges, international reaction was frantic. Japan's opposition Socialist party demanded a thorough investigation of the reports from Washington. They insisted on Parliament questioning Tanaka and two other former senior officials. The Government of Prime Minister Takeo Miki refused to take an immediate stance. The President of All Nippon Airways, Tokuji Wakasa, declared that "All Nippon had nothing at all to do with the money in question." Nevertheless, many Japanese politicians demanded that the United States "do a wholesale cleaning of this business."

Lockheed lost their $1.3 billion order from Japan for new planes because of the scandal. An antisubmarine-warfare build-up, encouraged by the United States on Japan, was set back for over a year. $1–2 billion in sales by other American aircraft manufacturers was also jeopardized. The Japanese Government Defense Agency had supported the arms industry by desiring an independent source of weapons and the most sophisticated arms technology; however, there wasn't a need for large quantities at the time in question. To manufacture the weapons would be more costly than to import them, and as a result Lockheed had sold nearly $800 million worth of aircraft to Japan in the past 15 years.

Marubeni Corporation, a trading company, had accepted over $3.2 million in payments from Lockheed. Their acceptance was deemed legal, but Marubeni's executives were accused of "advising" Lockheed to pay those bribes. One such executive, Hiroshi Ito, signed a Lockheed receipt for "100 peanuts," denying any knowledge of its meaning and claiming that he found the text to be somewhat confusing. Two Marubeni aides resigned, pleading ignorance of bribery. They threatened to sue A. Carl Kotchian, Lockheed's former vice chairman, for slander in giving testimony in Washington claiming Marubeni had passed bribe money on to influential Japanese politicians. Concurrently, Japanese government officials asked the US Senate Subcommittee to supply the names of politicians, officials and business executives alleged to have received the $12.6 million in commissions and bribes and all available documents. Miki personally contacted President Ford to ask for his assistance in the matter. The head of the Japanese Labor Federation asserted that the scandal should not be resolved "ambiguously" as had earlier issues. The Public Safety Commissioner made a rare political appeal to Miki, requesting him "to make clear the truth of the Lockheed contribution issue by doing everything in its (the government's) power." If this could not be successfully accomplished, it would leave the public with deep suspicions and encourage social disorder.

Later in February, large numbers of Japanese police conducted raids on 27 homes and a number of offices of the principal figures involved in the scandal. Gradually, the story of the bribes began to unfold.

In addition to recorded testimony from the U.S. Senate subcommittee and the Japanese Parliament, interviews with Japanese and American aviation executives and government officials disclosed the following: Lockheed's original allies in Japan included a pilot who helped devise the Pearl Harbor Attack; an American of Japanese descent who lost his United States citizenship during World War II; an ultra-nationalist publisher evacuated by the Allied occupation forces; and a member of Parliament who was later indicted on embezzlement charges.

Impact Abroad

When Lockheed's consulting arrangement with Kodama was arranged, his first instruction was for Lockheed to fire their original trading firm and hire Marubeni. Kodama had met Nonusuke Kishi while in prison serving time as a wartime cabinet officer and had established a close friendship with the man later to become prime minister. He also met Taro

Fukuda, who had lost his American citizenship when he worked for the Japanese government. He was an interpreter and later the publisher of Kodama's book, *I Was Defeated*. Contacted once again by Kodama, Fukuda became the public relations man for Lockheed.

In 1969, Lockheed gave Kodama his formal sales assignment: sell 3–6 Tristars to any major airline in Japan. Utilizing his personal contacts, Kodama engineered the sale to Wakasa who in mid-1969, had retired from his position of Deputy Minister of Transportation to join All Nippon as vice president and then president. As time progressed, however, Kodama relied more and more on money and less on personal relationships to facilitate Lockheed's sales.

In 1972, President Nixon called on the Prime Minister to suggest that the Japanese aircraft requirements be filled by Lockheed. Tanaka, in turn, called on Wakasa. Lockheed quickly moved the payment money on to Kodama, who personally stood to gain $5 million from the sales.

Japanese tax and police investigators studied income tax evasion and violation of the foreign exchange controls. Politicians tried to discover what investigators had discovered but not yet revealed. The Marubeni Corporation severed all ties with Lockheed in an effort to salvage their reputation but continued to deny any wrong doing on their part. Miki found himself under considerable pressure not to disclose all the facts because to do so would split the party. Mob journalism replaced investigative reporting, and the Japanese public found itself torn. One set of interests wanted the details fully revealed, partly to prove that the young democracy could withstand the turmoil. Another set of more traditional interests sought to resolve the controversy in private in traditional Japanese resolution fashion.

One result of Japan's persistent pleas for information discovered by United States sources was President Ford's offer to give the Japanese parliament access to the Senate Foreign Relations Committee findings. Shizuo Saito, a senior Japanese diplomat, was sent to Washington to explain the urgency of the situation to the American leaders and to get the true facts and emphasize the Japanese need for evidence. Saito emphasized that time was very important and discussions ensued on the most effective ways to deal with this controversy.

It was eventually learned that not only did Kodama receive approximately $9 million in bribes (and failed to declare $3.8 million in 1972 alone), but that the CIA knew of the Lockheed bribes since the 1950's. An employee had informed the American embassy of the payoffs, and, in turn, the embassy passed the information to the CIA. The latter, however, did not mention the matter to either the State Department or Grumman during the Lockheed/Grumman fighter aircraft competition.

By May, 1976, Defense Secretary Donald H. Rumsfeld had to intercede on behalf of Lockheed to help salvage their $250 million sale of patrol aircraft to Japan. As some of the sensationalism of the Lockheed disclosures died down, he proposed a government-to-government arrangement with the U.S. Defense Department as contracting agent for the sale. This would enable the United States government to provide guarantees to the Japanese government about Lockheed's financial ability to deliver the planes. Rumsfeld also emphasized the greater government control that would result in a closer scrutiny of marketing practices.

The Aftermath

By the end of the summer, there had been a total of 21 arrests in Japan:

6 All Nippon officials
7 executives of Marubeni, including the chairman
2 associates of Kodama
2 top Transportation Ministry officials
  Kodama
  Wakasa
  Tanaka and his secretary

Most of the Japanese charges stemmed from tax evasion, violation of the foreign exchange laws and perjury.

Takeo Miki refused to step down as Prime Minister despite calls for his ouster, claiming that he would remain until the Lockheed affair was settled. "The Worst Political Storm since WWII" was to be felt in Japan for some time.

During the last week of 1976, Takeo Fukuda, 71, of Japan's ruling Liberal Democratic Party, was unanimously chosen party president. A disappointed Takeo Miki bowed out as Premier.

Fukuda's first pledge was to "rebuild the party from scratch and (I) will stake my political life on accomplishing it." Regarded as a man of tenacity and ambition, Fukuda would now have to bring together a party terribly battered and in desperate need of a new strength.

His acceptance was great among Liberal Democratic leaders and influential businessmen alike. There had been fear that Miki would continue to oppose any new candidate, but he chose to quit without a struggle. He left a torn party, bruised by the exposure of corrupt members and the setback in December's elections for the Diet's 511-Seat lower house in which the Liberal Democratic majority dropped considerably.

Fukuda's greatest problem was the need to enliven his broad-based pro-American coalition and increase the performance of the declining Japanese economy. He stated his intention to form a committee to study party reform and study ways of redistributing the power held by aging power-brokers who controlled the Liberal Democratic Party since the 1950's. His first appointments to posts were cautiously made taking into interest all factions of the party. It was deemed unlikely that Fukuda would initiate any new foreign policy initiatives concerning the United States for some time.

Lockheed in the Netherlands

A. Carl Kotchian, former vice chairman of Lockheed, testified before the Senate Subcommittee on Multinational Corporations that Lockheed had funneled about $1.2 million in 1961 or 1962 to a "high official" of the Dutch government. Although Senator Frank Church didn't press Kotchian to identify him, during the course of a six-month inquiry the Senate subcommittee in executive sessions identified that high official as Prince Bernhard of Holland, husband of Queen Juliana.

The first connection between Lockheed and Prince Bernhard was made by the *Wall Street Journal* on December 4, 1975. A former Lockheed employee, Ernest F. Houser, who had worked in the West German sales office from 1961–64, was reported to have claimed that during the same period of time, Lockheed had arranged regular payments in the Netherlands with regard to the promotion of sales of the supersonic F-104 Starfighter. These payments were alleged to have gone to Bernhard. $1.1 million in bribes was said to be paid in connection with 138 of these jets.

Kotchian later testified that the company's cash "gift" was meant to "establish a climate of goodwill, a climate in which our products would receive considerable consideration." Although there existed no evidence that Bernhard had actually influenced Dutch aircraft policies, Dutch premier Den Uyl asserted that the Prince's behavior "has damaged the national interest and the consequences should be that he withdraw from all his positions."

The Prince resigned from his position as Inspector General of the Armed Forces along with the 300 other posts he held in military, public and business organizations and as director of KLM Royal Dutch Airlines. Premier Uyl, in a report to the Dutch Parliament, broadcast throughout the country, said that a three-member investigating committee had found that the Prince had "become involved in relationships and situations which are unacceptable." Although the Dutch government wouldn't press further criminal prosecution, for Bernhard had already suffered the "drastic consequences," it accused him of being open to "dishonorable requests and offers." The Dutch government believed exposure to be the best social guarantor of moral behavior. The Prince's actions showed "weakness, folly and greed" in a man who was so revered by the people for his interest in the public good.

Bernhard acknowledged in his own public statement that he hadn't been "critical enough in my judgment of initiatives and I have written letters that I shouldn't have sent." Those letters included Bernhard's complaints that his efforts weren't sufficiently appreciated by Lockheed. They were also used to confirm allegations against Bernhard who insisted that if he hadn't actually seen the letters, that he would not have believed that he could have written such things. While suggesting that the texts were proposed to him by others, he added that his memory sometimes failed him. Nonetheless, the letters made it clear that he was open to bribes for which he could maneuver deals to Lockheed's advantage. According to the Prince, the money went to the World Wildlife Fund, which he sponsored.

Lockheed paid out $300,000 twice and $400,000 once during the years 1960–62 through its representative in Switzerland, Fred C. Meuser, a close friend of the Prince. This money was deposited in a bank in Zurich. The Prince denied receiving payment from Lockheed in connection with negotiations between 1968 and 1974 for the Dutch purchase of the Lockheed Orion planes. The actual purchase never went through.

It was established, however, that during the early 1960's, Lockheed had considered paying off the Prince with a Jetstar "to create a favorable atmosphere for the sale of Lockheed jets in the Netherlands." The plan was rejected because of the complications and because the Prince refused it. Instead, he asked Lockheed to do something for his friend, Mr. Meuser, who had been demoted. Apparently, it was Meuser who received the money.

Lockheed had disbursed a sum of $62,000 without any explanation for the benefit of Prince Bernhard in 1965, according to the auditor's report. This money was presented on festive occasions, such as factory openings, anniversary celebrations, and similar events.

The corporation also offered Bernhard $500,000 in July 1968, in an effort to reverse the Dutch decision to purchase Breguet Atlantique planes rather than Lockheed's P3 Orion planes.

Other Countries

The list of countries in which Lockheed funneled payoffs included Scandinavia, South Africa, Italy, Turkey, Greece and Nigeria. Among these nations, it was Italy and its ruling Christian Democratic Party that received the most public attention for their Lockheed involvement. In the late 1960's the Italian Air Force bought 14 Lockheed C130 military air transport aircraft at a cost of $100 million. Documents supplied by the U.S. Senate committee pointed to payments to the prime ministers in office during the 1968–70 time span—Giovanni Leone, the President, Aldo Moro and Mariano Rumor. The latter, Mr. Rumor, was the one most widely indicted in the bribery questions. Following the formation of a new government in Italy after the disclosures, neither Rumor nor Moro were given positions in the new Italian cabinet.

The History of the Disclosure—The SEC and IRS

In June, 1975, the Securities and Exchange Commission started its investigation into "possible violations of the antifraud, proxy, and recording provisions of the Federal securities laws" by Lockheed. In August, the company informed the public that it had paid out at least $22 million to foreign government officials, political organizations and influential business contacts in order to secure sales, and $202 million in commissions since 1970. The company also revealed the existence of a $750,000 secret fund established "outside the normal channels of financial accountability." These disclosures followed the refusal of its auditors, Arthur Young & Co., to sign the company's proxy materials because some Lockheed executives declined to certify that the corporation had not operated illegally abroad.

Lockheed attempted to prevent United States authorities from receiving information as to who was involved or in what countries it had made the payments. However, in October, the SEC sued in federal district court to compel Lockheed to provide the names of recipients and produce all available documents pertaining to "payments in excess of $1,000 made to any person, group or entity employed by, affiliated with or representing, directly or indirectly, any foreign government . . . (or payments) to any government officials or political party directly or indirectly, from corporate funds" made by Lockheed between 1969 and 1974.

Lockheed proceeded to supply the SEC with 28 boxes of documents. The SEC's Division of Enforcement pursued the investigation of the payoffs overseas, and its Division of Corporation Finance reviewed Lockheed's proxy materials. The company had been under extreme pressure to refinance its debt, but it could not hold its annual meeting to seek shareholder approval for refinancing due to the SEC's refusal to clear the proxy material until terms were reached on a consent decree.

In February, 1976, the Senate Foreign Relations Subcommittee on Multinational Corporations chaired by Senator Frank Church (D-Idaho) began new hearings with the intention of mustering public support for congressional punitive action on the overseas activities of multinational corporations, specifically those exporting arms. The panel, along with the Senate Subcommittee on Multinational Corporations, subpoenaed Lockheed's auditors, Arthur Young & Co. The attorneys representing the auditors delivered masses of material to the committee before Lockheed could intervene. As it turned out, the boxes included many documents that Lockheed had not previously provided.

One of Lockheed's outside auditors informed the subcommittee that it had become increasingly concerned about the large commissions that were being delivered to foreign agents and had notified the board of director's audit committee in 1973. Because legitimate commissions were a standard part of doing overseas business, the auditors did not have precise evidence of any illegality.

The IRS decision to intensify and broaden its investigation of Lockheed's improper payments served to produce additional incriminating information. According to Treasury Secretary Simon, the IRS "intends to see to it that all those who have made improper payments and bribes do not profit through reducing their federal tax liabilities." Two new plans of action were instituted: (a) The IRS brought its international operations office into all of its corporate audit procedures; (b) the IRS was instructed to interview all corporate officers when conducting annual audits of corporate balance sheets.

Ramifications

"Notwithstanding the pillorying that we have been subjected to, somebody out there likes us."

Robert W. Haack
Chairman of the Board

On October 27, 1976, a refinancing agreement between Lockheed and its 24 lending banks was reached and plans were discussed for putting the proposal to work. The restructuring plans gave substantial stability to Lockheed's financial position. Its equity capital was increased from $107 million to $160 million while simultaneously its bank debt was reduced. According to the plan, the banks would convert $50 million of non-guaranteed loans into preferred stock. In addition, they agreed to extend the financing of the remaining $350 million in non-guaranteed debt through March 1981. Lockheed also managed to reduce its government guaranteed debt by $80 million.

Internally, A. C. Kotchian and Daniel Haughton resigned, reportedly under pressure. They called for the establishment of new standards of international business, emphasizing the defensive nature of Lockheed's payments. They made it clear that their resignations did not come willingly.

Employment at Lockheed was down slightly from 1975, but employees remained faithful and defensive of Lockheed and its practices. "Any big company has to give bribes to stay in business today. Lockheed got caught, so what else is new? Lockheed is just the fall guy," said an electrical equipment engineer.

Overseas, Lockheed signed up foreign commitments in the amount of $1,700,000,000, the largest amount signed up in the company's history. The most significant contract was the sale of the patrol aircraft to Canada. According to Haack, after much "imaginative and constructive thinking" and hard work, the deal was rescheduled and brought to fruition.

Also signed was an air traffic control order for Saudi Arabia that would amount to approximately $600 million. Negotiations for additional sales in the Middle East were also continuing.

Lockheed remained optimistic about selling aircraft to Japan. The company firmly believed that the country did require patrol aircraft and that Lockheed was the company to supply these planes. These were the same sentiments expressed in relation to Germany's possible purchase of aircraft.

Lockheed's executives emphasized that politicians and business people alike were capitalizing on the corporation's controversial situation. It was their hope that the new elections overseas would curtail some of the negative publicity and enable Lockheed to get a fresh start. The recession, gasoline shortages and fuel/cost squeezes had all affected the financial positions of the commercial airlines and negatively influenced their aircraft purchases. But the continued high level of defense budgets around the world served to give the company future hope.

SUMMARY: PROACTIVE RESPONSES
TO CHANGE

The image of corporate managers residing in glass and concrete castles, besieged by critics and the forces of change is an unfortunate stereotype but one that has its own grain of truth. In this and the three preceding chapters, we have seen a number of instances in which we might imagine a chief executive asking his lieutenants, "Can't you make the uncertainty go away?" And like good lieutenants, they sought to bring stability to an unstable world.

The proactive approach to dealing with the external environment essentially involves the efforts of the organization to alter, modify, or otherwise change factors and forces in the environment. In the case of Reserve Mining, we saw those efforts take the form of an attempt to delay or impede the implementation of identified public policy objectives. Reserve's use of the legal and administrative regulatory system to accomplish that purpose was consistent with the American legal system which permits appeals and petitions for review, and requires due process, though the company's pattern of behavior clearly demonstrated an operative policy of thwarting the accomplishment of legitimate public policy objectives. Unlike Reserve, the bottle bill opponents used a variety of tactics to change public opinion, all in service of an operative policy that involved defending existing property interests by altering the amount of public support for the bottle bill proposal. Perhaps the most dramatic case of corporate behavior designed to change the operating environment of an industry was the insurance industry's effort to prod Congress into passing a federal reinsurance plan that would protect the private carrier industry from excessive fire and crime insurance losses in urban areas. No less than the oil industry has secured favorable tax provisions in the past, or the domestic shoe industry, protection from foreign imports more recently, the efforts of the fire insurers to stimulate the political system to create change in the operating environment of that business is a common and familiar corporate response to external change. One can question the public value of such corporate actions, and whether the public interest is well served by such corporate responses to change, but the point is that those responses were both legal and made a great deal of sense to the managers of each company as a way of coping with change.

The most disturbing aspect of change, according to many managers, is the amount of uncertainty that it introduces into the normal operations of the organization. The Gulf Oil and Lockheed Aircraft examples illustrate the impact of political and business uncertainty on the behavior of operating and top level managers alike. In both cases, the operative policy of minimizing uncertainty in order to accomplish corporate purposes led to obvious violations of applicable law. That those actions could be defended on the basis of their "necessity" as means of preserving the corporate entity raises a serious issue of whether legal control of such institutions is adequate to restrain the creation of proactive strategies that involve changing the law itself. As we discussed in Chapter 1, among the motivational factors affecting corporate behavior are the values of the managers themselves. Apparently there are circumstances when the threat of uncertainty is perceived to be so serious that the objective of ensuring the organization's survival overcomes the manager's commitment to preserving the legitimate public policy of the society which charters and permits the organization to operate at all.

In short, proactive responses to environmental change are among the more conventional approaches to dealing with change. While it is neither illegal nor reprehensible for corporations to actively participate in formation of a nation's public policy, instances such as those described in the Gulf and Lockheed cases demonstrate the extent to which a proactive approach can be carried when the operative policy of the organization is the elimination of environmental uncertainty.

part four

interactive patterns of response

chapter eleven

politics and management

CRITIQUE OF THE ADAPTIVE AND PROACTIVE APPROACHES

The ubiquitous presence of external change, and the accelerating rate at which it affects organizations of all types makes it a central concern of modern management. It is unmistakable that change has been creating pressures in post-industrial business environments that require responses other than the conventional adaptive and proactive patterns. Our research has shown that in a variety of industries, facing different kinds of external change, responses that are predicated on organizational reaction (*adaptation*) to the public issue, or managerial efforts to alter or manipulate the environment (*proaction*) to defuse public issues are increasingly likely to fail. Successes, when they occur, tend to be much more short-lived than in the past. Public issues often reappear, in slightly different guises perhaps, or with slightly different constituencies. *This means that the conventional adaptive and proactive responses may be useful tactical approaches, but they are no longer effective strategic approaches to coping with change.*

One reason for the failure of the conventional adaptive and proactive patterns of response as strategic approaches to change is the increasingly political context in which managements and organizations perform. The assumption that managers should be free to run their firms as they see fit, without objection or interference from others is a proposition from another age. For a society that is increasingly organized in character and dependent upon organizations to perform important public services, the idea of the large corporation being as unfettered as Adam Smith's butcher and baker is as far removed from twentieth century reality as the purely local economy. It is the size of modern economic organizations, and the implications that such size has for a society, that creates the rationale for increasing public concern with organizational behavior and performance. New and changing public expectations are, ultimately, the template against which managerial action has to be evaluated for its effectiveness.

The greater the interpenetration between a firm and society, the more extensive the set of involvements and interdependencies flowing from that relationship and the greater the need for an organization to respond to change. While the precise set of involvements differs between each firm and the publics with which it interacts, it is clear that the ability or inability of any organization to respond to change in a timely and substantive way affects its status in society. Status, which is an organization's position in society or place in the scheme of things, creates sets of expectations among its relevant publics. The social legitimacy of the organization is safeguarded as long as it meets those publics' expectations. When expectations are not met, publics may act to either stimulate a favorable response through direct pressure or change an organization's status by changing the public policy which endorses the firm's legitimacy. Hence, what direct pressure on a management may fail to produce as a response, pressure through law, regulation, or legislation may accomplish. Throughout the cases discussed above, and others we have researched, it is the failure of managements to think imaginatively about external change that has produced the pressure for public policy action. Ultimately, the lesson seems to be that no management can afford to let the gap between public expectations of performance and the firm's actual performance become very large. Either corporate action or public action will have to occur in order to narrow the expectations/performance gap. The failure to narrow such gaps, one way or the other, is intolerable for a society because it signifies growing social fragmentation and conflict.

Managed organizations are learning mechanisms and when actions taken in response to a set of pressures and stimuli fail to produce results that are satisfactory in terms of achieving desired objectives, the organization can be expected to change its pattern of behavior. While a number of the cases discussed in earlier chapters illustrate this point, the illustration chosen to make the point in this chapter involves Aetna Life & Casualty. The firm had experienced some of the problems described in earlier chapters and had previously been quite successful using the conventional adaptive and proactive approaches. By the late 1960's, however, it had become apparent to a number of Aetna managers that the traditional approaches were no longer producing long term resolutions to public issues. Rather, as mentioned above, they had become tactics without a cohesive strategy to lend purpose. What evolved in that company's handling of the no-fault automobile insurance issue, however, was a distinctly new strategy (or pattern) of response. This new strategy recognized that public goals and corporate goals were both changing, though not at the same rate nor necessarily in the same way. Hence, some continuous public interaction was required if the automobile insurance crisis was to be resolved in any but a temporary way. These are the characteristics of the interactive pattern of response to change.

PUBLIC GOALS AND CORPORATE GOALS: AETNA AND NO-FAULT AUTOMOBILE INSURANCE

The Aetna Life & Casualty company has been an insurer of automobiles since the early 1900's, and automobile insurance has been an important line of business for the company since the 1920's. Throughout the 1960's and 1970's, the company has been a leading underwriter of automobile liability, collision, and comprehensive insurance coverages. The company's stature as a competitor is reflected in the data presented in Table 11-1. Its principal competitors during the 1960's and 70's have been Allstate and State Farm among the mutual insurance companies, and Travelers among the stock insurers.[1] Since the 1950's, the mutual companies had steadily increased their market share of the automobile insurance business and had set competitive trends in pricing and marketing.

The sale of auto insurance is an activity with important consequences for the insurance industry in the aggregate, and for individual casualty insurers. At the aggregate level, automobile liability insurance

---

[1] Stock insurance companies are owned by stockholders who own shares of stock and elect directors to manage the company. Mutual insurance companies are owned by policyholders, who also elect directors or trustees to manage the company. Dividends are paid stockholders of the stock companies; mutual policy holders receive dividends in the form of reduced costs for their insurance coverages.

TABLE 11-1
AETNA LIFE & CASUALTY, NET PREMIUMS,
SELECTED AUTOMOBILE LINES (IN THOUSANDS)

	1960	1966	1970	1974
(1) AUTOMOBILE BODILY INJURY LIABILITY				
Net Premium Written				
(a) Aetna	97,540	161,246	230,515	371,539
(b) Industry	2,563,913	2,286,223	5,494,148	8,513,997
(c) Aetna as % of Industry	3.8%	7.0%	4.2%	4.4%
Net Premium Earned				
(a) Aetna	93,477	154,293	228,246	370,849
(b) Industry	2,461,878	2,194,065	5,326,450	8,450,651
(c) Aetna as % of Industry	3.8%	7.0%	4.3%	4.4%
Profits				
(a) Aetna	−9,079	−13,617	−21,516	26,765
(b) Industry	−141,239	−195,252	−151,047	−46,227
Aetna Rank	#3	#4	#4	#3
(2) MISCELLANEOUS BODILY INJURY LIABILITY				
Net Premium Written				
(a) Aetna	43,729	43,497	81,882	163,849
(b) Industry	701,877	878,855	1,322,967	2,701,318
(c) Aetna as % of Industry	6.2%	4.9%	6.1%	6.1%
Net Premium Earned				
(a) Aetna	41,839	41,418	78,212	164,588
(b) Industry	663,304	880,461	1,244,142	2,644,613
(c) Aetna as % of Industry	6.3%	4.7%	6.3%	6.1%
Profits				
(a) Aetna	−1,145	5,567	−24,510	−18,292
(b) Industry	21,243	59,373	−71,749	−442,666
Aetna Rank	#1	#2	#1	#2
(3) AUTOMOBILE PHYSICAL DAMAGE LIABILITY				
Net Premium Written				
(a) Aetna	40,418	64,349	100,646	205,182
(b) Industry	1,117,796	1,553,131	2,371,865	5,341,603
(c) Aetna as % of Industry	3.6%	4.1%	4.2%	3.9%
Net Premium Earned				
(a) Aetna	39,505	60,987	98,730	201,453
(b) Industry	1,084,296	1,481,173	2,282,055	5,213,389
(c) Aetna as % of Industry	3.6%	4.1%	4.3%	3.9%
Profits				
(A) Aetna	950	−7,312	−14,354	−10,451
(b) Industry	23,812	−106,609	−271,408	220,687
Aetna Rank	#4	#4	#3	#3

	1960	1966	1970	1974
(4) AUTOMOBILE COLLISION				
Net Premium Written				
(a) Aetna	30,794	58,277	97,706	
(b) Industry	1,284,980	1,848,533	2,805,147	
(c) Aetna as % of Industry	2.3%	3.0%	3.5%	
Net Premium Earned				-a-
(a) Aetna	30,760	53,544	95,296	
(b) Industry	1,255,800	1,739,804	2,700,817	
(c) Aetna as % of Industry	2.4%	3.0%	3.5%	
Profits				
(a) Aetna	2,451	−3,620	−4,063	
(b) Industry	118,842	−40,469	−179,883	
Aetna Rank	#8	#5	#4	
(5) AUTO, FIRE, THEFT, COMPREHENSIVE				
Net Premium Written				
(a) Aetna	17,006	31,395	44,447	
(b) Industry	670,216	1,011,746	1,391,715	
(c) Aetna as % of Industry	2.5%	3.1%	3.2%	
Net Premium Earned				
(a) Aetna	16,706	29,423	43,760	
(b) Industry	640,358	959,129	1,329,661	-a-
(c) Aetna as % of Industry	2.6%	3.0%	3.3%	
Profits				
(a) Aetna	1,605	1,245	−3,443	
(b) Industry	44,094	64,042	−25,236	
Aetna Rank	#6	#5	#3	

Sources: *Best's Aggregates and Averages*
Note: -a- comparable information not available

had become as much a public necessity as the automobile itself by the early 1960's. With increasing automobile usage, however, accidents also increased and, in turn, injuries to persons and property. The need for security from the effects of liability to others for injuries caused by automobile use, and the presumption that a prudent person would insure himself against such liability, contributed to a deepening interpenetration between the industry and the public. In fact, this has meant that insurers were pressured to correct problems in the system in ways that would not impair the availability of liability insurance.

Background

The extent to which the automobile has become a vital part of American society tends to obscure the fact that its entire history is less than one hundred years in duration. In less time than that, automobile insurance has passed from a tentative new kind of coverage to a major line of business for many nonlife insurers; at the same time, it has been transformed from a regulated market matter to a major social problem. No issue in any line of the insurance business appears to have so deeply involved the interests of such a broad segment of the public and the industry as reform of the automobile insurance system did in the late 1960's.

Early automobile insurance policies provided coverage against the threat of fire, collision, and other physical hazards. Such policies provided that the policyholder ("first party") was to be reimbursed in event of loss. But since "third parties" were also injured by the operation of automobiles, there was an obvious need for liability protection as well. Under tort law, an automobile owner could be held liable for injuries to third parties and/or their property if he was at fault—that is, if his conduct fell below that of a reasonable man in the same or similar circumstances. This "fault system" depended, however, on the ability of the owner who was found liable to actually pay the injured third party. The courts could enforce the judgment only to the extent the liable party had economic resources which could be used to satisfy the judgment.

As early as the 1920's, the enormity of the automobile's impact in terms of death, injury, and property loss served to focus policy debate on the need for a system which would encourage the purchase of liability insurance. The outcome of this debate was the emergence of "financial responsibility laws." These laws, with the exception of the 1927 Massachusetts act which made automobile liability insurance compulsory, generally sought to encourage the public to voluntarily purchase such insurance. The situation worsened through the 1930's, however, and interest in compulsory laws grew throughout the 1940's and 1950's and led to a gradual strengthening of existing laws. By 1971 every state had a financial responsibility law, ranging from compulsory insurance to security deposit laws which required the equivalent of a bond in lieu of a liability insurance policy. The consequence of this movement was, as expected, that increasing numbers of liability insurance policies were being sold and that a public need was growing for some guaranteed access to liability insurance coverage.

As indicated above, the availability of insurance coverage was a problem in a number of insurance lines, including automobile liability insurance. The financial responsibility laws reflected a public consensus that no driver ought to be without liability insurance. But that consensus, and the financial responsibility laws themselves, did not answer the question of who would insure the worst risks in the driving population. Standard underwriting practices favored insuring those drivers with the fewest accidents and best claims experience. In other lines of insurance, especially high risks can be covered if the insured agrees to limit certain activities, correct special problems, or share in some part of any loss ("coinsurance"). Since those were options which were generally not viable in the auto insurance area, however, a coverage and cost dilemma arose. As long as insurers could not require high risk drivers to pay an appropriately high premium sufficient to meet underwriting requirements, the challenge was to cover such risks at acceptable cost levels. The attempts to meet these dual objectives ranged from sophisticated merit rating plans to assigned risk pool arrangements.[2] Still, the problems continued to worsen.

As the problems of the price and availability of automobile insurance mounted, pressure for reform intensified. Beginning in the mid 1950's, and continuing throughout the 1960's and early 1970's, a variety of technical underwriting solutions were developed including merit rating plans, safe driver training programs, assigned risk pools, and a surcharge or penalty system for especially hazardous risks.

Each technical solution seemed to generate its own new set of pressures as segments of driving public bore the impact of such changes. Although criticisms were numerous, it is likely that such technical tinkering with underwriting practices would have continued to characterize the industry's response but for the fact that large losses were being shown by insurers on their automobile business. Loss ratios rose through much of the 1960's and pressures arose within the industry for corrective action.[3] An obvious managerial solution was to raise premium rates and that was a course which was followed throughout the 1960's. Since rate increases were tempered by the need for prior regulatory approval in many states, a scenario developed whereby insurers announced proposed rate increases, customers objected, the state insurance department investigated, and a

---

[2] The courts also served to articulate the public policy aspects of financial responsibility legislation, especially the fundamental concern for accident victims. For example, the California Supreme Court ruled: "The entire financial responsibility law must be liberally construed to foster its main objective of giving monetary protection to that ever changing and tragically large group of persons who, while lawfully using the highways themselves, suffer grave injury through the negligent use of those highways by others." (Interinsurance Exchange of Automobile Club of Southern California v. Ohio Casualty Insurance Co., 58 Cal. 2d 142, 373 P. 2d 640.) This policy was also extended to prevent insurers from relieving themselves of coverage because of breach of policy conditions, such as notice of loss or failure to cooperate in all but the most extreme case of injury to the insurer. A New York appellate court ruled in 1969 that insurer prejudice must be shown in order to relieve the insurer of obligation because of the insured's failure to give notice: ". . . it becomes unreasonable to read the provisions unrealistically or to find that the carrier may forfeit the coverage, even though there is no likelihood that it was prejudiced by the breach. It would also disservice the public interest, for insurance is an instrument of social policy that the victims of negligence be compensated." (Allstate Insurance Co. v. Grillon, 251 A2d. 256.) The comment echoes Justice Cardozo who wrote "The final cause of law is the welfare of society. The rule that misses its aim cannot permanently justify its existence."

[3] Loss ratios refer to the amount paid out in satisfaction of claims in comparison to premium dollars received. In 1970, for example, loss ratios in the automobile insurance industry reached 64.7 percent.

compromise rate increase was approved. If the knee-jerk response of the underwriters was more restrictive underwriting arrangements, the knee-jerk response of the marketing-oriented managers was to increase auto insurance premiums.

Public Responses: Social Reform

Reliance on fault as a basis for distinguishing between those who will and will not collect the proceeds of an insurance policy is something of an anomaly in twentieth century insurance practice. Normally, one can claim the proceeds of a policy when a stated event occurs. Life insurance, fire insurance, accident insurance, and many other forms of coverage operate on some version of this principle. Automobile liability insurance, however, has traditionally relied on a "third party" system under which the insurer asks a potential claimant: "Were you at fault?" If so, recovery is barred.

In theory, the tort liability system serves the purposes of resolving social disputes in favor of the innocent party, enabling all to comprehend and anticipate the consequences of their actions, while also educating the public to that behavior which is publicly acceptable and unacceptable.[4] Given a public sentiment which supports the view that the innocent victim of another's negligence ought to recover damages for the injuries incurred, the tort system does fulfill the three social functions just mentioned. When the public sentiment supporting the system wanes or when the system fails to fulfill the social functions mentioned above, however, a breakdown of the system occurs. As applied to automobile insurance reparations, both public sentiment and the system's ability to fulfill its social functions diminished by the 1960's. The result was a public atmosphere in which proposals for radical modification of the system could receive a serious hearing.

Attempts to modify the tort liability system as it applied to automobile reparations had been made from time to time since the 1930's. A pioneering proposal with regard to a no-fault system of automobile compensation was the Columbia University Committee Plan, developed in 1932.[5] The proposal figured prominently in a no-fault plan adopted by the Canadian province of Saskatchewan in 1946. In the 1950's, the issue received some renewed interest in the United States, though no major legislative activity occurred before the mid-1960's.

[4] See Harold J. Berman and William R. Greiner, *The Nature and Functions of Law*, 3rd Edition (Mineola, N.Y.: Foundation Press, 1974), Chapter 1.
[5] For a discussion, see Willis P. Rokes, *No-Fault Insurance* (Santa Monica, CA: Insurers Press, Inc., 1971) pp. 51–52. Rokes also suggests that the earliest proposals involved the application of a workmen's compensation approach and were presented as early as 1919.

The catalyst for major public debate of a no-fault insurance plan in the 1960's was the Keeton-O'Connell proposal for a "Basic Protection Plan," originally presented in 1965.[6] The proposal suggested major changes in the law affecting victims of automobile accidents and attracted great attention throughout the latter half of the decade.

There were two main features to the proposal: (1) development of a new form of automobile insurance, called Basic Protection insurance; and (2) a change in the law which would eliminate claims based on negligence, within specified limitations. Basic Protection insurance was a combination of coverages already in existence and closely resembled medical payment insurance.[7] It envisaged a two-party claims system in which the insured or anyone else injured as a result of the ownership, maintenance, or use of the insured's vehicle would be compensated under the insured's policy. Two exceptions were those who were intentionally injured and those who were parties in other vehicles (who would be covered under the policies of the owners of those vehicles). To effect such a system, the plan would have to be compulsory, applying to all registered motor vehicles.[8]

The plan applied only to bodily injuries, property damage continuing to be adjusted on a fault basis. This provision reflected Keeton and O'Connell's view that the abuses of the negligence system were most serious in compensating the accident victim.[9] Most importantly, Basic Protection was intended to be an excess coverage—that is, there would be no payments made for losses reimbursed from other sources such as health or medical payment insurance.

The Keeton-O'Connell plan sought to preserve one aspect of the fault system with regard to personal injuries. A motorists' exemption from legal liability for negligence would be limited to $5,000 and for other injuries to $10,000. Where injuries caused expenses in excess of $10,000 for economic loss and $5,000 for pain and suffering, the Basic Protection plan would revert back to the negligence system.

The impact of the Keeton-O'Connell proposal was felt at two different levels. As an input into the public policy process, the plan was well publicized, in part because the authors were successful in publishing a large number of articles in the popular press, and in part because the pro-

---

[6] Robert E. Keeton and Jeffrey O'Connell, *Basic Protection for the Traffic Victim: A Blueprint for Reforming Automobile Insurance* (Boston, Mass.: Little-Brown & Co., 1965).

[7] See Rokes, *op. cit.*, p. 55.

[8] A special problem involved out-of-state autos entering a no-fault state and autos covered under a no-fault system which traveled to states with fault systems.

[9] The existence and widespread use of collision insurance is, in effect, a two-party system for property damage to the automobile. The insured collects from his own insurance company irrespective of who caused the damage. If the third party was at fault, the insured's insurer may proceed against him on a liability basis in which case the third party's liability insurance would come into play.

posal became a natural focal point in the discussion of all types of auto insurance reform. In a second and more technical context, the proposal served to stimulate the development of alternative proposals for major reform both from within and outside of the industry. By 1968, a number of alternative no-fault proposals had been offered by such companies as Insurance Company of North America (INA) and such groups as the American Mutual Insurance Alliance (originators of the "Illinois Experiment in Guaranteed Benefits"), and the American Insurance Association ("The Complete Personal Protection Automobile Insurance Plan"). Further proposals were made by various segments of the industry between 1968 and 1970.[10]

The public concern with the availability, price, and quality of automobile insurance had generally been diffused before Keeton-O'Connell. Their proposal served to focus diverse criticisms of the industry and weld discussions of the problems into a coherent attack on the system of fault reparations rather than peripheral attacks on availability, price, or quality matters. A source in one state insurance commission commented that "without Keeton-O'Connell, systematic reform of the automobile insurance business would have been years away." Experiments of the no-fault variety began to be implemented in public policy programs. Puerto Rico became the first U.S. jurisdiction to adopt a compensation plan for automobile victims when it enacted a "Social Protection Plan for Victims of Automobile Accidents" in 1968, to be effective in 1970. Massachusetts enacted the first state no-fault insurance plan in 1970, and by 1971, similar proposals had been introduced in a number of state legislatures.

Patterns of Response: The Aetna

The Aetna's response to the development of no-fault proposals occurred in three stages. The first stage involved the company's direct response to the Keeton-O'Connell proposal and led to a decision to undertake an internal analysis of the effects of a no-fault system on a sample of its own previously settled automobile accident cases. The second stage involved the company's disclosure of the results of its study and its cooperation with a federally sponsored study of the prevailing automobile insurance system. A third stage followed when the Aetna, at its own initiative, became the first major automobile insurer to actively promote the passage and implementation of no-fault automobile insurance legislation.

Before the mid-1960's, the Aetna had tended to support the type of technical responses favored by the industry as a means of correcting pric-

---

[10] A discussion and point-by-point comparison of these and other proposals can be found in Rokes, *op. cit.*

ing and availability problems. The Keeton-O'Connell proposal and the discussion it generated prompted the company to reexamine its position, however, and the management of the Casualty and Surety Division undertook an analysis of the new reform proposals. An internal divisional study was conducted under the supervision of William O. Bailey, then head of the underwriting department within the Casualty and Surety Division. The format which Bailey adopted was designed to concentrate on evaluating the impact of the Keeton-O'Connell plan on a sample of cases drawn from the Division's automobile claims settlement files. Each was reexamined with a view toward answering the central question of what effect a no-fault system would have had on the settlement of the case. The conclusion reached by Bailey and his staff was that had a system like that proposed by Keeton and O'Connell been in effect, average claims payments would have decreased in amount and a substantial rate reduction could have been passed on to policyholders. According to one of the staff members who participated in the study and divisional discussion of the findings, the analysis was convincing to even the most skeptical among the Casualty and Surety Division staff.

The staff report became a catalyst within the division for a re-thinking of the company's position about automobile insurance reform. As indicated above, an insurance company's management is especially concerned with loss ratios, the difference between premium flows (sales) on one hand and settlement flows (claims) on the other. In the case of automobile insurance, the narrowing between premium inflows and claims outflows was a major management concern throughout the 1960's. Recognizing the practical difficulties involved in the continuing escalation of premium rates, the Aetna's no-fault study was of importance as technical support for a course of action supporting reform. The net effect was that by late 1967, considerable support existed within the company for publicly advocating the no-fault concept in what seemed certain to be a major public policy debate.

The second stage of the Aetna's response occurred when the company made public its position on no-fault by cooperating with the Department of Transportation's 1968 study of automobile insurance,[11] and, at the same time, spurred the American Insurance Association's research into the merits of the Keeton-O'Connell plan. The result of the latter was that by October, 1968, the AIA announced that it had developed its own no-fault proposal; it thereafter moved for legislative enactment of such a no-fault plan by state legislatures. The result was that long before the

[11] See Department of Transportation, *Automobile Insurance and Compensation Study: Public Attitudes Toward Auto Insurance.* A Report of the Survey Research Center, Institute for Social Research, The University of Michigan for the Department of Transportation (Washington, D.C.: U.S. Government Printing Office, 1970).

D.O.T. study was concluded in 1970, the Aetna was on record as being in full support of the no-fault approach to automobile insurance reform.[12]

The Aetna's public endorsement of a specific no-fault proposal presaged the development of a third stage wherein the company took positive action to promote no-fault legislation. In 1969, no-fault legislation was considered in ten states. In each, the Aetna actively supported, through press releases and lobbying, those proposals which substantively approximated the AIA plan. The company was one of only a few insurers to support the no-fault legislation enacted in Massachusetts in 1970, and the company's affirmative posture has continued since then, involving lobbying on behalf of "genuine" no-fault proposals and against "counterfeit no-fault plans" that would impose limitations or restrictions on a first party indemnification system.

A further step was taken in 1974 when the company announced its support for a federal no-fault legislative package which would establish a national no-fault automobile insurance system for those states which failed to enact no-fault legislation or for those whose legislation failed to meet minimum federal standards. This action further set apart the Aetna from the rest of the industry on the no-fault issue, but was actually a continuation of the basic policy formulated in 1968. Recognition of the necessity for eventually having to support federal legislation was manifested as early as March, 1971, when William O. Bailey, Senior Vice President of the Casualty and Surety Division wrote to Olcott D. Smith, Aetna's Chief Executive Officer: "We will continue to seek legislation at the state level wherever this offers reasonable chance of success even though we recognize that federal action or federal sanctions may be necessary in the future to bring about a 'rational, equitable, and compatible reparations system for motor vehicle accident victims' throughout the United States."

Corporate policy formation involves two distinct dynamics, one of which is internal to the organization, the other external to it. The internal dynamic involves the interaction among the subsystems of the organization and the manner in which the company's posture develops as part of the "terms of trade" among the organization's components. The external dynamic involves the relationship between the organization and the relevant publics with whom its interests overlap, interface, or even interfere. A perceptive management will recognize the relevant publics with which the organization does have issues in common and will attempt to calculate the impact of its own actions on those publics.

---

[12] In a memoranda from Donald M. Johnson, then Senior Vice President of the Casualty and Surety Division, to all General Managers and Managers of Production Offices in October, 1968, the AIA proposal was announced and the company's endorsement given with a statement that Aetna executives and research people had been involved for over a year in the study group that recommended this course of action. Hence, "the Company fully endorses the AIA position and would back it with all means at its disposal."

The formulation of a corporate policy in support of no-fault reform primarily involved the Aetna's underwriters and managers. Initiative for the no-fault study came from the Casualty and Surety managers; support for a policy favoring no-fault reform depended on negating the objections of those relevant publics related to that division. In particular, account had to be taken of the impact of a no-fault system on the independent agents upon whom the company relied for its automobile business. Some fears existed among independent agents that a first-party indemnity system might enable the insurers to bypass the agents and deal directly with the public.[13] The Aetna sought to assuage such fears by publicizing its own intention to place greater reliance on the agents as client representatives in dealing with claims as well as sales matters.

An equally knotty concern was the effect of an AIA-like no-fault plan on the Aetna's other lines of insurance. A special concern existed that a no-fault system for bodily injury indemnification would duplicate applicable health insurance coverages. That raised the question of whether the public might not perceive a diminished need for medical insurance coverage which was sold as part of many automobile policies. (This is included under the "Miscellaneous Bodily Injury Liability" heading in Table 11-1.) After study, the company concluded that such a plan would allow coordination of benefits and would eliminate unnecessary duplication of coverage; as a whole, it would not result in any significant loss of revenue to other lines of business. The most significant impact would involve a substantial revenue loss for bodily injury liability insurance coverage. But since that had been an unprofitable line of business throughout most of the 1960's, a revenue loss was tolerable if a break-even or underwriting profit point could be achieved.

The coalition of technical and managerial interests supporting the no-fault policy within the company might not have prevailed had serious objections been raised by the company's top management. In fact, however, such a policy was readily endorsed at the institutional level. The plan was responsive to public demands for reform and had the potential of stimulating development of a system which could both serve the public's needs and utilize the capacities of the private carrier industry.

Whatever the intra-organizational dynamics involved in the formulation of new policy, the impact of action on relevant publics determines

---

[13] This concern persisted throughout the period of the 1971 hearings before the House of Representatives Subcommittee on Commerce and Finance. An important part of the testimony presented by the National Association of Mutual Insurance Agents, for example, related to the role of the independent agent in the marketing of automobile insurance. The development of programs for the mass marketing of insurance coverages reinforced the agents' fears. See U.S. House of Representatives, *Hearings before the Subcommittee on Commerce and Finance on Bills Relating to No-Fault Motor Vehicle Insurance, 92d Congress, April 1971.* Volume 1 (Washington, D.C.: U.S. Government Printing Office, 1971) pp. 271-273.

the ultimate effectiveness of a chosen management policy. Recognition of this fact can lead an astute management to anticipate or estimate the impact of various policy alternatives on the organization's relevant publics before finalizing a policy choice. This was the case when the Aetna's management considered the effect of the AIA no-fault plan on the independent agents who represented Aetna policyholders. Similar consideration was given to the impact on other relevant publics such as the Aetna's competitors (stock companies and mutuals), industry trade associations, state insurance departments, and state and federal legislators. With respect to each, Aetna's management attempted to anticipate the reaction to the company's endorsement of a no-fault plan, a calculation which was made more difficult since no other insurers had made similar policy commitments.

Formulation of a policy position also generates a set of issues relating to the implementation of policy. For the Aetna, the decision to support the AIA plan involved decisions about the extent to which the company would actively promote legislation and lobby on behalf of the plan. A more important consideration in practice was the point at which the Aetna would compromise in order to secure the passage of no-fault legislation. As experience was gained in the promotion of no-fault legislation during the 1969 and 1970 legislative sessions, it became apparent that opponents of no-fault legislation sought compromise on the question of the "threshold" limit beyond which an injured party could resort to the tort liability system. In 1967, for example, the Massachusetts State Senate defeated a Keeton-O'Connell "Basic Insurance Protection" bill that would have established a $10,000 threshold and deducted all collateral source recovery. The "Personal Injury Protection" plan which was finally enacted in 1970 set a $2,000 threshold for tort suits and deducted only wage continuation payments. Moreover, where the 1967 plan eliminated pain and suffering suits under $5,000, the 1970 law permitted such suits where a medical loss exceeded $500. The position which the Aetna finally adopted was that any compromise that would result in a de facto retention of the tort system would be unacceptable. Thus, only an extremely high threshold figure (one as high as the financial responsibility law itself imposed) would be an acceptable compromise. This position, and the passage of a number of "counterfeit" no-fault plans which actually retained the tort liability system, ultimately led the company to publicly support the establishment of federal no-fault standards.

INTERACTIVE RESPONSES TO CHANGE

The Aetna's response to the issue of automobile insurance reform illustrates a number of important points about managerial responses to change. First, response to change is itself a process involving continuous management perceptions of the environment, action taken in light of such change, and the evaluation of effects. The Aetna's own market losses in the auto insurance lines and the continuing public pressure for insurance reform contributed to management awareness of the seriousness of the matter. The Keeton-O'Connell proposal may have been the high point in this stage for Aetna's management for it seemed to galvanize the casualty and surety division into making the internal study of a no-fault system's impact on loss settlements. That study was also the transition from an awareness stage of response to an action stage. It was during this second stage that the Aetna's response to no-fault differed from the conventional responses it pursued in the case of variable life insurance and fire insurance protection for the inner city. In the case of no-fault, the internal study served to seriously raise the question of the company's public involvement within the division and to raise the possibility of new kinds of alternatives. This openness to an examination of the merits of no-fault proposals had the effect of allowing the public's reform demands to become internalized within the management of the casualty division. The results of the study then supported the proposal from the technical underwriting perspective; lastly, the coalition of managerial and underwriting personnel secured top management support for the chosen course of action, public support of no-fault legislation. At that point, Aetna's top management prompted development of the AIA plan. Eventually, the company even broke away from the AIA per se, and stood alone as a spokesman for federal no-fault standards. This transition to a positive, initiative-taking posture signified the movement into a third stage of response, a stage which was not reached in either the life insurance or inner city insurance instances.

The no-fault auto insurance case highlights the process by which certain by-products of the market process have important consequences on society and become important public concerns. The Aetna's response involved both an awareness of this secondary impact and several forms of action designed to positively interact with society to resolve the dilemma. To be sure, the company had a real interest in resolving what for it was an important business problem. It had incurred underwriting losses despite rate increases and selective underwriting while public pressure itself was mounting to limit both of these alternatives. The important point is that the Aetna not only reacted to change, but attempted to integrate prevailing public values into its own decision making. It chose a course of action that would not simply react to, or manipulate the environment, but would positively interact with the public goals. It had, in effect, internalized the public values for reform.

The Aetna's decision to actively support a public policy transformation of the rules of the game by which auto insurance system would be administered was neither a reaction to environmental change, and hence, adaptive, nor an attempt to manipulate the situation and effect a change in the environment for its own purposes (proactive). In those states where no-fault auto legislation was enacted, liability rates for drivers were reduced as much as 15–20 percent in the first year. The 1974 data presented in Table 11–1 indicate the continuing problems facing the Aetna and the industry in the physical damage lines where no-fault had not been applied. Indications that no-fault has been improving the settlement of bodily injury claims from auto accidents is clear, if not overwhelming and congressional support for a federal plan has grown.[14] These results have prompted the Aetna to continue its support and active encouragement of genuine state no-fault plans and federal no-fault standards.

[14] A review of the no-fault experience can be found in *Barron's* "No-Fault Insurance: The Evidence is Mixed, But the Drive is On," August 25, 1975, pp. 3 ff.

chapter twelve

managing external affairs

PERCEPTIONS OF CHANGE

The environment in which managed organizations operate has both objective and subjective characteristics. Demographic information such as population statistics are relatively objective in nature, as are the number of competitors in an industry or the names of substitute products. We have already discussed a number of situations in which *managerial interpretation* of such objective factors has differed among competitors in the same industry. Gerber's response to the birth rate decline suggested in population statistics was one example of a management that perceived an objective element in the environment, but was prepared to interpret and act on an interpretation quite different from that of others. A similar argument can be made about managerial interpretations of facts in such cases as Lockheed, Gulf Oil, Reserve Mining, all of which were discussed in earlier chapters.

Apart from the objective environment, and interpretations thereof, there is also a subjective environment that exists only as it is perceived by others. There are many kinds of environmental change which are not inherently either threats or opportunities. Rather, the character of the change is almost entirely a "perceived character," depending on the observor and the observer's interests.[1] The Civil Rights Act of 1964 might be considered a case in point. Certainly, members of minority groups in the United States generally perceived this legislation as an opportunity to advance the achievement for equal opportunity in employment, schooling, and public services. Managers of such organizations as the National Association for the Advancement of Colored People (NAACP) and the Urban League no doubt perceived the legislation as an advantageous environmental change. To managers in firms, government agencies, and other employers, the legislation may well have been seen as a new environmental requirement, compliance with which would have to be determined over time. To managers of certain "target organizations," however, which had become the special focus of attention in debate over employment opportunities, that legislation may well have been perceived as a direct threat to their on-going operations. The point is that the legislation had no inherent character, but depended on the perceptions of others to identify it as an opportunity, a requirement, or a threat.[2]

One aspect of the relationship between corporations and society that is particularly given to varying interpretations is the existence, nature of, and extent to which companies possess and wield *power* in local communities. In one sense, it is easy to assume that organizations—especially large organizations—possess significant power in a local community. Similarly, an organization that has power necessarily uses it, doesn't it? Yet, interviews with managers of firms in local communities show a far more complicated and complex relationship. To be sure, power exists. Corporations have a status or position in a community and, like individuals, have a certain stake in the decisions which the community makes. But corporations also have roles that flow from their status as the largest employer in a

---

[1] There is a growing body of organizational behavior literature that is beginning to recognize the importance of this "perceived" environment.

[2] We recognize, of course, that the congressional sponsors of the legislation intended that it create opportunities for minorities. Nevertheless, the history of United States legislation is replete with laws enacted for one purpose that have been interpreted and implemented in ways wholly contrary to legislative intent. A classic example is the Sherman antitrust act which the legislative history indicated was not to be applied to labor unions. Nevertheless, the U.S. Supreme Court applied the law to a union, finding it guilty of violating the Sherman Act's provisions. Ultimately, this led Congress to enact the Clayton Act which explicitly exempts labor unions from its terms.

town, a major taxpayer, or some analogous position. The community, on its part, *expects* specific corporations to act in particular ways and render certain kinds of performance. The company/community relationship is not a one-sided relationship in which power is exercised unidirectionally by the corporation on the community. Rather, the community and the corporation interpenetrate one another, influencing each other and the processes by which they continue to interact.

In many organizations, relations with the local community have been the area generally understood when "external affairs" are mentioned. As we shall see in the case discussed below, such a conception can evolve into a much broader set of considerations when management applies basic principles of goal setting, program design, and evaluation. Unlike the discussion of core economic activities which has characterized cases in the preceding chapters, where "external affairs" are taken to mean any external public, the following discussion of the evolution of Aetna Life & Casualty's community affairs function begins with issues far removed from the Aetna's core business activities, but eventually brings these peripheral activities into the mainstream of the company's management concerns. Some would refer to these as "social responsibility" matters that have been internalized. Upon reflection, it seems evident that such a conception fails to recognize the critical relationship between those matters which are disposed of in the marketplace (e.g., resource procurement, distribution of output) and those for which there is no market mechanism (power, community influence). An alternative approach which recognizes the inherent connection between all public issues affecting the firm, whatever their genesis, revolves around the distinction between an organization's primary and secondary involvements.

PRIMARY AND SECONDARY INVOLVEMENTS

That technical core of productive activities that represent the heart of the enterprise cannot be sustained without the support services of the managerial subsystem of the organization. Whether it involves procurement of resources, coordination of multiple technical activities, or the distribution of output, the managerial subsystem performs the critical administrative functions that enable the entity to operate. Taken together, the technical activities and the administrative activities that are necessary to their accomplishment represent the organization's primary involvements with society. Thus, raw material and personnel procurement, production, marketing, and distribution all require interaction with society and are the primary way in which the organization's involvements arise. In the normal course of events, these primary involvement activities have consequences

and impacts on the external environment that are noticeable and significant. Because they are directly linked to or flow from the primary involvement activities of the entity, these consequences—or secondary involvements—must also be a concern of the management of the enterprise.
In fact, it now appears that the top managers of many businesses (the institutional subsystem as we referred to it in Chapter 1), spend upwards of
50 percent of their executive time on the management of these "external
affairs." If nothing else, it is now abundantly evident that the management
of external affairs is not a matter at the periphery of the business of the
organization; it is an activity that runs to the core of an organization's legitimacy in a society that is constantly changing. That legitimacy, in turn,
is measured by the organization's ability to meet the expectations of performance which its many relevant publics hold. If not easily managed,
these are nevertheless matters which are critical and therefore demand the
best efforts of the top managers that comprise the institutional subsystem.

The case below presents a secondary involvement situation in which
the need for careful management of external affairs arises from the company's status or position in a local community. This case, using Aetna Life
& Casualty as an example, presents in detail the evolution of an external
affairs function within a large service industry firm.

The history of Aetna's external affairs management, especially as it
relates to social and community conflicts, is essentially the story of an institutional concern with the company's legitimacy in terms of meeting the
expectations of local publics. Over the course of a decade, those concerns
evolved from a community-focused set of ad hoc actions to a programmatic and institutionalized response. Finally, the increasing concern with
secondary involvement aspects of the relationship served to raise, and
lead the company to act on issues that touched its primary involvement
activities as well. Hence, we see an evolution of external affairs management from relatively indirect consequences on the community flowing
from the company's presence and size, to an involvement with matters
having a more direct relationship with the company's activities on the national, as well as the local community level.

SOCIAL ROLES:
AETNA AND COMMUNITY AFFAIRS

There are few aspects of a company's relationship with society that are
clearer in fact, yet unexplained by conventional management theory, than
a firm's impact on its local community. Factually, employment statistics
and contributions to the regional production of goods and services are
market oriented indicators of impact. But few indicators articulate a firm's
influence on local laws, community development efforts, or provisions of

services. There is no real doubt that such influence exists, and that it is an understood part of the fabric of social life in a community, but there are limited ways of measuring such effects. Normally, influence is exercised on an ad hoc, issue-by-issue basis; hence, on a day-to-day level, the amount of influence which a firm or organization wields may be distorted, appearing to be overwhelming in some instances, muted in others. The overall dimensions of such power seem to remain obscure—or at least be-clouded—in the absence of longitudinal study.[3]

The concept of interpenetration, and the notion that the firm and society are social systems which influence each other, permits a systematic analysis of a firm's relation with its community in the context of its other involvements with society. As pointed out in my study of the insurance industry, it was found that the nature of the interpenetration between a firm and society varies with the scope of the relationship, the salience of specific issues, and the continuity of the entity's dealings with relevant publics.[4] For Aetna Life & Casualty, the scope of its interpenetration has been broad because of the multiple line character of its business, its national and international operations, and the size of its assets, premium levels, and insurance in force The salience of such issues as providing insurance for the inner city and no-fault automobile insurance has also heightened management awareness of the company's interpenetration with society. In this case, the Aetna's relationship with its hometown community will be examined in some detail. That relationship, and especially the manner in which it changed during Olcott Smith's tenure as chairman (1960–1972), highlights both the influence of a firm in a local community and the manner in which community change influences the enterprise.

Dimensions of Interpenetration

The Aetna has been headquartered in Hartford throughout its history and has become one of the metropolitan area's largest employers, sources of personal income and tax revenues, and purchasers of local services. In 1970, for example, the Aetna employed nearly 8,500 people in its headquarters office; this amounted to over 2 percent of all jobs (325,000) in the capital region of the State of Connecticut and 28 percent of all insurance related jobs in the region.[5] This status represents power within the

---

[3] Robert Dahl's study of political influence in one city remains a classic model in this regard. Yet to be written is a comparative study of corporate influence in local communities. See Robert Dahl, *Who Governs?*, New Haven: Yale University Press, 1962.

[4] See J. Post, *Risk and Response: Management and Social Change in the American Insurance Industry*, D. C. Heath, 1976.

[5] Derived from information provided by Greater Hartford Process, Inc.

community,[6] power which is viewed by some as imposing important responsibilities upon the firm.[7] The firm is not the only source of power,
however, and a broad set of non-market pressures, concerns, and interests
is typically found in the local community environment. The diversity of
factors involved in the community power equation is usually so substantial, and so constantly changing, that it constitutes a major area of management concern whether the intention is to adapt to or manipulate that
environment. In the case of the Aetna, the company's involvement with
the Hartford community appears to have undergone considerable change
during the 1960's, occasioned in part by the community and in part by the
company itself.

Interpenetration between an organization and a host community,
like that between an industry and society, need not be consciously recognized by a company's management at each stage of its evolution. Indeed,
an organization's managers may not recognize the extent of the interpenetration until severely pressured to do so by social conflict which touches
the firm. Since a community has an ongoing life of its own, and the
firm—especially the large firm—is an integral part of that vitality, it is
more difficult to separate community change from the firm's response
than in other situations. What is possible, and what a longitudinal analysis
of the company/community relationship facilitates, is an identification of
those periods in which critical transitions from one type of relationship to
another are effected.

Before the 1960's, the Aetna's community involvements were significant in such areas as employment, but modest with regard to matters such
as community development. Moreover, management perception of the
scope of its community involvements was also narrow; although its market operations were national in scope, its voluntary non-market activities
were strictly confined to the Hartford community. Hartford hospitals,
charities, and civic organizations had benefited from the Aetna's philan-
thropy. No formal policy guided this involvement however, and the affili-
ation of top executives with local organizations seems to have been the
guiding principle in the disbursement of charitable contributions. Occasionally, a new group would receive the benefit of the Aetna's largess, as
in 1963 when, on Christmas day, the large Roman Catholic church across
the avenue from the Aetna's home office was destroyed by fire. The company promptly invited parishioners, including the Bishop of the Hartford

---

[6] In this regard, see E. Epstein, "Dimensions of Corporate Power," Parts 1 and 2, *California
Management Review*, Vol. XVI, No. 2 and No. 4, 1973–74.

[7] Obviously, management need not agree with the contention that it has power, the dimensions of that power, or the responsibilities that other groups would impose on it. For a discussion of the proposition that responsibility equals power see K. Davis and R. Blomstrom,
Business, Society, and Environment: Social Power and Social Response, McGraw-Hill, Inc., 1971.

diocese, to use the company's large auditorium as a temporary home. The invitation continued for several years until a new cathedral was erected on the old site. Apart from such exceptional circumstances, the Aetna's urban profile was a low one and the pattern of its involvements can be described as random and ad hoc, lacking both formal policy and consistent practice.

The city of Hartford is near the geographic center of the State of Connecticut. It is the state capitol, and historically, it has been a major commercial center. Surprisingly, the city originally flourished as a seaport during the colonial period, despite its location some 50 miles north of the point where the Connecticut River enters the Long Island Sound. The marine activity created a natural need for insurance underwriters, and the business developed on the Hartford docks in much the same manner as in New York, Boston, and Baltimore. Hartford's status as a seaport declined, but its prominence as a center of insurance ascended throughout the 1800's. In the 1970's, the headquarters of such large insurers as the Aetna, Travelers, Connecticut General, Hartford Fire, Phoenix Mutual, and Connecticut Mutual are still located in the Hartford metropolitan area.

Hartford is the hub of a 29-town area known as the Capitol Region of Connecticut. In 1940, about 335,000 people lived in this region; by 1970, the population exceeded 670,000 and population projections estimated another doubling by the year 2000.[8] As in other cities, much of the existing population growth was absorbed by suburban communities surrounding Hartford, leaving the city itself to a population dominated by neighborhoods of middle income and lower income families. Concentrations of poor families and blacks and Puerto Ricans grew within the city throughout the post-World War II period. Within the city's population of 158,000, unemployment rates rose to between 20 and 30 percent throughout much of the decade of the 1960's. The center city, including the core business district, was following a pattern evident elsewhere of becoming an island of wealth surrounded by poverty, decline, and decay.

Some neighborhoods had been suffering from decades of cumulative neglect by 1960. The situation was further aggravated by increasing concentrations of blacks and Puerto Ricans in certain areas of these neighborhoods. A foursided conflict situation began to emerge, involving the suburbs and the city, the black population, the Puerto Rican population, and the inner city white population. By the early 1960's, it had become evident to a number of government, community, and business leaders in the Hartford area that action was required to first stabilize, then improve, a deteriorating social environment.

Some attempts at local redevelopment had in fact occurred in Hartford. Perhaps the most publicized of these projects was a plan sponsored

[8] Data derived from *The Greater Hartford Process*, Hartford, CT: Greater Hartford Process, Inc., 1972, p. 7.

by the Travelers Insurance Companies to revitalize several square blocks adjacent to the main business district of the city. The plan involved razing a cluster of small ethnic neighborhoods, to be replaced by a newly constructed commercial and office building complex that would provide office space, create new job opportunities, and attract shoppers back to the center city area on a regular basis. The Constitution Plaza project, as it was called, involved an expenditure of more than $200 million and did provide a stimulus for new downtown redevelopment. But the public opposition to the razing was considerable and made clear the latent hostility among neighborhood groups toward the dominant influence of the local banks and insurance companies.

Public opposition, in the face of a clear need for civic improvement, served to convince a number of business and political leaders that substantial redevelopment of the city could not be planned and implemented without broader public participation. Moreover, the view that urban problems were not just city problems, but regional problems, was ascending at the time. A number of urban laboratories and urban design projects had been started at major universities by the early 1960's, and public awareness of a regional approach to urban development was beginning to take effect.

In Hartford, the impetus for action came from the business community. The decay of the city, the erosion of property values, the changing population patterns of the local labor market, and the hostility of some segments of the population toward other segments were evident and unmistakable. But action, in the form of destroying and rebuilding, could not be done unilaterally as the Constitution Plaza project had also made clear. To redevelop the city, and to plan for the future of the regional area, a new means was required that would be sufficiently participative to facilitate a community consensus on the need for, and the direction of change. This idea germinated during late 1963 and the early part of 1964; in April of 1964, the first tentative steps toward a new response to community redevelopment were taken.

Patterns of Response: The Ad Hoc Phase

On April 22, 1964, 150 "community influentials" from the Greater Hartford area met in the dining rooms of the Aetna Life Insurance Companies to discuss a program for metropolitan cooperation which would enable the community to identify, understand, and develop solutions for regional problems. The consensus of that meeting was that a larger conference, complete with agenda, research papers, and expert inputs be held in the Hartford area. In an editorial, The Hartford Courant lauded the idea and noted: "The Conference is without a plan. There are no preconceived answers. Least of all is there a plot to set up a metropolitan government.

The idea is simply a common search by the core city and its satellites for a freely chosen and freely determined future."[9]

To characterize this conference, with its participative mode and its progressive theme, the coalition looked to the traditional New England town meeting, a forum in which all citizens were allowed to voice their opinions. The conference was to be called "Town Meeting for Tomorrow" and it was held in November, 1964. For three days, 500 delegates were organized into working seminars that grappled with an agenda of regional planning issues, concerns, and problems. Background studies had been prepared and distributed in advance, providing a general context for the discussions.[10] At the conclusion of the three days, a resolution was adopted that called for the establishment of an organization to continue discussion of matters of regional concern, to identify matters of highest priority, to conduct studies on such issues, and to work toward solutions. The work of the conference had produced a document, but had also generated a new set of forces in the Hartford community that might conceivably serve as a basis for attacking the problems of community and regional development.

One of the key figures in the Town Meeting For Tomorrow was Olcott Smith, chairman of the Aetna. The Aetna's top management had been involved from the start with the Town Meeting idea. An instrumental connection had been with the Hartford Chamber of Commerce, whose president, Arthur Lumsden, was a prime mover in the regional revitalization drive. Lumsden was an accomplished solicitor of corporate support for the Chamber, and the insurance companies were high on his list. Smith was persuaded of the merit of the Town Meeting and was named General Chairman; Travelers' president, Sterling T. Tooker, was also convinced and was selected to deliver the keynote address at the Town Meeting. Presidents of other insurance companies were asked to contribute as seminar members during the meetings. What Lumsden sought, and got from such leaders was participation, financial support, and commitment. Local insurance companies underwrote much of the cost of the Town Meeting and have continued to support the organizations that have been formed to carry forward the plans of what is now called the Greater Hartford Process.[11] In 1972, the *Wall Street Journal* reported that the business

---

[9] Quoted in the opening remarks of Olcott Smith, Chairman of the Town Meeting for Tomorrow.

[10] These studies included the following titles: "Skepticism and Cautious Optimism in the Minority Community of Greater Hartford"; "Governmental Reorganization: Prospects for Action"; "Politics of Regional Planning"; "Regional Problems and Public Opinion in Greater Hartford"; "Policy Implication of Regional Planning."

[11] Several corporations have been formed to actually undertake the redevelopment plans for the capitol region. In 1972, a major redevelopment plan was prepared under contract, by the American City Corporation, developers of Columbia, Maryland, one of the first "new towns" built during the 1960's.

community had underwritten over $6 million of planning costs and that it was committed to another $7 million for the next six years.[12]

The commitment which the Town Meeting for Tomorrow stimulated in Olcott Smith was not confined to regional planning matters. In some respects, it appears to have been a consciousness-raising experience for him. He was brought face-to-face with the multitude of relevant publics whose cooperation was essential to community improvement. That experience could not permit successful executives such as Smith to believe that Hartford was, or could be, a homogenous community.

The latent conflicts which the Town Meeting brought to the foreground in Hartford emphasized points that other industry leaders had been making for some years. In particular, exposure to the influences of such life insurance "statesmen" as James Oates, chief executive of the Equitable Life Assurance Society and Orville Beal, chief executive of the Prudential, both of whom had long been preaching a doctrine of social responsibility within industry councils, further sensitized Smith to the needs of urban communities. Also, between 1964 and 1967, Smith was involved in the federally sponsored Plans for Progress campaign to increase minority employment. Following on the heels of the 1964 civil rights legislation, the campaign involved voluntary corporate efforts to open new job opportunities for minority group members.

In summary, the Town Meeting for Tomorrow was the highlight of a first phase in the Aetna's changing recognition of the dimensions of its relationship with the community. The action taken between 1963 and 1967 was still largely ad hoc in nature and prompted by external stimuli. It was becoming clear to Olcott Smith, however, that such stimuli were not random in nature; they were clustered, and of the same type, and they demanded from the Aetna—and perhaps all companies—more than a transitory response.[13]

Programmatic Responses

Cognizance of the scope and continuing nature of urban problems did not, by itself, stimulate the Aetna into an initiatory posture. Although the company's institutional subsystem was sensitive to urban problems, and responsive to requests for support and assistance, there was neither a continuing institutional response nor a means of incorporating the institutional subsystem's sensitivity into the continuing operations of the managerial and technical subsystems.

By 1967 a way developed for Olcott Smith and the Aetna's institutional subsystem to elicit a continuing response from the investment

[12] "Businessmen, Politicians Seek to Renew a City and Help Suburbs, Too," Wall Street Journal, July 26, 1972, p. 1.
[13] See discussion, Chapter One, regarding the evolution of environmental conditions from placid to turbulent.

department of the company. One of the principal areas of secondary involvement between an insurer and society is the impact of corporate investments. Such an impact is especially felt in the housing market which depends heavily on life insurers for mortgage funding. During the 1950's life insurers had invested heavily in FHA-insured housing, but by 1967 there was evidence from executives within the industry that such support had virtually dried up. Moreover, housing starts in general had declined. In 1966, they were less than 1.3 million, the lowest rate since immediately after World War II. Of importance to urban areas was the fact that only about 70,000 of those units were subsidized for low-income families. In an effort to stimulate building, the U.S. Department of Housing and Urban Development had discussed possible programs for injecting substantial resources into housing with life insurance business representatives during the summer of 1967.

The Rent Supplement Program was one federal program which offered a potential for providing greater amounts of housing to low and middle income families. Under the plan, a family would pay one-fourth of its gross income for rent; the government would subsidize the balance between that and the rental value of the facility. The problem was that the program only applied to FHA-insured apartments under Section 221(d)3 of the Federal Housing Act. Mortgage money for 221(d)3 housing came solely from Fannie Mae (Federal National Mortgage Association), then an agency of the federal government. In 1967, however, Fannie Mae's funding for 221(d)3 mortgages had nearly run out. Thus, one possibility for the life insurance business was to provide mortgages to Section 221(d)3 projects at a market rate of interest, thereby freeing Fannie Mae to purchase below-market interest rate mortgages. This would encourage the Rent Supplement Program and assist the federal government's housing programs.

Another alternative was for the industry to cooperate with the FHA in directly dealing with blighted areas. For many years the FHA had "redlined" or excluded deteriorating areas from mortgage consideration on the basis that its purpose was to function as an insurance mechanism to guarantee economically sound housing, not as a social welfare agency. In July 1967, however, the FHA announced its intention to insure single family mortgages in blighted areas. A risk-pool was created to cover unusual risk possibilities involved in such financing. If the life insurance industry could direct needed mortgage money to blighted areas, with FHA guarantees, it might be possible to put an end to the "redlining" practice. According to several sources, HUD officials argued forcefully on behalf of such an effort.

By early August of 1967, industry officials were considering a substantial investment program as a means of encouraging the building of low- and medium-priced apartments which would be eligible for rent

supplements, and also, as a means of providing mortgage funds for families to purchase homes in blighted areas. Underlying both goals, of course, was an assumption by industry officials that jobs and decent housing were related, and that by making additional routes to home ownership available, both the housing and job markets would be improved.

By the time industry leaders were able to settle on the dimensions of such a program, the 1967 summer riots in Detroit and Newark had taken scores of lives and caused millions of dollars of destruction. At an August 3 meeting, the industry's Joint Committee on Urban Problems heard Orville Beal, chairman of the Prudential, propose a program whereby the life companies would collectively make available a lump sum of money for direct urban development projects at a lower than market rate of interest, protected by a government guarantee. Apparently it was Mr. Beal who presented the idea of a $1 billion fund. The leadership embarked on a drive to sell the idea to member firms, and to the real estate finance committees that had to approve such a commitment in each company.

The drive was successful and it enlisted over 160 life companies to pledge up to one percent of their assets in order to meet the billion dollar goal. Because more companies agreed to participate than was originally anticipated, the requisite pledge from each was reduced to about two-thirds of one percent. The largest companies—Prudential and Metropolitan—thereby ended up with a pledge of about $157 million each while the smallest participant had an actual pledge of about $100,000.

The life insurance industry's Urban Investment Program was announced at a White House meeting on September 13, 1967, and received considerable press coverage and publicity. It was an explicit acknowledgement of the secondary involvement aspects of the industry's operations and was the first effort by a single industry as a whole to use its resources for the purpose of ameliorating a major social and economic problem.

For the industry, the Urban Investment Program was an action prompted by representatives of the institutional subsystems of the member firms. To secure the pledge of each company, the institutional subsystem within each organization had to convince the relevant investment and administrative departments of the need for the pledge. Moreover, the pledge would have to be implemented at the investment department and administrative levels, a condition further demanding a strong coalition. Naturally, the riots and social conflagration made the action a timely one. But timeliness alone did not create a compelling rationale for such action. As the institutional subsystems of the casualty carriers had been able to veto the abandonment of the inner city fire insurance market favored by managerial and technical interests (see Chapter Seven) so, too, were the managerial and technical interests within each life insurer able to veto an unequivocal commitment to blighted area investment by the institutional subsystems. The FHA guarantee was especially important in this regard,

for it provided the safeguard that satisfied underwriting objections to such investment because of higher than normal risks and administrative objections because of the lower than market rate of interest return.

Once the pledge was made, it became the responsibility of each life insurer to actually make the investment of the allocated funds in blighted areas. The Aetna had pledged $40 million as its share of the billion dollar total and began the process of systematically implementing the program by late 1967. Tensions had run high in Hartford, as well as Newark and Detroit, during the summer of 1967 and sporadic rioting and violence had occurred with unsettling frequency. The volatility of the local situation, coupled with the experience he had been exposed to in the industry meetings, led Olcott Smith to see a real need for the Aetna's active and substantial involvement in urban matters. To administer the company's pledge and coordinate the disbursement of funds, the Aetna hired Sherrill Luke, a black lawyer interested in community development, as director of urban affairs. Luke also had a second charge however; in addition to his responsibility to seek appropriate investment opportunities to which the pledged funds might be directed, Luke was to recommend projects or opportunities for the company to make other significant contributions to community improvement. It was in this way that the Aetna, through Smith and Luke, moved away from the ad hoc approach of the past toward a systematic and programmatic method of dealing with community involvement.

In due course, the company's $40 million pledge was dispersed in line with Luke's recommendations and the criteria of the program. That experience was the genesis of the Aetna's urban affairs program. But it was Luke's second objective—recommending special projects—that moved the Aetna toward a distinct and self-sustaining urban affairs program.[14] Special project recommendations included the "adoption" of an inner city high school in Hartford's north end, a project which began in 1968; also, the company funded a capital development project in the amount of $25,000 for construction of a community center, a commitment made in 1968 for a facility that was completed in 1970. The philosophy which Luke espoused in searching for such special projects was one of looking for situations in which the Aetna's support would assist an activity which itself would have a useful long-term community impact. The community center, for example, had no immediate impact but did constitute an important long-term community resource. The company's overall goal, therefore, was to promote development within the community by funding projects not otherwise likely to receive support.

[14] The special projects were funded on a basis entirely apart from that of the Urban Investment Program. In many cases, funding for special projects was drawn from the company's charitable contributions budget. Later, such funding would come from the urban affairs department budget.

From the perspective of a firm's response to social change, this initial stage in the development of an urban affairs program at the Aetna is notable because it represents a transition from the ad hoc responses of the past to a programmatic stage in which a policy was consciously articulated for community involvement. Whatever criticisms might be voiced about the specific projects which were either funded or rejected by the company, it is clear that an important shift had been made away from the informal ad hoc approach of the past.

During the period between 1968 and 1970, the Aetna continued to focus its urban activities in the directions suggested by Luke. A second billion dollars was committed by the life insurance industry, with a special purpose being the financing of job-creating investments. The Aetna pledged another $40 million to the program. Additional community projects were also funded by the company, including the sponsorship of several new community groups. Projects were still evaluated on an individual basis, but the concept of long-term community development established a criterion against which those projects could be judged. A more basic policy shift had also occurred. Whereas the company had once operated on the basis of an informal policy that commended personnel not to encourage the community to seek Aetna assistance, by the late 1960's a formal policy existed which encouraged the community to solicit the company's resources and assistance.

Creation of a Structure

The Aetna's urban affairs activities continued along these lines until 1971 when another change occurred. At that time, Smith, upon the recommendation of Luke and others, sought to bring together the Aetna's diverse external affairs programs under a single administrative head. (This was a practice which was consistent with the pattern Smith established in effecting other structural changes during his tenure as chief executive.) In July, 1971, the Corporate Social Responsibility department was created. Under the administration of a Vice President, the department consisted of three major sub-units: equal opportunity affairs, public service programs, and urban affairs. Implicitly, at least, the continuing importance of the matters involved in these areas and the need for a coherent and continuing approach to their management had been recognized.[15]

The third, or structural stage in the development of the Aetna's re-

[15] The Aetna was apparently the first insurance company to adopt corporate social responsibility as an official title for such activities. At an October, 1971 conference of life insurance industry chief executives it was decided that the Urban Investment Program would be terminated. An industry Clearinghouse for Corporate Social Responsibility was established. At that time, the Aetna was the only company with an existing corporate social responsibility department.

sponse to non-market aspects of its interpenetration with the public linked the main areas of external affairs. Three sub-units were created within the Corporate Social Responsibility (CSR) department with the following general responsibilities:

(1) The *public service* programs unit is responsible for the administration of the company's charitable contributions programs; it also has responsibility for providing technical assessments and background information to the board of directors on proxy voting matters relating to shareholder matters involving companies in which the Aetna has an investment interest.

(2) The *equal opportunity* unit has two sections, each under the direction of a manager. Equal opportunity *compliance* is concerned with meeting the company's responsibilities in the hiring, training, and employment of minority and women employees; equal opportunity *program development* is concerned with the formulation and implementation of programs designed to open new positions throughout the company for women and minority employees. Each manager has responsibility extending to all Aetna offices.

(3) The *urban affairs* unit is also headed by a manager who administers a separate urban affairs budget, coordinates the funding of urban projects with other charitable contributions the company may be making, and directs the company's actual urban activities in Hartford and other cities.

The managers of each sub-unit report to the Vice-President of Social Responsibility who, in turn, reports to the Senior Vice President for Corporate Planning. The Corporate Social Responsibility department also reports regularly to a special committee of the company's board of directors.

Edwin E. Knauft was recruited from the personnel area to assume the position of vice president of the CSR department. Among the first tasks he faced was the selection of a manager for the urban affairs unit, Sherrill Luke having left the Aetna by that time. The position was an especially important one because the urban affairs unit had the least specific mandate of the three units in the department. In the wake of the life insurance industry's termination of the Urban Investment Program, it was unclear what direction the Aetna's urban affairs activity would take. The danger which some saw was that the substantial commitments undertaken by the company during Luke's directorship would not be carried forward without the industry's program as a foundation. The urban affairs unit needed a person who could conceptualize and define the role of the unit, as well as administer an existing program. After a lengthy search, the company approached Glenda Copes, a community organizer for Hartford Process and immediate past president of the Hartford NAACP. In March, 1972, she was named manager of the urban affairs unit.

From Structure to Strategy

It is frequently argued in the management literature that an organization's structure follows from the strategy adopted by its top management.[16] The organizational history of insurance firms generally supports the idea of an evolving organizational form which was designed to effectively implement the technical goals of underwriting and investment growth, the administrative objectives of coherent and standardized sales and claims practices, and the institutional need for cultivating a climate of public support for the private insurance industry. In most regards, strategy has preceded structure. The Aetna's experience with urban affairs however, suggests that where matters are not well understood by top management, a structure must be created from within which a strategy can emerge.

To the extent that urban problems involve inner city areas, inhabited by the poor and by members of minority groups, there is a natural association between a firm's equal employment responses and any affirmative urban action it may undertake. In the case of the Aetna, this commonality eventually led to re-focusing of charitable contributions, and an integration of equal opportunity, public service, and urban affairs efforts into a single set of related urban-oriented activities. This non-market strategy did not evolve, however, until *after* the CSR department was formed. Prior to that time there was only cognizance of the problems and recognition of the need to develop a strategy. Formation of the CSR department reflected a perceived need for coordinating a variety of non-market matters under a single administrative head rather than the design of a structure to effect a predetermined strategy.[17]

Treating the creation of the Corporate Social Responsibility department as a matter of structure, not strategy, raises a number of interesting questions. First, if strategy is considered to be the plan for the organization's future, and structure the means of effecting that plan, what did Aetna's top management perceive the relationship to be between these

---

[16] A. D. Chandler's *Strategy and Structure* (Cambridge, MA: M.I.T. Press, 1962.) is the classic reference in this regard.

[17] Chandler, *op. cit.*, has written: "Strategy can be defined as the determination of the basic long-term goals and objectives of an enterprise, and the adoption of courses of action and the allocation of resources necessary for carrying out these goals." (p. 13) Structure refers to "the design of the organization through which the enterprise is administered. . . . It includes, first, lines of authority and communication between the different administrative offices and officers, and, second, the information and data that flow through these lines of communication and authority." (p. 14)

non-market matters and company's total or grand strategy? How were non-market concerns to be related to market matters in terms of policy, operations, and resource allocation? Were they to be adjuncts to market matters or an integral part of the market strategy? If they were to be a part of the market strategy, how would they be integrated with market matters? If they were not to be a part of the strategy, did Aetna's top management intend a separate non-market strategy? Finally, how would the department be affected by basic allocation decisions?

These questions were apparently not of great concern to Aetna's top management in 1972. Their purpose was to unite major non-market matters under a single department structure, and, in turn, integrate the new department into the decisionmaking mainstream as had been done with other new departments in the past. The action had symbolic as well as substantive effect. According to several employees who were involved, before the CSR department was created it was unclear within the company just how serious matters such as equal employment were to be taken. Policy statements had been made by Olcott Smith, to be sure, but the implementation of policy was uneven among operating departments.[18] A separate department whose charge included the enforcement of such policy directives was apparently perceived as a top management decision to seriously pursue the implementation of equal opportunity policy. That, however, was an administrative decision, not a matter of strategy.

The condition of the urban affairs unit differed considerably from that of the equal employment and public service units. Whereas the latter had fairly well-defined purposes, an immediate task for Glenda Copes was the conceptualization of an appropriate role for the urban affairs unit. The industry's investment program had been terminated, but the company, through Smith and Knauft, seemed determined not to allow the Aetna's urban involvements to expire. The focus and future direction of such activities was nevertheless unclear and the new manager of urban affairs was immediately obliged to deal with the question of the unit's mission and purpose.

Although the three sub-units had different sets of tasks, it was also clear that some coordination of purpose and activity was essential to the CSR department's success. A "social responsibility" study had to be developed for presentation to top management and the board of directors by

---

[18] One of the best known of Smith's policy statements was made in a letter to employees following the assassination of Dr. Martin Luther King, Jr. in April, 1968. Regarding equal employment he wrote: "Aetna Life & Casualty has sought through programs of affirmative action to help the disadvantaged earn a better life. The Company is taking steps to intensify such efforts." Regarding a call for personal employee involvement in community needs, he wrote: "Responding to Hartford's needs will take an appreciable amount of personal time and may also involve some use of business time. The Company is willing to make time available to you . . ." Memoranda to home office employees, April 19, 1968.

late summer of 1972. Many of the social responsibility aspects of any future company strategy depended upon the department's ability to focus on the dimensions of the company interpenetration with the public and present a coherent concept of response. The need was intensified at the time because Olcott Smith had announced that he would be succeeded as president by John Filer in July, 1972.

In summary, between 1968 and 1972 the stimulus for the Aetna's activities was within the company (per Sherrill Luke) and a preference for longer term, programmatic activities (e.g., high school sponsorship, Urban Investment Program, community building projects) began to emerge. It was during this period that the concept of a major commitment by the Aetna to urban involvement began to emerge.

A Strategy for Urban Affairs

Continuing a theme first developed by Sherrill Luke, the new urban affairs unit endorsed the concept of stable, well-organized community organizations. Ms. Copes paid particular attention to committing the Aetna to community projects and organizations which would not be short-term. The short-term community group is one which is founded for a narrow purpose and succeeds for a brief time in accomplishing those goals. Typically, however, lack of interest and/or funds forces the organization to disband. Luke and Copes both believed that the vitality of inner city neighborhoods depended on the existence of community organizations which could survive temporary funding setbacks and which could offer continuity of purpose and effort to local neighborhoods. By indicating their intention to assess groups seeking financial assistance in terms of their ability to systematically plan activities, prepare annual budgets, and audit, as well as develop, programs, the Aetna attempted to spur the creation of viable community organizations that would not fade away once the Aetna's financial support diminished. This approach led the urban affairs unit to provide considerable advisory service to community groups, including guidance about alternative sources of funds.

The urban affairs unit has been involved with the distribution of funds to community groups, but a premium has also been placed on projects where the company's internal operations and non-financial resources can be put to use. The high school which the Aetna adopted in 1968 still receives funds from the company but also uses Aetna facilities as an internship training site; computer services have been shared with a number of groups; other physical facilities and personnel assistance have been made available to needy groups. An important aspect of this line of activities has been the creation of a program whereby Aetna personnel can, on a time release basis, contribute a share of their work hours to community service.

The establishment of these "nuts and bolts" activities constituted an important first step in the building of a continuing urban affairs program. Once established, the program moved into a second phase where the urban affairs unit began to "reach out" to the community and solicit suggestions about activities or programs in which the Aetna might financially or otherwise participate. The first "reach out" attempts were directed toward Hartford's black community. It soon became apparent that while the black community was becoming adept at soliciting assistance, other ethnic groups were not. Efforts were made to establish relations with other ethnic groups in the city. In the words of one recipient group, "The Aetna was trying to be color blind in its assistance."[19]

Throughout most of the 1960's, the Aetna's urban activities were concentrated in the Hartford area. Following the creation of the Corporate Social Responsibility department, however, attention was given to the implementation of Aetna policies in locations other than the home office. The equal employment unit was concerned with compliance requirements at the local office level as well as at the home office. Requests for charitable contributions were also national in scope, thereby forcing the public service unit to look beyond Hartford.[20] The urban affairs unit was slower to adopt a national focus for its programs, a result that was deliberate in nature.

The decision to concentrate the company's major efforts in the Hartford community was premised on the need for administrative control believed necessary for effective implementation. The cultivation of working relationships with community groups demanded staff time that was generally not available in local offices. In Hartford, staff was allocated for this purpose; elsewhere, the responsibilities would have to be assumed by local managers.[21] One difficulty lay in the uneven enthusiasm of local managers for developing the type of inner city associations the urban affairs program contemplated. Since the urban affairs staff in the home office itself was quite small, numbering only Ms. Copes at the professional level, the idea of field office "specialists" was not considered feasible.

Since it was essential for the urban affairs unit to conceptualize its role, establish appropriate programs, and structure a set of activities for

[19] By mid-1974, when these interviews were conducted, the company's goal had become one of establishing overall funding parity among black, Hispanic, and white ethnic community groups.

[20] In 1972, 29 percent of Aetna's contributions went to charities outside Connecticut; by 1974, 51 percent was directed outside Connecticut. Total contributions in 1974 amounted to $2.83 million, an increase from $2.3 million in 1973, and $1.3 million in 1972. Approximately 45 percent were related to health and welfare, 24 percent to civic groups and projects, 22 percent to educational ends, 4 percent to cultural matters, and 5 percent miscellaneous.

[21] These were mostly general agency managers, with responsibility for sales and claims service.

the company, a strategy was conceived that involved the development of project ideas on a pilot basis in Hartford to be followed by evaluation and eventual export to field office cities. Given the constraints on the department and the urban affairs unit, however, few practical alternatives existed. On balance, the allocation of more resources for urban activities would not have resolved the relative lack of managerial expertise with programs of the type which Sherrill Luke and Glenda Copes had each advocated.[22]

The full range of the company's urban involvements is, of course, not defined by its contributions of funds or personnel to community betterment. Indeed its most vital influence on an urban community may follow from its investment, employment, and underwriting decisions—that is, the company's *primary involvement* with society. Recognizing the impact of such activities on urban areas, the urban affairs unit has become involved in encouraging the company's operating divisions to examine the urban impact of their own activities (secondary involvements), minimizing adverse impacts and increasing positive impact where possible. Specifically, the unit attempts to point out the urban impact of the operating department and encourage formation of a departmental response.

There are inherent difficulties in attempting to promote change among operating departments. Unlike equal opportunity matters, for example, there is no legal requirement involved which compels managers to respond. When the proposed change comes from the urban affairs unit, only general company policy supports change. In fact, actual responses depend upon the department's "output," the interests of its staff, and the internal impact of the proposed change. For example, a mortgage and bond department is generally reluctant to deal with the small mortgages and loans ($25,000–50,000) that are important to a local urban community. In a department that deals in millions on a daily basis, it is difficult to raise special concern over a $25,000 mortgage. A minority loan specialist could be appointed to concentrate on such loans. Yet, in a department where authority and responsibility are measured by the size of the accounts one manages, a specialist in small loans might expect to be stereotyped as a "nickel and dime manager," a reputation that is unlikely to enhance career prospects.

Alternatives exist. The company has explored the creation of an al-

[22] By early 1974, a number of programs were being tried in field office cities. Specifically, field offices were receiving a 40 percent match of grants to local United Fund campaigns; special projects were being forwarded to the urban affairs staff for possible funding; and the company had begun an experimental "flat grant" program in which a pool of funds is established for each field office to be distributed in the local community on the basis of need. It is contemplated that future pools would be based on an employee "head tax" formula, the company contributing a specific amount per employee.

ternative structure arrangement, such as the establishment of a MESBIC, which would allow the mortgage and bond department to continue to think in millions, but which would also permit the funding of a large loan account which MESBIC personnel could administer for the benefit of local communities. There are problems with such an approach, of course. To some extent, it allows the mortgage and bond department to avoid the issue of minority and inner city investment; it thereby allows the department to avoid factoring social impact information into its primary activities. Yet, in terms of overall corporate performance, it does suggest that alternative means of effecting desired objectives must be explored in non-market as well as market matters.

Since late 1972, therefore, a fourth stage has been evolving in the activities of the urban affairs unit. Efforts have been made to reach out to the community and solicit possible new involvements; urban programs which have proven successful are being exported to field office cities for testing and implementation; and efforts are being made to integrate urban concerns within all of the Aetna's operating divisions. There has been a broadening of the company's concern with its secondary involvements from those flowing from its community presence to those consequences of its primary involvement activities. Through the course of this process, the company has learned much about its interactions with the public and the effective management of external affairs.

chapter thirteen

developing interactive responses

INTERACTIVE STRATEGIES OF RESPONSE

One overall conclusion that stands out from the study of corporate responses to external change is the increasing vulnerability of conventional adaptive and proactive approaches to change. As discussed in Chapter 11, there are circumstances and situations in which organizational reactions and efforts to change or alter aspects of the environment may be useful *tactics* in the process of coping with change. These approaches are, however, not satisfactory approaches to the longterm management of change. They are "fire-fighting" techniques, and while there are occasional fires that need to be fought, the underlying managerial need is for an approach to change that minimizes the number and severity of corporation-society conflicts. Hence, in this final chapter we turn to an explicit consideration of new *strategies* of corporate response to change.

As the two preceding chapters have pointed out, there are instances in which managements have proven remarkably imaginative in dealing with a changing environment. The examples of the Aetna Life & Casualty company's responses to no-fault auto insurance proposals and its responses to issues raised by its role in community and urban affairs are not isolated examples of an interactive approach to managing the fit between changing public goals and corporate goals. In the cases we researched, significant examples of this pattern were found in all industry groups (i.e., natural resources, manufacturing, trade, communications, and financial) with respect to various types of public issues. Even in such classic conflict situations as gun control, companies were found which exhibited behavior designed to narrow the gap between changing public expectations and actual corporate performance. For example, in the same referendum election discussed with regard to the Massachusetts bottle bill (Chapter Seven), there appeared a proposal to ban the private ownership of handguns. Advocacy was sharp and sustained on both sides of the question. Gun manufacturers have long opposed any form of legislation or control over guns. In 1976, however, Smith and Wesson, a well-known maker of firearms, publicly announced support for a federal system of owner-licensing. As the first company to take such a position, Smith and Wesson has been sharply attacked by other industry firms and by pro-gun groups throughout the country. Yet, in the overall context of public expectations, opinion polls regularly indicate overwhelming majorities in favor of some form of control over firearms. In the near-term, Smith and Wesson will have many "fires to fight" as pro-gun groups threaten boycotts and other punitive action. But who is to say that in the overall context of public credibility, Smith and Wesson has not adopted the most imaginative posture in the industry? They have not called for the licensing of guns, per se, but rather for the licensing of *owners*. Some hard-core anti-gun advocates will claim Smith and Wesson's position is a sham; pro-gun advocates will claim it is a sell-out. Perhaps that criticism is the best indication that the company really has moved to close the gap between public expectations and its performance. By standing alone, its credibility as an independent and responsive actor is greater than that of any other firm in the industry. That is the nature of the interactive approach—not to "make friends," but to take positions that are responsive to changing public goals.

Is this concept of an interactive strategy toward change a chimera, an illusion that cannot really exist? Certainly, the cases used as illustrations in the two preceding chapters suggest that firms can create strategies that are responsive to their publics' expectations. One can also think back to some of the earlier chapters and recall other organizations that took more interactive and anticipatory approaches to change: Gillette in the flourocarbon controversy, advertisers such as Eastman Kodak in the television violence instance, and the Coors Brewing Company with respect to the bottle bill legislation. It is usually difficult to know what opportunities exist for interactive responses in a particular situation without comparing the patterns of action actually exhibited by a number of firms facing the same environmental conditions. Hence, the last case illustration we will use presents a comparative analysis of the responses of five firms to what has been called the "great bottle feeding controversy." Note that this public issue has evolved for more than seven years in its life history, during which time manufacturers have adopted sharply different approaches to the controversy. It is also a complex controversy, involving issues of appropriate technology, changing public values, economic interests, and public policy development in industrialized and less developed nations. It thus links many themes raised elsewhere in this book. But most of all, it speaks for the managerial need to search for imaginative responses to change.

COMPARATIVE RESPONSES: THE INTERNATIONAL INFANT FORMULA INDUSTRY

Infant formula was developed in the early 1900's in the United States as a medically acceptable alternative form of food supply for newborns. For 30 years, the product was primarily used in hospital settings. The popularity of formula feeding as a scientific and convenient approach jumped dramatically after World War II, and by the late 1950's, as many as 75 percent of all American babies were being fed infant formula for part of their first year of life. The rising popularity of infant formula, and a high birth rate were favorable market conditions for the manufacturers, but by the 1960's birth rates began to decline in the United States, and constituted an environmental change with serious effects on the infant formula manufacturers.

The international market for infant formula also grew rapidly during the post–World War II era. Although a number of food companies had sold breast-milk substitutes in Western Europe and North Africa before that time, many of these products were evaporated milks or powdered milks that are not comparable to the nutritionally equivalent infant formulas. As prosperity returned to Europe and multinational firms expanded operations in Africa, South America and the Far East, infant formula became an increasingly popular "food of choice" for the children of the expatriot American and Western European population.

The large numbers of wealthy and middle-class persons able to afford infant formula in the United States and Europe made mass distribution and promotion of such products a widespread and acceptable phe-nomenon. In the nations of Africa, South America and the Far East, how-ever, the number of wealthy customers was fewer, and the size of the middle class was notably smaller. Distributors often were the channel through which the product reached those who sought it and were anxious and able to buy it. In an effort to expand sales, distributors, and sometimes the manufacturers themselves, began to promote infant formula to broad segments of the population. It is the promotion which reaches the poor and those only marginally able to afford the product in less developed na-tions that has created the great infant-formula controversy.

There are two separate kinds of problems associated with the pro-motion and use of infant formula in LDC's. First, the product is usually sold in powdered form and must be mixed with local water. In social en-vironments where inadequate sanitation and water supply are major con-tributors to disease, this exposes infants to the very real threat of disease. Secondly, infant formula is an expensive product, which can consume much of a low income family's disposable funds. Critics argue that since the formula is never quite as good as mother's milk, both the child and the family would be better served by using their limited funds to meet the family's more general nutritional needs.[1] Dr. Derrick Jelliffe (1971), for-merly director of the Caribbean Food and Nutrition Institute in Jamaica, found that it would cost $73 to feed an infant processed foods (milk-based infant formula, cereal-based infant food, and babies' vitamin drops) for the first six months of life, or nearly $2.75 per week. Of those Jamaicans having jobs at the time, 40 percent were earning less than $11 per week.[2] Yet, according to Jelliffe, this was the very class that the promotional mes-sages were reaching.

These observations helped stimulate major concern about infant nu-trition among profession nutritionists by the early 1970's. Alan Berg, au-thor of *The Nutrition Factor*, made the point that the decline of breast feeding over the past 20 years has caused the average age of children suf-fering from severe malnutrition to drop from 18 to 8 months in some areas in the world.[3] A study in Trinidad (1972) showed that over 70 percent of the cases of severe malnutrition in Port-of-Spain involved children under one year of age; and the Pan American Health Organization reported that deaths from malnutrition now peak as early as the third and fourth months of life.[4]

---

[1] See Alan Berg, *The Nutrition Factor*, (Washington, D.C.: Brookings Institution, 1973).
[2] V. G. James, "Household Expenditure on Food and Drink by Income Groups," paper pre-sented at Seminar on Natural Food and Nutrition Policy of Jamaica, Kingston, Jamaica, 1974.
[3] Berg, *op. cit.*
[4] See R. Puffer and C.V. Serrano, *Patterns of Mortality In Childhood*, (Washington, D.C.: Pan American Health Organization, 1973).

A number of important actions evolved from this professional concern. In November, 1970, the World Health Organization (WHO) and UNICEF sponsored a conference in Bogota, Colombia, to focus discussion on the issue. Industry representatives were invited to participate, along with nutritionists and government officials. According to participants, the atmosphere began with open hostility toward the industry, a number of nutritionists accusing the latter of unconscionable marketing conduct. Some measure of reconciliation was achieved by the end of the conference, and a succeeding conference was planned. A second conference was held in Geneva in 1972 under the auspices of the UN's Protein Advisory Calorie Group (PAG), and a statement was drafted with regard to the promotion of special foods, namely infant formula and powdered milks. The statement (PAG Statement #23) was revised and issued in November, 1973, in the hope that it would generate a consensus among nutrition experts, the industry and the governments of the LDC's as to a future course of action that would resolve the problem of infant formula marketing practices vis-à-vis infant malnutrition. This line of institutional activity continued when the World Health Assembly, governing body of WHO, unanimously adopted a resolution which identified misleading sales promotion as a cause for declining breast feeding and urged nations to take action to review and regulate marketing practices.

Although news of the Bogota conference, PAG Statement #23 and the World Health Assembly resolution was reported in the popular press, widespread interest in the issue did not develop until more journalistic treatments of the problem occurred. In the United States, Greiner's report on promotional practices was published in 1975.[5] The Greiner report was a collection of advertising copy (some over 40 years old) and assorted data ostensibly linking the manufacturers of infant formula to the product's overpromotion and misuse. Although the data collection was erratic and specific conclusions frequently suspect (indeed, the report includes some data wholly unrelated to infant formula), Greiner's document served as a basis for a number of newspaper articles that helped focus public attention on the industry.

In Great Britain, a report entitled *The Baby Killer* was published in 1974 by War On Want, a charity organization with worldwide activities, which discussed the problems of infant feeding in less developed nations and was especially critical of Nestles Alimentana, S.A., the Swiss multinational food company, and Unigate, Ltd., a British firm.[6] Within a year, public action groups in Switzerland, France, and Germany were raising

---

[5] Ted Greiner, *The Promotion of Bottle Feeding By Multinational Corporations: How Advertising and the Health Professions Have Contributed*, (Ithaca, N.Y.: Cornell International Nutrition Monograph Series, No. 2, 1975).
[6] Michael Muller, *The Baby Killer*, (London: War On Want, 1974).

anew the issues posed in *The Baby Killer* and confronting Nestle in a variety of public forums. These actions eventually led Nestle to file suit in Switzerland alleging injury due to defamation and libel, caused by a translation of *The Baby Killer* entitled, *"Nestle Tötet Kinder"* (Nestle Kills Babies).

The publicity which these activities generated gradually began to raise the issue to a higher and broader level of public awareness. In the United States it was the filing of shareholder proposals at annual meetings of the three United States companies—Abbott Laboratories (Ross Laboratories), American Home Products (Wyeth Laboratories), and Bristol-Myers (Mead Johnson Laboratories)—that put the pressure squarely on the management of these firms to respond in a public way.

Industry Orientation

Producers of infant formula products have two basic orientations, which reflect different histories of product development. In the United States, the principal sellers of infant formula were founded on the successful efforts of medical researchers to prepare an infant food substitute for mother's milk. By the late 1920's, Ross Laboratories, Mead Johnson, and Simulated Milk Associates (SMA) were in the business of producing and selling human-like infant formula. In the late 1920's, SMA was acquired by Wyeth Laboratories, a Philadelphia pharmaceutical company. Wyeth, in turn was acquired by American Home Products in the 1930's. Ross Laboratories concentrated on infant formula research and production; it was eventually acquired by Abbott Laboratories, a pharmaceutical company, in 1964. Mead Johnson also remained in the infant formula business and built on its research base, developing in addition to Enfamil, the well-known low calorie food, Metrecal, in the 1950's. When Metrecal lost its market in the late 1950's, Mead Johnson floundered and Bristol Myers, another pharmaceutical firm, acquired the company. While Wyeth has more direct pharmaceutical sales than either Ross or Mead Johnson, all three have brought a pharmaceutical research orientation to product development and marketing of infant formula. Indeed, during the 1960's, a number of special "sick baby" formulas were produced by these companies for children with special dietary and health requirements. While the "sick baby" segment of the market is insignificant in comparison to the "well baby" segment (perhaps 2 percent of total sales volume), the existence of such specialized products is attributable to the research orientation of the industry.

The second orientation to the industry is a food processor approach which is characteristic of such firms as Nestle and Borden. Both Nestle and Borden began in the evaporated milk business in the 1860's. Through the early decades of the 1900's, new uses were found for the canned milk products which Nestle sold in Europe and Borden sold in the United States. One use to which the evaporated and condensed milks were put was infant feeding. As this market segment expanded, and as medical research indicated that the humanized infant formulas were nutritionally superior for infants, both food companies sought to retain their share of the infant food market by introducing infant formula products which were either developed internally (Nestle) or whose rights were purchased from others (Borden). Nestle introduced its famous formula, Lactogen, in the 1920's. Borden, on the other hand, did not introduce its infant formula product, Bremil, until the 1950's. The approach to the market of these two firms is similar to other food companies. Sales are generated through heavy advertising, with a special reliance on mass media such as newspapers, radio, and television. Brand identification is cultivated through such advertising, and price sensitivity is the key to preserving brand loyalty.

To summarize, industry orientation derives from the genesis of the competitors' entry into the market. The pharmaceutical orientation emphasizes research as a basis for the infant formula product and it is marketed through the medical marketing approach used to build the sales of other pharmaceutical products. The food processor orientation emphasizes the consumer goods aspect of the product, and entry into infant formula production was necessitated by the competitive threat of new products and the need to retain market share. The marketing of infant formula by food companies has been like that of other food products, emphasizing consumer advertising and brand loyalty.

Business Strategy

There are several routes to commercial success in the infant formula business and these are reflected in the basic business strategies adopted by the firms mentioned above. In the United States, Ross Laboratories and Mead Johnson emerged as the survivors in an industry battle to win pediatrician endorsement and recommendation of infant formulas to new mothers. By the 1960's, the two firms accounted for approximately 90 percent of the domestic infant formula business, Ross' Similac accounting for 55 percent, Mead Johnson's Enfamil products for about 35 percent. So entrenched were these sellers in the domestic market that Nestle, the acknowledged worldwide industry leader with 50 percent of the market, did not attempt to penetrate the United States market. As the United States birth rate leveled off in the 1960's, however, both Ross and Mead Johnson were forced to look outside the United States for major growth opportunities. Ross chose to look to industrialized nations where disposable income was high and where there were prospects for market penetration. Canada, Europe, and North Africa became major foreign markets for Ross' Similac, Mead Johnson looked primarily to the Caribbean where export was relatively easy and control could be exercised without major difficulty. Puerto Rico, Jamaica, and the Bahamas became important Mead Johnson export markets. This inevitably led Mead Johnson products to be used in a social environment including significant elements of poverty and illiteracy. Jelliffe's early charges of "commerciogenic malnutrition" were based, in part, on observations that involved Mead Johnson products in Jamaica. Ross, on the other hand, seemed to have adhered more closely to strategic criteria of high disposable income levels and sizable middle and upper classes in selecting those developing countries in which it marketed Similac.

Wyeth Laboratories was not a major seller of infant formula in the United States before World War II, but it had begun to sell internationally. Following the war, the company's presence as a pharmaceutical manufacturer established a base from which infant formula was marketed by affiliates in Latin America, Europe, and Southeast Asia. The affiliate arrangement is comparable to a set of operating subsidiaries whose actions are coordinated by top management. This was especially important to Wyeth since the company was establishing production facilities on a regional, and sometimes local basis. When an international marketing division was created, the sale of formula, as well as other products, became significantly more aggressive with corresponding increases in worldwide market share. Today, Wyeth probably accounts for 10–15 percent of worldwide sales.

Nestle is the only seller of infant formula that has adopted, as its basic business strategy, the concept of significant presence in every national market. Throughout the developing nations of the world, Nestle looms as a major seller of infant formula products. Its worldwide market share approaches 50 percent, and its penetration in individual national markets exceeds 70 percent. The sales concepts of market development (e.g., Nestle introduced dairy herds in a number of Latin American nations), aggressive sales promotions, and intensive advertising have characterized the company's efforts in infant formula as they have with other food products. So prominent is Nestle, that when the War On Want study (*The Baby Killer*) of bottle feeding in Africa was published, Nestle was the principal firm the author criticized.

Borden's business strategy differs from the others described in this chapter in two ways. First, it developed an infant formula product relatively late in the life history of the industry (1950's), and secondly, it did not attempt to develop a significant market share in any single national market. Hence, the company has not been a major seller of humanized infant formula. However, one serious health problem in developing nations is that the population often uses products other than infant formula for bottle feeding purposes. In Borden's case, its leading powdered milk product (Klim), which is not an infant formula, has been alleged to be mistakenly used as a food fit for infants. Borden has marketed Klim aggressively as a powdered milk product, and it seems that one consequence has been consumer misuse of the product for infant feeding. In 1976, Borden announced that it was stopping all advertising of the new humanized infant formula (New Biolac) it was selling in Taiwan and Hong Kong, because it could only successfully sell this new product with a heavy mass media advertising expenditure. For Borden, therefore, the strategic decision has been to abandon the infant formula milk market and concentrate on the powdered milk business.

Industry Responses

The five companies mentioned above have differed in significant ways in their response to the controversy. In chronological phases, the following responses have characterized each of the companies discussed.

Phase I: During the early 1970's, the principal response to professional concern and criticism was industry participation in the conferences sponsored by PAG. Ross Laboratories, Wyeth Laboratories, and Nestle each sent representatives to these meetings. Borden and Bristol-Myers were not active in these conferences.

Phase II: In November, 1975, representatives of nine international manufacturers met in Zurich, Switzerland and decided to form an international council to be known as the International Council of Infant Food Industries (ICIFI). Nestle, Wyeth, and Ross participated, along with two other European and four Japanese companies. Borden and Bristol-Myers chose not to join the group. The ICIFI members adopted a code of marketing ethics which obliged members to recognize the primacy of breast feeding in all of their product information and labelling, to include precise product use instructions, and to eliminate in-hospital promotion and solicitation by personnel who were paid on a sales commission basis. Ross withdrew from ICIFI and criticized the code as being too weak; the company then adopted its own more restrictive code, including a provision prohibiting consumer-oriented mass advertising. Wyeth and Nestle remained in ICIFI; Borden and Bristol-Myers neither joined ICIFI nor adopted any marketing code. Additional criticism of the ICIFI code by PAG has led to subsequent incremental changes in the code, generally reinforcing the "professional" character of sales activities, but not proscribing all consumer-oriented mass advertising.

Phase III: In 1977, Ross Laboratories announced its intention to commit $95,000 to a breast feeding campaign in developing nations and also budgeted $175,000 for a task force to conduct research on breast feeding, infant formula, and LDC's. The company also announced a plan for continuing review of the situation with its critics. ICIFI has now begun work

TABLE 13-1
INFANT FORMULA SELLERS
PRODUCER ORIENTATION AND BUSINESS STRATEGY

PRODUCER*	INDUSTRY ORIENTATION	MAJOR MARKET	MAJOR AREA OF LDC MARKETS	BUSINESS STRATEGY
Bristol-Myers (Mead Johnson)	Pharmaceutical	Domestic United States	Caribbean and Central America	Export business; Geographic proximity to U.S.: Excess production from U.S. plants; use of distributors;
Abbott Laboratories (Ross Laboratories)	Pharmaceutical	Domestic United States	Rapidly developing African and Southeast Asian (e.g., Nigeria, Taiwan)	Export from European plants; High income product marketed to upper classes; market via own sales force; limited use of distributors;
American Home Products (Wyeth Laboratories)	Pharmaceutical	Selective world markets (e.g., Canada, Gt. Britain, S. Africa)	Southeast Asia; Latin America; Africa;	Complement to drug sales efforts; use of Wyeth affiliates (subsidiaries) to market; preference for local or regional production;
Nestle	Food Processor	Europe; Africa; Latin America; Asia: Not in U.S.	Worldwide	Sell full line of food products in all nations; Full line local food processing plants; Established first dairy herds and milk industry in many nations; Product evolved from early milk products;
Borden	Food Processor	Worldwide	Latin America	Independent food product marketed via distributors; Powdered milk is not an infant food; Participates in joint ventures with other food processors (Nestle);

*Subsidiary in parentheses

with the World Health Organization in preparing educational materials to be used in LDC's to encourage breast feeding and maternal and child health care. ICIFI is also committed to supporting scientific research about breast feeding, infant formula and the status of maternal and child health in LDC environments.

Throughout all three phases, pressures have been exerted by industry critics through the courts and, in the United States, the stockholder resolution process provided for under the Securities and Exchange Commission regulations.[7] In Switzerland, Nestle sued the group that published *Nestle Kills Babies* for defamation. The court allowed testimony on the underlying facts of the controversy, thereby allowing great publicity of the trial to occur. Eventually, the court ruled that members of the group had to pay damages for defaming Nestle's name in the pamphlet title. However, the court also told Nestle that it should carry out a "fundamental reexamination" of its infant formula marketing activities, pointing out that the decision in favor of Nestle was a technical one, not a vindication of the firm's marketing behavior. In the United States, shareholder resolutions were filed at Abbott Laboratories, American Home Products, and Bristol-Myers in 1975, 1976, and 1977. A resolution was filed at Borden in 1977. Dispositions of these are shown below. No resolution has ever received more than 6 percent of voting shares; in the Bristol-Myers case, however, such institutional investors as the Ford Foundation and Rockefeller Foundation have abstained or voted against the management. In cases where resolutions have been withdrawn, a compromise with the shareholders filing the resolution has been achieved.

INFANT FORMULA SHAREHOLDER RESOLUTIONS			
	1975	1976	1977
Abbott	withdrawn	vote	withdrawn
Am. Home Products	withdrawn	withdrawn	vote
Bristol-Myers	vote	vote	(See text)
Borden	no filing	no filing	withdrawn

Bristol-Myers management opposed the shareholder resolutions in 1975 and 1976. The company's 1976 proxy statement contained statements which were thereafter alleged to be false and misleading by critical shareholders, and a lawsuit was filed on alleged violations of securities laws in

---

[7] Rule 14a(8) of the Securities and Exchange Commission provides that shareholders have the right to submit proposals for consideration at the annual stockholders meeting. Management may either accept the proposal or oppose it; in the latter case, proponents may request an SEC review and decision as to whether the proposal must be included. In this instance, resolutions have called for disclosure of marketing practices and abandonment of specific promotional activities.

the spring, 1976. Borden negotiated a settlement of the resolution filed in 1977, the company agreeing to modify certain advertising messages and tightly oversee marketing of its powdered milk product so as to minimize misuse as a formula product.

Determinants of Operative Policy

The industry orientation which each firm has toward the infant formula market certainly seems to have shaped the perceptions of each toward the market ("infant food" versus "scientifically prepared infant nutritionals") and the controversy. The ability of each firm's management to respond to the controversy, in turn, appears to have been constrained by the business strategy which that firm pursued. Thus, industry orientation and business strategy have been important determinants of the *operative policy* adopted by each company. In the real world of management decision making, it is operative policy, not stated policy, that defines the true priorities and interests of a corporation.

The heart of the critics' case against the infant formula manufacturers has been that the marketing and promotional practices of the firms have induced purchases from mothers for whom the product is not a necessity. There are direct and obvious correlations between the orientations of the firms and the marketing, advertising, and sales concepts which each employs. The food companies traditionally sell food products by large scale consumer advertising efforts. It is not surprising, therefore, that they perceive a need for some mass advertising opportunity if they are to successfully penetrate a market. The pharmaceutical firms, on the other hand, can market their products to physicians and medical clinics through their medical detail staff. Since they are associated with the promotion of drugs, as well as formula (though they do not promote both simultaneously), the pharmaceutical manufacturers have an entree in medical settings not readily available to food company salesmen.

Not surprisingly, the orientation of infant formula sellers has also affected their willingness to restrict or change marketing practices. Abbott (Ross) Laboratories and American Home Products (Wyeth) have both been willing to endorse codes of marketing ethics which restrained or prevented consumer oriented advertising. Abbott's own code prevents such advertising and AHP's internal policy restricts advertising to medically-oriented professional promotion. Nestle, on the other hand, has argued on behalf of some consumer advertising opportunities, including educational messages. The permissiveness of the ICIFI code in this regard can probably be attributed to the interests of the member food companies. While some specific consumer sales practices were restricted (e.g., uniformed mothercraft personnel), the opportunity for new kinds of consumer-oriented advertising has been retained in the code. The threatened limitation on promotional practice may also have been a contributing factor in Borden's decision not to join ICIFI for the company continues to heavily advertise its powdered milk products. The only case in which orientation does not shed significant light is Bristol-Myers, where the pharmaceutical orientation belies strong resistance to any participation in ICIFI or adherence to restrictions on marketing practices.

Business strategy does help explain Bristol-Myers' stonewalling approach to the infant formula controversy, however. The company's strategy has been to build on its significant United States market base and export to the Caribbean and Central America. This has been its dominant geographic sphere of influence in the international industry, though it now also sells heavily in the Philippines. The company's basic business strategy in these LDC markets seems to be to sell to anyone who will purchase the product. To cultivate this sales activity, the company has endorsed uniformed mothercraft personnel, mass consumer advertising, and even allowed its personnel to solicit in hospital settings *after* the rest of the industry had largely abandoned such practice. As late as 1975, Bristol-Myers was adamant in its refusal to recognize the legitimacy of the critics' allegations that real health problems were associated with bottle feeding in LDC environments. In terms of what Bristol-Myers had at stake in this conflict, it can be concluded that its international business depended upon dominance of a geographic market where export was easy and relatively inexpensive. For Bristol-Myers, their stake in the prevailing multinational corporation/LDC market relationship was very high. It is not surprising, therefore, that their approach to the conflict has involved resisting all efforts to alter the prevailing relationship.

Business strategy also helps to account for Borden's response to this controversy. The company's orientation as a food processor meant that it had a high stake in preserving its ability to advertise to consumers directly. In 1976, the company began to test market an infant formula product in two Southeast Asian developing nations. The product was to be a means for Borden to penetrate the under-six-months age group which requires a modified milk product. After six months, children can medically tolerate the powdered milk (Klim) which is the company's principal milk product. Hence, the infant formula would be a lead-in product which would then permit switching to powdered milk at about the six-months age. So intense has criticism of the mass advertising approach become, however, that Borden's management concluded that it would not be able to successfully advertise because of public criticism. Caught in this dilemma, Borden chose to withdraw from the infant formula business and has agreed to support breast feeding campaigns in LDC's. If bottle feeding abates, the company's management is hoping that they will then have an equal chance to attract customers at the six-months point, since the other competitors (especially Nestle) will not have been able to build brand name loyalty. Hence, what was once a set of conflicting interests with industry critics has been transformed into a set of common interests. In light of the realities in both the business and political environments, Borden has adopted an accommodation strategy toward this conflict.

Business strategy has also been a factor in the responses of Nestle, AHP (Wyeth), and Abbott (Ross) Laboratories. Nestle began, somewhat like Bristol-Myers, in a stonewalling mode of response. Pending the trial in Switzerland, it announced it would not make public statements about the matter. Its stakes in the prevailing relationship were extremely high and Nestle appeared unable to acknowledge (publicly or internally) that its product might be associated with a serious social issue. Public pressure eventually moved Nestle out of the extreme stonewalling posture toward a "shared responsibility" position when it joined ICIFI in 1975. In the views of some industry observers, Nestle was a reluctant participant in ICIFI. The trial in the Swiss court, however, added an additional dimension of pressure even though it was the company that was suing for defamation. The court's admonition to undertake a fundamental reexamination of its marketing practices, while not legally binding, helped move Nestle toward a more responsive posture. At the least, their enthusiasm for ICIFI as the vehicle for dealing with criticism has significantly increased. This movement at Nestle has served to bring it toward a more interactive approach, a position which AHP (Wyeth) has occupied since 1975 (i.e., "shared responsibility"). Wyeth's stakes are significant, but it has been seeking to identify areas of common interest with its critics. Hence, the company has strongly endorsed further medical research into related matters of infant and child care in LDC environments. Nestle has now adopted a similar posture.

Finally, Abbott (Ross) Laboratories abandoned the "shared responsibility" posture when it became apparent that the ICIFI code would not ban mass advertising. The company has since adopted a posture that recognizes its own high interests in the matter, but in a way that now seeks to build on perceived common interests with industry critics. The decision to support breast feeding campaigns in LDC's with a direct grant for public education messages is consistent with the business strategy of trying to sell only to high-disposable-income families while encouraging low-disposable-income families to breast feed. There is an implicit assumption that high-income women will still choose to use infant formula for a variety of convenience and status factors, and that the danger of losing a few choice customers is less than the cost of public criticism and possible pediatrician backlash. Abbott has therefore gambled on "taking the high road" in this controversy; it is an approach that fits both their orientation and their business strategy.

Figure 13-1 illustrates the kind of positioning just discussed in terms of the "stakes" of each company in maintaining the prevailing relationship with LDC markets and whether the company has "mostly conflicting" or "mostly common" interests with the industry critics. Among these, the "collaborative" and "shared responsibility" approaches fit the interactive pattern of response; "stonewalling" represents a strategy of resisting environmental change (alter the environment by refusing to change!); and Borden's "accommodation" approach is mostly a reactive approach to the issue.

FIGURE 13-1

Approaches to coping with Social Conflict

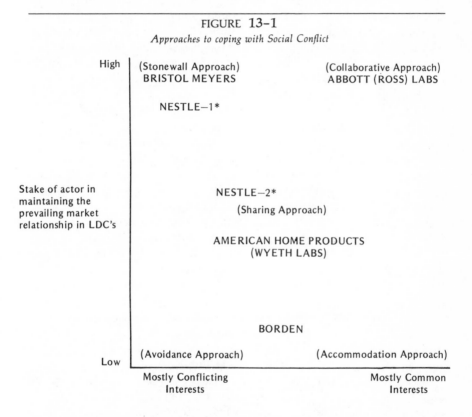

Conflicting versus Common Interests in Relationship with Industry Critics.

*Nestle - 1 refers to approach before Swiss court decision;
Nestle - 2 refers to approach following Swiss court ruling.

[8] This scheme was adapted from one presented by Kenneth Thomas, "Conflict and Conflict Management," in *Handbook of Industrial and Organizational Psychology*, ed., Marvin Dunnette (Chicago, Ill.: Rand-McNally & Co., 1976), pp. 889-935.

STRATEGIC APPROACHES
TO COPING WITH CHANGE

The responses of the five firms in the infant formula situation illustrate both different strategies of response to external change and different degrees of corporate socialization. The impact of infant formula promotion and use in the environments of less-developed countries is a complex matter, neither entirely detrimental as the critics charge nor wholly positive as the industry might argue. Indeed, it is an excellent example of the complicated secondary involvement effects that can occur when a product that is quite acceptable in one social environment (industrialized nations) is widely used in a significantly different social environment (LDC's). There seems to be no easy way out of this conflict, given the sellers' continued interest in selling their product and critics' interest in a broad return to breast feeding. Is it possible to narrow the gap between evolving public goals that favor breast feeding as a means of reducing infant malnutrition and corporate goals that favor sales of infant formula?

The deadlock which seems manifest in the previous question is not intractable. First, it seems clear that the firms must *recognize* the existence and legitimacy of the critics' concern about a very real infant malnutrition problem in LDC's. Yet, the lengthy refusal of Bristol-Myers to even acknowledge the existence of a problem bespeaks a stonewalling strategy that resists any socialization whatever. This seems to be a strategy designed to widen the gap between public expectations and corporate performance, not narrow it. And court actions to drive the critics away (proactive tactics) also seem unlikely to close the expectations/performance gap. Thus, cognizance of the legitimate concerns about the problem are the first step in a socialization process that will harmonize corporate goals and public goals.

Consideration of evolving public goals, and critics' arguments, in the evolving business strategies of the corporate actors is a further stage in the process of responsiveness. Borden certainly seems to have manifested such a consideration in its decision to abandon the sale of infant formula products in LDC's, and to concentrate instead on the sale of its powdered milk products. This seems to recognize the company's "distinctive competence" as a milk producer, not an infant formula manufacturer. In so doing, it has emphasized an interest in directing its corporate activities toward ends that are not in conflict with the evolving goals of the LDC's.

Similarly, the decisions of Nestle, Wyeth Laboratories, and Ross Laboratories to modify their marketing and promotional activities represent tactical adaptations to near-term pressures. The creation of ICIFI, however, and that organization's efforts to *positively* interact with critics, international health agencies, and the governments of LDC's signal a more imaginative and creative approach toward harmonizing corporate goals and public goals. This collective "shared responsibility" approach to dealing with the issues raised by critics is a strategy for coping with change, the success of which will depend on whether the underlying competitive strategies of the member firms can be adjusted to narrow the expectations/performance gap. For the food processing firms which depend on consumer advertising for product promotion, constraints on mass media advertising present a real problem. Borden resolved the problem by avoiding the dilemma; Nestle's stakes are much larger, however, and it now faces a problem of either finding a way to conduct its infant formula business without mass advertising or pursue its business strategy of food selling without selling infant formula. The pharmaceutical companies can probably eliminate consumer advertising without significant harm, given their medical marketing staffs. Thus, there is a serious competitive problem for each of the firms in the industry. Integrating new external concerns into the business strategy of the firm is not always an easy task. As this case shows, however, given a certain amount of managerial imagination, the task of being responsive while also framing a successful competitive strategy is not impossible. The value of an interactive strategy in this context is that it holds the promise of helping the firm preserve its legitimacy as a useful and desirable social actor.[9]

An affirmative effort to correct the problems about which the critics have complained is also evident in the Ross Laboratories strategy of collaborative corporate/government activity. The company's commitment to prepare, supply, and subsidize the broadcast of public service announcements encouraging new mothers in LDC's to breast feed their infants is more than just a strategic reaction to change. This is a positive initiative-taking strategy to reduce the magnitude of the problem in LDC's. If low-income mothers heed the messages, there is the prospect that infant malnutrition rates will decline. More importantly, Ross has a business strategy that is founded on sales to upper income groups whose resources are sufficient to permit infant formula use without adverse health consequences. Even if some of these upper-income mothers do choose to breast feed their infants, the use of formula as a supplement seems likely among women who have employment opportunities and a need for the convenience that infant formula can provide.

This comparison of strategic approaches to a single, albeit complex, public issue illustrates the opportunities that exist for managements to

---

[9] In the infant formula example, it appears that nutrition policymakers in LDC's are nearing consensus on the social preferability of breast feeding. One approach that several managers have discussed is to emphasize the role of infant formula as a *supplement* to maternal feeding, not as a replacement for it. Although this might create some temporary loss of sales, some believe it will not have a serious long run impact on nations where births are still increasing.

abandon the conventional reactive and proactive approaches to change in favor of more imaginative responses. It may be, as some managers have said in the infant formula case, that no matter what they do, the critics will still find new bases for challenging their corporate performances. That may be frustrating, but it underscores the fundamental theme of this entire research project and book: *that social expectations are constantly changing, and that the effective management of external affairs continues to be the most challenging facet of modern management.*

TOWARD MANAGERIAL IMAGINATION

Many writers have commented on the escalation of corporate criticism that has occurred throughout the 1970's. For managers whose careers began in the 1950's, and who are now in the prime of their executive years, public disenchantment with business and business institutions is particularly frustrating. The 1950's really marked the end of a major period in the evolution of corporate America. Historian Louis Galambos has written that between 1880 and 1940, American society generally accommodated the evolution of the large corporation, letting itself be shaped and formed by the interests and purposes of the corporate sector.[10] While public opinion about business was always mixed, Galambos concluded that anti-business sentiment was not extreme and that this permissive environment facilitated the expansion of big business and the emergence of large scale bureaucracies.

But if the *accommodation process* that Galambos described characterized the period of corporate emergence that ended in the 1950's, the last two decades have to be considered a' period of corporate questioning— that is, a time when the social will to accommodate has been reversed. The questioning of technological change, political challenges to unregulated business activity, and social protests accompanying "normal" corporate activities signify the existence of a new process by which the changing values of the larger society are forced upon the institutions of society. Elsewhere, Lee Preston and I have referred to this as the socialization of the modern corporation.[11]

The sample of cases researched for this project clearly indicate that firms do undergo a *socialization process* as an ever-changing society seeks to find ways of influencing corporate behavior, challenging power and size, and raising the level of corporate performance. Evidence of the process is abundant as firms become more sensitive to, and adept at, recognizing

[10] Louis Galambos, *The Public Image of Big Business in America, 1880–1940*, (Baltimore, Md.: John Hopkins University Press, 1975).
[11] Lee E. Preston and James E. Post, *Private Management and Public Policy*, (Englewood Cliffs, N.J.: Prentice-Hall, Inc., 1975), Chapter 4.

new expectations, comprehending their implications, and internalizing the values they represent. All in all, the socialization of the modern corporation appears to be a social process that is beginning to have a recognizable and central effect on the management of large organizations. If this is as lasting a phenomenon as the evidence seems to suggest, it strengthens the case for a more interactive approach to the management of change.

More than a year before the 1976 American presidential election, Max Ways wrote an article in *Fortune*, the popular business magazine, entitled "Business Needs A Different Political Stand."[12] The thrust of the article was that doctrinaire conservative political positions by business didn't square with the reality of corporate courting of governmental favors. Such a stance, according to Ways, will not be tolerated by a public that has found the means and methods of imposing political controls on business institutions. He concluded, "It is only by showing a willingness to cooperate with the American people in the *management of change* that business may regain the political influence it once had."[13] (Emphasis added.) Nevertheless, there was no noticeable rush of corporate managers to endorse populist candidates in the months that preceded the election.

There were ways in which some change in approach was manifested however. The Mobil Oil Corporation's advocacy advertising on issues of major public policy debate (e.g., energy, full employment, and pollution) became a standard part of the "op-ed" pages of newspapers around the nation. And a growing number of firms seemed to take seriously an idea advanced by John W. Hill, a public relations executive, who wrote that businessmen must come to understand the inner mind of the public and make their case in terms of what that public can understand.[14] The language of corporate management is not the public's language, nor the terms in which the public mind thinks. To communicate effectively, there is a need to disclose more, in forthright and clear ways, about matters that are of public concern. Disclosure and a willingness to take public positions can be the keystone of an interactive approach to coping with new social expectations.

The cumulative lessons of the cases studied point to a few conclusions about the socialization process that are basic to the interactive pattern of response. First, it is critical that an organization be cognizant of the publics which it affects and with which it interacts, including society as a whole. Secondly, it is important that such interests be taken into account as the organization pursues its own market and economic objectives.

---

[12] Max Ways, "Business Needs A Different Political Stand," *Fortune* (September 1975), p. 96 ff.

[13] *Ibid.*, p. 193.

[14] John W. Hill, "The Business of Business . . . The Government of Business," *New York Times*, OpEd, October 6, 1976.

Thirdly, as to those matters where the firm has secondary involvements with external publics, it is critical that the organization attempt to internalize the goals and purposes of those publics (public policy goals). If this can be done, then the preferred state of organization/environment relations which the firm is trying to reach will also be that state which is preferred by its relevant external publics. In this way, the organization is socialized toward directing its efforts in ways that serve public policy objectives as well as corporate policy objectives. This cannot be accomplished by simply adapting to external change, or attempting to alter the public purposes, but by actively being involved in the simultaneous evolution of corporate and public policy goals. That is the new challenge to the managerial imagination.

appendix

a note on
theory and
empiry

INTRODUCTION

There has been a longstanding, not always
muted conflict among academic students of
management about the need for, possibilities
of, and methodology appropriate to the study
of management policy. Although the study of
management policy has progressed substantially since the 1950's, there are still occasional
stories of deans who ask "what is it?" and departments that are disbanded because an adequate answer was not forthcoming. How is it
that policy, unlike marketing, finance, or organizational behavior has suffered this fate?
While the answer undoubtedly has as many
facets as there are schools of business or management offering the subject, one contributing
factor seems to be the tenuous relationship
between policy research and policy theory. Indeed, the most devisive influence in this whole

275

area may be the fragmentation of opinion among faculty teaching in the area about the research/theory relationship.

There are two extreme views of the relationship between policy research and theory. One, "sui generis situationalism," argues that each policy incident is a unique experience that can be understood after it has occurred, but is not likely to be replicated in the future. Hence, no significant theoretical propositions can be divined from the study of these atypical situations; each is "sui generis," as the lawyers say, one of a kind. The alternative view is that policy, like other academic areas, lends itself to testable hypotheses built on objective data and information. Hence, narrow research questions need to be framed, research bases constructed, and hypotheses articulated and empirically tested. Proponents of the first view argue that the empiricists generally produce narrow questions that permit quantitative analysis but fail to yield real understanding of the complexity of policymaking. The empiricists counter that the *sui generis* approach produces anecdotal evidence at best, trivial insights at worst. To compound the problem, these basic positions exist in both the business policy and business and society wings of the management policy field. Little wonder that deans are frustrated by the whole subject!

Henry Mintzberg has made the simple, yet insightful observation that all fields of research have an interplay between deductive models and inductive observation.[1] Especially as it applies to the study of the corporation and its external social environment, there is a back-and-forth movement between the development of models based on prior experience and evidence and the testing of those models against new empirical cases and evidence. The truth of Mintzberg's observation is best seen in the evolution of research into the study of patterns of corporate response to change.

WHERE IGNORANCE LIES

Kenneth Berrien has argued "(i)t is only by erecting conceptual frameworks that we discover where ignorance lies, and take appropriate steps to fill the gaps."[2] The necessity of conceptual models to illuminate areas where gaps in knowledge exist can be illustrated by a brief recounting of the way in which the "interpenetrating systems" model evolved. In 1972, Lee Preston and I began to address ourselves to the literature of the corporation-society area. But the idea of doing a literature search of the area proved both difficult and frustrating. Try as we might to organize it, the

[1] Henry Mintzberg, "Policy As a Field of Management Theory," *Academy of Management Review*, vol. 2, no. 1 (January 1977) pp. 88–103.
[2] Kenneth Berrien, "A General Systems Approach to Organizations," in *Handbook of Industrial and Organizational Psychology*, Marvin Dunnette, ed., (Chicago: Rand McNally & Co., 1976) pp. 41–62, quote from p. 60.

literature seemed to go off in so many directions, embracing so many issues and topics, that it seemed to defy synthesis and order.

In time, we identified the views of several major authors—Adam Smith, Karl Marx, Milton Friedman, and John K. Galbraith—around which the literature clustered; but, it was still necessary to search for a means by which each view could be criticized and evaluated against the others. We eventually chose to "translate" each of the key conceptions into the common language of systems theory.[3] Our central assumption was that the firm and society were social systems, related to one another in some not yet fully understood way. In this framework, the similarities and differences between the market model and the exploitation model became sharp and clear—each saw an "exchange process" between the firm and society, but differed on the relative benefits accruing to the various subsystems through the process of exchange (consumer surplus versus surplus value!). Galbraith's concept of a technostructure dominating social values could be viewed as a suprasystem dominating many individual social systems (firms and other organizations). And the legal model could be seen as a process by which the suprasystem (society) established the rules of the game for each of the social units within it. Some evidence suggested that each of these views did indeed have a grain of truth in it. Our problem lay not in choosing among them (for no one choice could explain the "deviant" situations explained by the other models), but in finding an integrating conception.

The systems literature provided what was to become both an alternative way of viewing the corporation-society relationship (model), and a set of concepts that could embrace all of the inductive evidence that seemed to support one or another of the extant models. The new concept was that of *interpenetrating social systems.* According to Talcott Parsons,[4] social systems are interpenetrating when they not only influence one another but also *mutually* influence the processes by which they continue to interact over time. As applied to the study of the corporation and society, this concept permitted an emphasis on the process of corporation-society interaction without predetermining what form that interaction must take. It facilitated an analysis of behavior that reflected both social conflict and harmony; and, unlike other models, the presence of either harmony or conflict between the corporation and society was not the primary theoretical concern. Rather, this model focused attention on the *processes* of interaction (market and public policy), the kinds of behavior exhibited by corporations and other social actors, and the patterns of response by

[3] Lee E. Preston and James E. Post, *Private Management and Public Policy* (Englewood Cliffs, N.J.: Prentice-Hall, Inc., 1975) Chapter 2.

[4] Talcott Parsons, "An Approach to Psychological Theory in Terms of the Theory of Action," in *Psychology: A Study of Science,* Sigmund Koch, Ed., (New York: McGraw-Hill Book Co., 1959) vol. 3, pp. 612–711.

which harmony or conflict evolved. A framework for understanding the processes of interaction was the gap in knowledge that the interpenetrating systems model sought to fill.

TESTING A FRAMEWORK

The need for a holistic framework in designing research becomes clear when one looks at a specific case. A brief personal example illustrates the point. Until several years ago, the bulk of studies in the corporation-society area focused on a specific social issue and its impact on a particular industry and member firms. Interfirm comparisons had been made, but no one had studied how the management of a single firm simultaneously responded to many different issues, each at a different stage in its own life history. The beginnings of a corporate responsiveness model, as articulated by Ackerman and Bauer,[5] Preston and Post,[6] and Votaw and Sethi,[7] had suggested a process involving managerial awareness of an issue, commitment toward response, and actual implementation. However, this model had not been tested in the context of a single firm facing many issues.

To analyze this question, it was necessary to find a candidate firm that would allow itself to serve as the research case. Once such a firm was found and the study initiated, it became clear that the responses of the firm to different issues could not be comprehended without knowing something about the factors motivating its management, the role of the firm in the industry, the historical development of the company, and the history of the industry itself. To understand these, in turn, one had to look at other historical analyses of the evolution of the industry and the many competitive trends that had shaped it during that time. The result was not a narrow study of a specific question, but the pursuit of an elephant! To understand how the management of Aetna Life & Casualty responded to an agenda of public issues in the early 1970's, it was necessary to go back to the very beginning of the American insurance industry and trace two hundred years of market trends, public policy trends, organizational trends, and regulatory trends. It was only against the backdrop of this continuous industry and social history that one could analyze the nature and character of the Aetna's responses to change in the 1970's.[8]

---

[5] Robert Ackerman and Raymond A. Bauer, *Corporate Social Responsiveness: The Modern Dilemma* (Reston, VA: Reston Publishing Co., 1975).

[6] Preston and Post, *op. cit.*

[7] Dow Votaw and S. P. Sethi, *The Corporate Dilemma* (Englewood Cliffs, NJ: Prentice-Hall, Inc., 1973).

[8] James E. Post, *Risk and Response: Management and Social Change In The American Insurance Industry*, (Lexington, Mass.: D. C. Heath, Inc., 1976).

THEORY BUILDING:
PATTERNS OF RESPONSE

The study of the corporation and society relationship has attracted scholars who are interested in both the applied aspects of the relationship (e.g., conflict management) and the more theoretical. Any theory that would deal with this field, however, must ultimately confront the reality of extensive and continuing corporation-society interaction. According to Robert Dubin, an applied theory necessarily has to have the real world as its point of origin: "It is exceedingly difficult to say something about the real world without starting in the real world. Observation and description of the real world are the essential points of origin for theories in applied areas . . ."[9] Documentation of the interaction between corporations and society is extensive, and the many volumes of observations, anecdotes and case studies are regularly supplemented by the continuing tale of interaction told in the pages of the *Wall Street Journal, New York Times* and local newspapers throughout the world.

The extensiveness and the richness of this inductive base does not guarantee theoretical formulations, however. What is required for the central theoretical conception of which Preston[10] wrote, is a creative leap from the data base to a conclusion from which other deductive propositions might emerge. Dubin's essay, "Theory Building in Applied Areas," makes the point in the following manner:

> "Theories . . . represent levels of generalization beyond a statistical summary of data points. Any generalization which starts from the data points generated by observation and description is arrived at through an inductive process. . . . What further conclusions the researcher wishes to draw from the correlation depends upon his skill and cleverness in reaching an inductive generalization at a level higher than the correlational conclusion . . . (In this way) we have reached an inductive conclusion that is already removed from the data base from which it originates. . . . (H)aving started from sound observation and description, we could well be on the road to developing a new theory."[11]

The search for a creative generalization, in Dubin's context, has infrequently been successful in the study of the corporation and society. It is ironic that while there seems to be relatively little argument in academic circles about the importance of the field, only parsimonious encouragement is given to theoretical scholarship. Yet the need for such an investment of scholarly effort is apparent. Our vast data base does not, by itself,

[9] Robert Dubin, "Theory Building in Applied Areas," in *Handbook of Industrial and Organizational Psychology*, Marvin Dunnette, ed. (Chicago: Rand McNally & Co., 1976, pp. 17–39).
[10] Lee E. Preston, "Corporation and Society: The Search for a Paradigm," *Journal of Economic Literature*, vol. 13, no. 2 (June 1975) pp. 434–453.
[11] Dubin, *op. cit.*, p. 18.

make clear where the information is lacking. If anything, we probably have too much raw material and unstructured data and insufficient ways of organizing it.

One purpose of the patterns of response research has been to establish a set of behavioral categories, conceptually and theoretically distinct, into which the body of observations of corporate behavior could be placed. The interpenetrating systems theory raised behavior to the foreground as an important matter for research. In *Risk and Response*, two familiar behavior (adaptive and proactive) models were articulated and a third model derived from the study of how the management of one firm simultaneously responded to multiple environmental issues. Articulation of the interactive behavior model represented the kind of creative leap from the data to which Dubin referred. Further testing of these models was the next research step.[12]

BROADENING THE DATA BASE

The existence of three distinct patterns of response to change at Aetna Life & Casualty was confirmed by the actions of other firms in the insurance industry. Nevertheless, it was not clear whether the patterns were unique to the insurance industry, or applicable to other industries and corporation-society relationships. There was a clear need to test the patterns of response concepts against a larger body of empirical data. If the patterns were to be a set of useful analytical concepts, their existence had to be demonstrated in a broad variety of environmental change cases.

Because environmental change touches the core of management activity and policy decision-making, there was reason to believe that patterns of response similar to those identified in *Risk and Response* would be found in other industries, and with regard to other types of environmental change. Having found some similarities in the manner in which an organization coped with change, irrespective of its economic or social character, the question remained whether these patterns would exist under various kinds of environmental change. To push this line of research forward, a subsequent study was constructed to test the patterns of responses hypotheses. A series of "high salience" issues in a variety of industries was drawn from conflicts reported in the popular press. This pool of cases has been supplemented with a number of historical cases of organization/environment conflict. The sample has been segmented by the type of underlying environmental change, utilizing four categories of change: economic, technological, sociocultural, and political.

---

[12] A full discussion of the relationship theory between the interpenetrating systems and the patterns of response research can be found in James E. Post "The Corporation and Society: Research On Patterns of Response To Change," in *Research in Corporate Social Performance and Policy*, Lee E. Preston, ed., vol. 1 (Bridgeport, Conn.: JAI Press, 1978).

The sample of environmental change cases researched for this purpose is indicated in Table 1, with an indication of the principal firm or industry group involved. In some instances, cases were selected on the basis of the company's involvement in a conflict issue; in other instances, a known environmental issue was the basis for inclusion, and the behavior of one or more firms was then analyzed. An indication of the number of firms studied, and the pattern(s) of response exhibited by each is indicated in Table 3.

Both firms and environmental change issues were selected with an eye toward creating a sample that included a variety of industry groups. This system of categories, along with reference to specific cases, is presented in Table 2.

RETURNING TO THEORY

The empirical studies which are the foundation of this book have been concerned with both corporate performance and corporate behavior, and the special effect that social change has on both. The sample was constructed for the purpose of examining whether or not the three patterns of response to change existed in a variety of industry settings and with respect to a variety of public issues. The study was *not intended* to answer such theoretical questions as (1) under what conditions does each of the three patterns of behavior arise? or (2) what results or success are directly attributable to each of the patterns? These are logical questions flowing from the patterns of behavior research, but they have not yet been answered.

The patterns-of-response study has suggested a framework for looking at these further research questions. Throughout this book there has been an underlying argument about the relationship between corporate performance, behavior, and social change. The theory that underlies the book, and the selection of actual cases presented in the various chapters, can be presented as a series of propositions, which in turn, flow from the research done to date and provide an agenda of sorts for future research activities.

Proposition # 1. Organizational performance is multidimensional in nature. The performance of managed organizations cannot be measured by profitability or any single measure alone.

Profits have probably never been the only criteria by which managers, stockholders, or the public evaluated the performance of corporations. But if they ever were sufficient, that time was surely long ago. Corporations are chartered by society for social purposes—they are given a license to act within a broad set of behavioral constraints that constitute the legal rules of game. But a corporation can lose its charter if it regularly

TABLE 1. CODING OF CASES IN SAMPLE

NATURAL RESOURCES INDUSTRIES (01–09)

01 Reserve Mining, environmental pollution
02 Gulf Oil, business activities in S. Korea
03 Mobil Oil, advocacy advertising
04 Georgia Pacific, clear cutting operations
05 Strip mining legislation, multiple firms
06 Mobil Oil, Rhodesian boycott violations

MANUFACTURING INDUSTRIES (20–49)

20 Allied Chamical, Kepone incident
21 Gillette, fluorocarbons and ozone layer
22 DuPont, fluorocarbons and ozone layer
23 DuPont, toxic substances legislation
24 Bottle Bill, various firms
25 Polaroid, equal opportunity
26 Lockheed, business practices overseas
27 Infant formula promotion in LDC's, multiple firms
28 Gerber Products Co., demographic changes
29 Proctor and Gamble, Pringles and nutrition
30 ITT, Hartford Fire merger settlement
31 ITT, political activities in Chile
32 Smith and Wesson, gun control
33 Tobacco industry, health hazards
34 United Brands, business practices overseas
35 B. F. Goodrich, polyvinyl choloride hazards
36 Northrup, business practices overseas
37 Gulf & Western, business practices
38 SST, pollution issues
39 Coffee cartel, various firms
40 Quaker Oats, nutrition information
41 South Africa, manufacturing firms
42 U.S. Political contributions, various firms

FINANCIAL AND INSURANCE INDUSTRIES (50–69)

50 Aetna Life, inflation and life insurance
51 Insurance industry, fire insurance crises
52 Aetna Life & Casualty, no-fault auto reform
53 Aetna Life & Casualty, community affairs
54 Redlining, various banks
55 EFTS, various banks
56 Citicorp, Arab boycott
57 Citicorp, South Africa dealings
58 Bank of America, data disclosure
59 Medical Information Bureau, data disclosure

UTILITIES (70–79)

70 New Hampshire Public Service, pollution
71 American Electric Power, advocacy advertising
72 Kerr-McGee, nuclear safety
73 Electric supply dependency, various firms

COMMUNICATIONS (80–89)

80 TV Violence, various firms
81 Children's TV, various firms
82 RCA, portrayal of women and minorities
83 Cable television, competitive impact
84 CBS, accuracy in broadcasting

TRADE (90–99)

90 Universal Product Code, various firms
91 Sunday Blue Laws, various firms

---

ignores and violates those rules or if society decides that the intended social purposes are not being fulfilled by corporate activity. Changing the rules of the game by legislation, administrative ruling, and judicial decision is both legitimate and well understood as being legitimate by managers and the public alike. And decisions about what types of economic activity should be left to the competitive marketplace, which to a regulated marketplace, and which to government enterprise are also being constantly made. Hence, changes in the rules of the game and decisions about the appropriate means of accomplishing certain public ends are both influenced by the present performances of business firms and the public expectations of what those performances should be.

Proposition #2. Public concern with an organization arises as gaps develop between the *actual performance* of the entity and the performance which is *expected* by its relevant publics.

A social issue exists, according to this conception, whenever a gap develops between what the organization's relevant publics expect its performance to be and the organization's actual performance. Whether the issue is pollution, minority employment, product safety, labelling, or any of a thousand others, that issue begins to develop an independent life history when some group of persons and/or organizations take note of it and begin to seek change with respect to the matter. Publics become relevant to the organization when there is a crossing of the interests of the group and the interests of the organization.

It is also important to recognize that not all relevant publics are constituencies. It is wrong to think of the organization's relations with the society in terms of constituencies for two reasons: first, constituencies suggest some dependency of the organization upon the group, a condition

TABLE 2. CLASSIFICATION OF CASES (by code number)
TYPE OF UNDERLYING ENVIRONMENTAL CHANGE

INDUSTRY GROUP	ECONOMIC	TECHNO-LOGICAL	POLITICAL	CULTURAL VALUES	N =
Natural Resources	04, 06	01	02, 03	05	6
Manufacturing	26, 28, 30, 36, 37, 38	20, 21, 22, 23, 33, 35	24, 31, 34, 39, 42	25, 27, 29, 32, 40, 41	23
Financial and Insurance	50, 51, 54, 57	55	53, 56	52, 58, 59	10
Trade	91	90			2
Communications	81	83	84	80, 82	5
Utilities	73	72	71	70	4
N =	15	11	11	13	50

which plainly does not exist when issues are in the early stages of their development (When does a group become a constituency? What is it before then?). Secondly, constituencies imply some permanence in their relationship to the organization. In fact, groups are frequently formed to contest an issue with an industry or firm and then evaporate when the issue fades. The concept of relevant public carries no implication of permanence, but rather, makes clear the fact that not all publics are relevant to the organization at the same time or in the same way. The relevance of publics to the organization changes constantly and the term constituency fails to capture this dynamism. Hence, it is the expectations of the society at large that are important, because under proper conditions, any segment of that society can compose itself in such a way as to make it a relevant public for the corporation.

Proposition #3. The stimulus or motivation for change in organizational behavior can derive from the pressure of changed legal rules of the game, pressure from the firm's relevant publics, or from the initiative of management.

The reasons for an organization's acting as it does are not always obvious. From empirical evidence, it appears that any organization behaves as it does because its managers choose for it to act in a certain way (purely voluntary situation), because it is under some degree of pressure from one or more of its relevant publics (partially involuntary situation), or because the rules of the game compel certain action. Frequently, there are combinations of stimuli at work, as for example when certain publics press an organization to strictly comply with a new piece of legislation or administrative ruling (e.g., residents of an area previously affected by now-illegal smoke emissions). Lastly, it is important to note that management has its greatest decision-making discretion with regard to an issue during the period before any overt pressures build up in the environment. We know that there is a pattern in the life history of social issues which involves changing social expectations, politicization of the issue, the creation of legislation, and eventual enforcement by litigation of the law. As each stage progresses, the degree of managerial discretion becomes significantly less. Hence, there is a point beyond which organizational behavior is directed by external sources rather than internal management.

> *Proposition #4.* An organization's response to changing demands and expectations for performance will vary with a variety of factors related to its overall status or position in society.

As the life history of every organization evolves, it develops a series of relationships with other elements and components of the environment. We can speak of this as an evolving *interpenetration* between the managed organization and the society. Among the variables to which we can look in assessing the extent of the interpenetration are the scope of the firm's activities (e.g., the number of products, markets, and geographic areas in which it operates), the continuity (or life history) of those relationships, the size of the organization in particular product and geographic markets, and dependency of other social units on the organization (e.g., the number of employees, the number and volume of local supplier's contracts, etcetera). Although traditional economic models of relationship between managed organizations and society emphasize the market process as the framework within which interpenetration occurs, we know that the relationship between organizations and their environments has numerous non-market dimensions and occurs in the public policy process as well as the market process.

> *Proposition #5.* Because of their position in the society, organizations have various *social roles*, which, along with motivation and status, influence their behavior.

Empirical observation confirms what school children learn about their local community and environment: people and organizations develop a framework of roles over time which enable the community to function in a smooth and expeditious manner. The largest employer, the only bank, and the local hospital each acquire a status, and specific roles in the community that identify what behavior is appropriate and what performances ought to be rendered. No less than in the local community, the

TABLE 3. PATTERNS OF RESPONSE BY FIRM

SAMPLE CODE #	FIRMS	PATTERN(S) EXHIBITED
01	Co-1	Proactive
02	Co-1	Proactive, Adaptive
03	Co-1	Interactive
04	Co-1	Adaptive, Proactive
05	Co-1	Adaptive
06	Co-1	Adaptive
20	Co-1	Proactive, Adaptive
21	Co-1	Interactive
22	Co-1	Adaptive
23	Co-1	Adaptive
24	Co-1	Adaptive
	Co-2	Adaptive
	Co-3	Proactive
	Co-4	Interactive
25	Co-1	Adaptive
26	Co-1	Proactive
27	Co-1	Adaptive
	Co-2	Proactive, Adaptive
	Co-3	Adaptive
	Co-4	Interactive
	Co-5	Interactive
28	Co-1	Adaptive
	Co-2	Proactive
29	Co-1	Proactive
30	Co-1	Proactive
31	Co-1	Proactive
32	Co-1	Interactive
33	Co-1	Adaptive
	Co-2	Proactive
	Co-3	Interactive
34	Co-1	Proactive
35	Co-1	Adaptive
36	Co-1	Proactive
37	Co-1	Proactive
38	Co-1	Adaptive
	Co-2	Proactive
39	Co-1	Adaptive
40	Co-1	Interactive

41	Co-1	Interactive
	Co-2	Adaptive
42	Co-1	Adaptive
	Co-2	Proactive
	Co-3	Proactive
50	Co-1	Adaptive
51	Co-1	Proactive
	Co-2	Adaptive
52	Co-1	Interactive
53	Co-1	Interactive
54	Co-1	Adaptive
	Co-2	Adaptive
55	Co-1	Adaptive
	Co-2	Proactive
	Co-3	Proactive
56	Co-1	Adaptive
	Co-2	Proactive
57	Co-1	Adaptive
	Co-2	Proactive
58	Co-1	Interactive
59	Co-1	Proactive
70	Co-1	Adaptive
71	Co-1	Proactive
72	Co-1	Adaptive
73	Co-1	Adaptive
80	Co-1	Adaptive
	Co-2	Adaptive
	Co-3	Interactive
	Co-4	Adaptive
81	Co-1	Adaptive
	Co-2	Adaptive
82	Co-1	Adaptive
	Co-2	Adaptive
83	Co-1	Adaptive
	Co-2	Adaptive
	Co-3	Proactive
	Co-4	Interactive
84	Co-1	Adaptive
90	Co-1	Proactive
	Co-2	Adaptive
91	Co-1	Proactive
	Co-2	Adaptive
	Co-3	Interactive

"industry leader" is a role in product markets for both goods and services. Although we can easily enough recognize roles that organizations fill in markets, in communities, and in economies, there is very little systematic research about what occurs when role occupants fail to adequately render that social performance which conforms to the expectations of its publics. Are new role occupants sought out? Are remedial steps taken? Are new rules of the game promulgated to force performance that conforms to expectations? While the reader probably has some intuitive feeling about the answers to those questions, the fact remains that insofar as we are concerned with macro organizational roles, research opportunities abound to confirm or reject intuitive hypotheses.

Given these basic propositions, our theory can be stated in fairly simple terms. First, a firm's *performance* as an actor in complex societies varies with its *behavior* in response to environmental change. This change can be perceived as being a threat, an opportunity, or a new requirement. Organizational behavior will vary depending on the perception of the environmental change. Secondly, issues of corporate performance arise as a gap develops between the organization's actual performance and expectations of what that performance should be. As this gap grows, momentum develops for transforming the issue into a public issue which may then proceed through a life cycle process involving increasing politicalization. Thirdly, corporate *behavior* in response to social change will also vary with the social *status* of the organization; with the type of *motivational factors* at work; and with the *roles* the entity fills in the competitive and social environment.

Such a theory is obviously in its infant stages, and yet it represents the outgrowth of previous research and analysis in this area. Looking both at what has been accomplished and what remains to be done in this field, there is little doubt that research opportunities in the field of management policy have barely been comprehended, much less exhausted. In a world where such complex problems as those discussed in this book are the cutting edge of both corporate policy and public policy, there is a challenge for academicians that is every bit as great as that facing their practitioner counterparts.

index